DANCING *with* GOD

Dedicated to my father,
Taylor L. Baker Jr.,
who, in a courtroom filled with the lost and the poor,
strove to mete out justice with compassion
to les misérables of the world
and
to my mother,
Kay Jett Baker,
who went beyond teaching the children in her life
their three "R's" to sharing the joy of dance and laughter.

—KAREN

DANCING *with* GOD

The Trinity *from a* Womanist Perspective

Karen Baker-Fletcher

ST. LOUIS, MISSOURI

Cover art: Fotosearch
Cover and interior design: Elizabeth Wright

Visit Chalice Press on the World Wide Web at
www.chalicepress.com

10 9 8 7 6 5 4 3 2 1 06 07 08 09 10

Library of Congress Cataloging-in-Publication Data

Baker-Fletcher, Karen.
Dancing with God : the trinity from a womanist perspective / Karen Baker-Fletcher.
p. cm.
Includes bibliographical references and index.
ISBN-13: 978-0-8272-0633-5
ISBN-10: 0-8272-0633-X
1. Womanist theology. I. Title.

BT83.9.B33 2006
231'.044–dc22

2006023310

Printed in the United States of America

Contents

Acknowledgments

The more one writes, the more one realizes that one never writes their best work alone. I appreciate many people who offered suggestions, comments, criticisms, and other forms of support during the time I wrote this book. First, I am grateful for Katie Cannon whose "unshouted courage" encourages me to keep walking with head and heart in divine grace, dignity, and courage. Strong editors are a gift, and I could not have completed this book without the advice of my editor at Chalice Press, Trent Butler. Many thanks to the Scholarly Outreach Committee at Perkins School of Theology for providing a grant in 2004 to assist in finishing the book, which provided the extra incentive I needed knowing that administrative and faculty colleagues were supportive of this project. Deborah Williams and Andrew Eubanks, my research assistants, were helpful with proofreading and locating books.

During the summer of 2004, I read Joyce King's work, *Hate Crime: The Story of a Dragging in Jasper, Texas* (Pantheon, 2002) and began drafting an initial theological analysis of the information she provides in her work. King's book and the lecture she presented as a 2004–2005 Honors Lecturer for the Honors lecture series at the Hughes Trigg Center, Southern Methodist University, October 2004, are invaluable contributions to understanding the horror of hate crime and the presence of healing grace in communities affected by it. King is a healer, and her love for the Byrd family and for others in her commitment to healing are contagious to those who hear and read her work.

The poem "Sacrificial Food" by writer/dancer/producer Vanessa Baker and the choreography for the poem by Vanessa Baker (performed to the song "Strange Fruit" sung by Billie Holiday and written by Jewish school teacher, activist, and songwriter Abel Meeropol) inspired attention to the healing power of the dance of the Spirit throughout this book. Monica Coleman, an African American woman and Whiteheadian theologian, thoroughly reviewed the method chapter and the chapters that provide theological analysis of the dragging of James Byrd Jr. in 1998. Along with Theodore Walker Jr., Marjorie Suchocki, and John Cobb, she has been influential in persuading me that since my theology is already relational, I should engage in intensive conversation with process metaphysicians and theologians.

Theodore Walker read the task, methodology, and context chapters in their roughest drafts. I am thankful for the frank suggestions that he and Coleman offered. Dwight Hopkins offered very helpful suggestions regarding the chapters on the dragging of James Byrd and the comparison of *han* with the blues. Sharon Welch and Joerg Rieger were helpful readers regarding the chapter on dance and postmodernity, which at that point was dancing rather wildly in the chapter on task and method and did not have a space of its own. Charles Wood, in response to my queries regarding whether or not it is necessary to create a metaphysical argument for the Trinity provided several articles he has written on John Wesley's sound analysis of the issue.

Garth Baker-Fletcher and Evelyn Parker reminded me to be forthright about the role of holy indignation and righteous anger as theological categories in any discussion of cycles of hatred and unnecessary violence. Marjorie Suchocki, John Cobb, Catherine Keller, Donna Bowman, and Tom Oord have been encouraging colleagues as I engage Whiteheadian thought and process theism without becoming a process theist in a strict sense. Thank you for your openness. Joerg Rieger, thank you for your input and encouragement in response to an early draft of chapter 1. Billy Abraham, I thank you for the evangelical common ground we share and our common position of being difficult to "pigeon-hole."

Many thanks to Dean William B. Lawrence and Marjorie Procter-Smith of Perkins School of Theology, who understood my writing schedule and need for quiet time away to focus on research and writing during my sabbatical in spring 2005. I extend further appreciation to Ross Murfin, provost of Southern Methodist University, for approving my request for a research/writing sabbatical for spring 2005. I am grateful for my students in "Interpretation of the Christian Message" (Systematics), whose questions move me to keep teaching and writing.

My family has been very gracious toward me. My mother and father, Kay J. Baker and Taylor L. Baker, alerted me to the lynching case of James Cameron in Marion, Indiana, and to the fact that he has written a powerful testimonial in his book, *A Time of Terror* (TD Publications, 1982). Taylor Baker also alerted me that Indiana had had some slavery, although most know it as a location of the Underground Railroad and that Cameron founded the Black Holocaust Museum in Milwaukee, Wisconsin. My cousins Karia and George Bunting listened patiently as I talked about the various stages of writing this book month after month. My aunt Verna Baxter and cousin Lynne Donna McCollum helped clarify the significance of addressing the theme of healing in a world of crucifixion. My husband and my children, Garth, Kristen, Kenneth, and Desiree Baker-Fletcher, patiently put up with my sitting at a computer or reading books for hours on end just about every day. Garth is a good listener and understands me well. As a writer, I can't imagine having a more thoughtful companion.

I owe several Mom and Kids times to all three of my children. For Back to School Night, I blushed to see that while all the other children had drawn pictures of their mothers doing family things, Desiree's picture showed me writing at the computer. Thanks, Desiree, for reminding me to spend some time with you, too. Spending time with you clears my mind to make room for more creativity. Kenneth, working on science projects with you gave me a fresh perspective on creativity and science. Kristen, I enjoy reading your essays. Dez, you write great poems! Thanks, Dez, for helping me cook when I felt like cooking. Thanks, Kenneth, Kristen, and Garth when I was just too absorbed to think about it. Your cooking sustained me many times. You are a great family, and I love you!

Finally, thanks and glory to God, my everlasting inspiration and source of strength for all that I feel called to do. I belong to two church communities. I appreciate both churches for understanding that I am called to learn and minister within interdenominational depth and breadth. St. Luke "Community" United Methodist Church, pastored by Rev. Dr. Zan Wesley Holmes when I first arrived in Dallas and pastored by Rev. Tyrone Gordon since July 2002, is a constant source of spiritual strength, comfort, and empowerment for me, my family, and the wider Dallas community. I appreciate the Spiritual Leadership Class that Pastor Gordon and Rev. Dr. Michael Greene taught during the spring and summer of 2005. This class and the Spirit-led discussion with so many other members of St. Luke kept me spiritually centered.

My second church community is Grace Outreach Center in Plano, Texas, which also keeps me spiritually centered through its emphasis on praise and worship, its down-to-earth biblical teachings, interdenominational emphasis, and commitment to intercultural community in esteeming and valuing others. Thanks to Pastor Gerald Brooks for reminding us all that "This is what heaven is going to look like!" Thanks to Pastor Tyrone Gordon for reminding all that this is what God is all about–just be Christian and know that God is the liberating God of all peoples!

Preface

It is important for readers to know that the approach to theology I employ here is integrative in several respects. Womanist theology does not separate theology from real-lived, concrete, existential concerns. Womanist approaches to theology, generally speaking, are interdisciplinary. Therefore, the reader should not look for this volume to take an approach similar to types of Trinitarian theology that separate the study of God from ongoing, concrete, historical, and current social concerns. In a womanist approach, *God is social.* Therefore, theology–the study of God–is inherently social. It is concerned with *both* who God is in relation to God's self *and* who God is in relation to creation. A Christian womanist, I am deeply influenced by the Trinitarian understanding of nineteenth-century Wesleyan African American women evangelists such as Jarena Lee, Zilpha Elaw, Julia Foote, and Amanda Berry Smith. The specific influence of these women on the Trinitarian nature of my theology is the subject of another book. Here I am concerned that if we are created in God's likeness, then we are called to fully reflect God's own just, loving, compassionate, communal nature. Most simply, I see God as divine community whose aim is for authentic community on earth as in heaven.

Who are "womanist theologians"? I define "womanist" in greater depth in the body of my work. For now, the reader should know at least this much: Womanist theologians and scholars of religion are women of African descent, and in Alice Walker's definition, global women of color, who endeavor by *wholistic* approaches to further the healing and wholeness of entire communities, male and female. Womanist theology does not abstract constructive theology from concrete existence. Womanist theology is inherently integrative and relational. Womanists take seriously the experiential knowledge of God among women of African descent and, for those who retain Walker's inclusion of "women of color," global women of color. Given the fact that womanists draw on real-lived experience within these communities, those without such experience cannot be said to be womanist. There are, however, many advocates of womanist thought who engage in similar work. Also, relational theologies of various types are influenced by and include womanist thought, finding that it enriches and enlivens the work of theology as a whole. If womanist theologians are making theological claims that are true, then we are among the many theologians who contribute to understanding universal truth, not simply one particular culture, in what we have to offer. My hope is for the womanist theology I and other womanists write to influence all types of relational peoples and theologies around the globe, interculturally, across genders, and beyond all that threatens to divide us.

In this book, I engage in intercultural theological construction and analysis as a Christian, relational womanist. I enter into dialogue with diverse types of relational theologians, from diverse cultures and faith backgrounds. I encourage others to do so, because why shouldn't twenty-first-century Christian theology learn from theologians of diverse backgrounds and cultures, who are not simply interesting "others" but who are divinely gifted members of the body of Christ upon whom we are interdependent? Moreover, why shouldn't theologians who are committed to rigorous scholarship give credit where credit is due for angles of vision into the truth of God's nature within the body of Christ, from whatever culture the contribution to Christian faith may come? For me, this is a gift of womanist attention to being divinely created in freedom and equality.

I am free to include the contributions of women of African descent and other women of color in my work. *And,* I am free (not coerced in a way that excludes the contributions of such women) to embrace the gifts of divine revelation that I share in common with peoples from other cultures, including some of the insights from Euro-American culture, that are consistent with womanist attention to praxis, the interrelatedness of body and spirit, and the integration of ontological and existential concerns.

While some womanists are also liberation theologians, this is not true for all of us. I, like Delores Williams, find that God liberates, but God does not always liberate–at least not in the sense that some would have us imagine in terms of liberation from oppressive institutions like slavery, segregation, sexism, racism, classism, hatred of and violence against gays and lesbians, ableism, genocide, terrorism, war, and so forth. So, what is God doing in the meantime, given that liberation has been and is an ongoing process that rarely comes to us as immediately as we desire? If God is not absent, then in what way is God present? As a cruel, unmerciful, noninterventionist God? Or is God everlastingly present in this universe and all possible universes, persuasively inviting us to receive God's vision for quality of life and survival resources to stay on spiritual "battlefields" as participants in divine justice? Williams's work emphasizes that God does not always liberate in the way or in the time that we would like, but also God provides quality of life. God provides vision for survival resources and concrete survival resources in the midst of our existential, concrete, physical, and spiritual lives.[1] The implication I draw from her work is that God is omnipresent in creation's struggle for life abundant and for the full realization of freedom, justice, love, and wholeness on earth as in heaven.

The emphasis of my own womanist work is that even when God does not liberate us in the time or way that we want, God encourages us to continue struggling for healing and wholeness from hatred and violence.

Even when God does not deliver victims from sinners who act violently and with fatal results, God is present as a healing and "whole-making" reality in the lives of survivors–family, friends, community, society, the globe. Moreover, God, who is omnipresent, dynamically invites and persuades us into healing relationship with God and the rest of creation to participate in God's creating, restoring, and healing activity. We witness the dance of the Trinity in the testimonies and social activism of Christian survivors who have lost loved ones to hate crime and lynching like the families of James Byrd Jr., James Cameron, and Mamie Till-Mobley. Coretta Scott King was yet another survivor of hate crime in the form of assassination, whose immense work I cannot give full attention to in this volume but whose Christian faith was a witness to God's omnipresent healing power in the universe.

How might we understand God's response to hatred and violence? Where is God in the lives of those who lose loved ones or barely escape losing themselves and loved ones to racialized hate crime, lynching, rape as a form of hate crime, acts of terrorism, war, and other types of violent sin? To consider God's response, I briefly examine the "immanent Trinity"–who God is in relation to God's dynamic self in three distinct persons as "agents," or better, "relations." I consider the divine dance–God's dance within the divine community. Then I attend to the problem of fallenness to another kind of dance–the dance of sin, woundedness, and suffering. Third, I return to the Trinity, specifically the *economic* Trinity–the relation of divine community to the broken yet intrinsically interrelated creation-community we humans call "the world." I specifically attend to the work of Christ and the Holy Spirit in the healing dance of the Trinity. I endeavor to offer a Trinitarian analysis of the problem of evil and the divine promise for healing, as I base my analysis in an understanding of divine community–God as the Trinity. Finally, while some in the guild are still inclined to assume that womanist theology is "really ethics," womanist theology *is theology* as theology was understood until very recently. Not until the modern period, with its artificial and excluding categorizations of creation, people, and thought were theology and ethics separated into exclusionary disciplines. One of the gifts of earlier historical theology is that it was more interdisciplinary than much of theology in the modern era. As modernity ends to enter a new creation, with all the gifts and problems that are emerging with it, we are aware that earlier theologians were more correct about taking a multidisciplinary approach to the study of God than the modern world knew. Theology is about the source of all life, is concerned with that source and all life it creates, and therefore theology is necessarily interdisciplinary.

My work is always about what God does in creation and in the midst of all peoples. Without God who loves us into loving God, there is no hope for this world. Therefore, I write about God's persuasive, inviting, ever-present, loving activity. It is about the grace of divine community and the call to all creation to receive restoration to communion with God. It is about the loveliness and beauty of the dance of God in the midst of this "ball of confusion." It is about God's love and compassion for this earth with all its creatures and for us human creatures with our beautiful and ugly ways.

In Christ,
Karen Baker-Fletcher,
Dallas 2006

Introduction

At least since the story of Job in the Hebrew Bible, people of faith have dared to ask God for an explanation for the presence of evil and suffering in human experience. Victims of war, terrorism, hurricanes, holocausts, tsunamis, rape, hate crimes, and other forms of extreme violence require a faith that is filled with courage. Stella and James Byrd Sr., whose son was lynched by dragging in 1998, and the mother of Emmett Till, Mamie Till-Mobley, suggest that such faith comes from a power greater than the individual human spirit.

In the presence of extreme violence, faith is sorely tested. When faith survives and thrives to the point of being a source of healing for others, it manifests itself as a form of courage. If all that is created comes from God, then courage must come from God. But how does one attain this courage in a world of violated relationships? If the courage to confront the complexities of existence in its beauty and its ugliness is found in the dance, pulse, touch, heart, and breath of God, then who is God? In a world of crucifixion, how might human creatures find courage to receive the promise of healed, whole relationships with one another, the rest of creation, and with God? *Dancing With God* offers integrative and relational reflection on Christian intercultural worldviews and on divine response to unnecessary violence across regional, national, global, cultural, ethnic, gender, ecological, ability/disability, and other bounds that human beings use as excuses to harm others.

Academic, Literary, and Pastoral Influences

Dancing With God is influenced by a diversity of theologians. It engages some of the contributions of Whiteheadian and Hartshornian process theism, the more traditional open and relational Wesleyan Christian understanding of Thomas J. Oord, the womanist theology and ethics of Delores Williams, Joanne Terrell, Katie Cannon, and Emilie Townes, as well as Korean understandings of suffering and woundedness among the sinned against in the theologies of Andrew Sung Park and Chung Hyun Kyung.[1] When I published *Sisters of Dust, Sisters of Spirit* in 1998,[2] I began developing a more relational and integrative understanding of God. Initially process theologians wanted to claim me, including me as an intuitive Whiteheadian and encouraging me to read the writings of Alfred North Whitehead and Charles Hartshorne. Process theist colleagues and mentors hope that I will declare myself as either Whiteheadian or Hartshornian. They have warmly welcomed me in their conversations

Given my own Wesleyan, biblical, traditional, and Trinitarian emphases, the integrative and relational approach I employ has most in common with the work of Thomas Jay Oord, not simply in its engagement with process theism, but also in its conserving of historical Christian theological claims. Oord is an evangelical relational theist who engages in dialogue with Whiteheadian process metaphysics. He lists five affirmations found in global evangelical theology: (1) "The Bible is principally authoritative for matters pertaining to salvation"; (2) "a conversion from sin, made possible by Jesus Christ, is necessary for full salvation"; (3) "Christians should be active in the midst of a decadent culture, attempting to evangelize and transform it"; (4) "Christian formation (labeled variously as 'Christian spirituality,' 'holiness,' 'discipleship,' 'Christian morality,' 'growth in Christ,' etc.) is indispensable to the Christian life"; (5) God is perfect in love, almighty, without beginning or end, one (although Trinitarian), personal, free, omniscient, the Creator and Sustainer, both transcendent and immanent in relation to the world, the ground of hope for the final victory of good over evil, and the proper object of worship.[3]

As for the authority of scripture, not all process theists employ scripture as the primary source of authority. It is possible to do so, and nothing in process metaphysics would prevent it. Regarding conversion through Jesus Christ, Oord observes that Whiteheadian metaphysics is more inclusive of a diversity of religious possibilities, yet "Evangelicals in the Wesleyan theological tradition have typically affirmed that God's prevenient grace provides a measure of light for salvation to all peoples."[4] Regarding Oord's discussion of the third affirmation of personal and social evangelism, it is important to examine distinctive understandings of this holy work in African American Christianity and culture. Oord observes that process theists tend to be liberal on issues of sexual orientation and abortion while evangelicals tend to be politically conservative. These categories of liberal and conservative do not always fit African American Christian thought with its distinctive attention to both personal and social salvation, its inspiration by cultural emphasis on "the Spirit" and charismatic/Pentecostal influences, and its cultural, both/and appreciation for the presence of the Spirit in secular and sacred spheres as well. Historically, Black bodies suffered sexual abuses during slavery and segregation and continue to suffer from the media's ongoing stereotypes of Black sexuality as pathological. This history makes African Americans feel suspicious when Euro Americans make sexuality a political issue. This holds true for all African Americans regardless of varieties of African American individual and collective stances regarding sexual orientation and abortion. Some are "conservative," some "liberal," and some are just loving everybody regardless and leaving such matters in God's hands with the understanding that God is greater and more loving than human creatures about why people are different from one another in any area of their lives.

My own position is the latter. Our first task as Christians is to love God with all of our heart, strength, mind, and soul. The second is related to the first–to love our neighbors as ourselves, regardless of whether or not we fully understand why human beings are so very different from one another. We've all been pulled out of all kinds of ditches by the good Samaritans of our time–those we were taught to question, avoid, view as profane, scorn, look down on, feel uncomfortable with, or even hate. Like the lawyer who questions Jesus about who his neighbor is, such events lead us to stop judging the people society has taught us to judge and to prayerfully examine our own capacity to participate in divine love toward the least of these instead (Lk. 10:25–37; Mt. 25:31–46).

African American Christians tend to give greater attention to social-historical problems of racism, sexism, and classism. While some African Americans have taken the position of Euro-American evangelical Republicans on the issues of gay marriage and abortion, the majority are still keenly disappointed in the failure of Republicans *and* Democrats to commit fully to economic, gender, and racial liberation. Like many other American Christians who are in the middle of debates between "left" and "right" Americans, African Americans resent the superficial use of religion as a Machiavellian "divide and conquer" ploy to emotionally bait American voters.[5]

Oord observes that it is around the fifth area that we find the most mutual criticism in process theist and evangelical theist dialogue. Indeed the type of integrative, relational theology I am proposing *conserves* orthodox and evangelical understandings of divine omnipotence and omniscience. I do, however, define these terms in a relational and integrative understanding in light of process theistic understandings. I employ the terms "conserve" and "conserving" in this work rather than "conservative" intentionally.[6] The term conservative has been co-opted in popular culture to signify an oppositional political stance. Likewise, the term "liberal" has been co-opted to signify an oppositional political stance. The term "moderate," for many, has come to indicate little more than indecisive compromise, having lost its deepest biblical meaning of balance or "moderation in all things." Therefore, I find that in our present cultural climate, none of these terms is helpful for describing the work at hand, because they simply lead to division and confusion. The term "moderate" in its biblical sense, however, is the one I find most fitting.

Oord employs process theism while also respecting the Wesleyan and biblical witnesses. I employ the term "conserving" in relation to Oord's work and my own to refer to a type of theology that maintains key influential tenets in Christian doctrine: resurrection, healing, effective prayer, Trinitarian understanding of God, and the primacy of scripture. Process theism does allow for such "conserving." Contrary to popular misunderstanding, Whiteheadian metaphysics, in particular, is very clear that conserving past influences is key to present and future becoming as each entity, which is both a society and an individual, selectively integrates past influences into its becoming. "Open and relational theology," however, conserves more elements from past Christian traditions and biblical texts than some Whiteheadians can philosophically accept. Our theology, like "open and relational theology," is more comfortable with greater levels of mystery and tolerates the discomfort that comes from having fewer scientific answers better, perhaps, than some Whiteheadians.

Moreover, while the present theology has common interest and some overlap with Clark Pinnock's "open theism," it revises and maintains the omniscience of God in a way that is, in the author's intention at least, more in keeping with traditional understandings.[7]

John Wesley wrote that "Seeing our ideas are not innate, but must all originally come from our senses, it is certainly necessary that you have senses capable of discerning objects…not those only which are called 'natural senses', which in this respect profit nothing, as being altogether incapable of discerning objects of a spiritual kind, but spiritual senses, exercised to discern spiritual good and evil." Moreover, for Wesley we are born with this spiritual sense.[8]

Integrating John Wesley's understanding of a "spiritual sense" of the divine with Whiteheadian findings regarding evidence of internal experience of the divine in all creation is very helpful. Therefore, whereas some evangelicals would like to throw out the baby with the bath water when it comes to Whitehead, it makes far more sense to consider what Whiteheadian physics and metaphysics have to offer regarding internal feeling and experience of God in all creatures. It is rather exciting that science and scripture agree on this point. As for Wesley's theological influence, I do not explicitly discuss Wesleyan thought here, but it is part of the background that has shaped my theology given that I am a Wesleyan Christian, with a Trinitarian understanding that has much in common with nineteenth-century Wesleyan, holiness women like Zilpha Elaw, Jarena Lee, Julia Foote, and Phoebe Palmer.[9] It is important to be open to the mystery of divine revelation that we Christians have inherited from the past and that continues in the present. This conserves the revelational influences of the past and ongoing divine revelation in our present. At the same time, there is an openness to engaging theology with postmodern science, along with particular insights of postmodern metaphysics in its understanding that God is certainly and literally relational. Moreover, there is an eye to the future and to the possibilities available in God that we have not yet experienced.

While I greatly appreciate process theists' attention to Whiteheadian, Einsteinian, and quantum physics, I have come to the conclusion that I am too committed to Christian orthodoxy to become an orthodox Whiteheadian or Hartshornian. The type of theology I propose here may be closer to open theism. This theology is orthodox neither in relation to process-relational theism, nor in relation to open theism. I use the term "orthodox" in reference to a certain type of process theist argument that is critical of orthodox Christianity. Classical process metaphysicians have developed their own sense of right doctrine based on Whitehead's work. As Suchocki puts it, there are "classical" and "modified" Whiteheadians.[10] Strict Whiteheadians may find some of my orthodox Christian claims heretical in relation to the metaphysics of Alfred North Whitehead. This is intentional on my part.

The theology of *Dancing With God* is closest, in several respects, to what Oord calls "open and relational theology." God as Wesley describes God, Oord writes, "is worthy of awe." God for Oord "is the primary agent effecting those miracles Christians should legitimately consider authentic." Some are more especially revelatory of divine love than others. God persuades "gently and strongly," is "almighty, perfectly loving," and should not be considered "culpable for failing to prevent the genuine evils occasioned by essentially free creatures." While some might argue against Oord's "free will theism," Oord is Wesleyan and with Wesley emphasizes the role of divine grace in persuading or calling the lost to choose God over evil. For Pelagius, grace plays a far more dubious role and the human *will* is emphasized, leading to works righteousness and willfully practicing Christian discipline. For Wesley and Oord, grace makes it possible to live a Christian, spiritually disciplined life.[11]

My objective is simply to propose that God is relational and integrative, while also conserving key doctrines such as the Trinity and divine revelation. At this early juncture, I am only willing to say that I employ a type of relational and integrative approach that appreciates the findings of contemporary physics since Whitehead along with the witness of classical Christian tradition, scripture, and experience in the body of Christ that resonates with the biblical witness throughout the ages. The theology I propose is *a type of relational and integrative theology.*

In some respects what I propose shares common ground with the type of thought that Howard Thurman sought to develop in his lifetime, particularly in his book *The Search for Common Ground,* in which he weaves the nontheistic process insights of Henry Nelson Wieman into a theistic understanding of community living in unity, or what some call unity in diversity.[12] Alice Walker wrote a complimentary endorsement for the back of an anthology of Thurman's writings: "In those long midnight hours when morning seemed weeks, if not years, away, the words of Howard Thurman have kept watch from me."[13] Like Thurman and Walker, I feel that my own work is difficult to categorize into one school of thought or another. This is intentional on my part, because like Walker and Thurman, I am attracted to understandings of truth that appear in works of diverse authors and traditions. I have chosen to focus on a particular understanding of Christianity here, explicitly conserving key orthodox understandings, more so than either Thurman or Walker. Christianity is at the core of my spirituality. To pretend otherwise, would be deceptive. At the same time, I endeavor to write theology that clarifies what I find valuable in Christianity and implicitly what I find valuable in the works of others. If there is prevenient grace in God and if there is no place where we can flee from God's Spirit, then surely the Spirit has been instructing others around the world for thousands of years. Here I am implicitly cognizant of wisdom in other traditions. Clarifying where places of similarity and difference are, however, is not a central theme in this book. Where appropriate I have noted similarities and differences with this Christian theology and Walker's pagan spirituality, for example. I hope to give more explicit attention to such similarities and differences in a later work.

As a "womanist" or "Black feminist" theologian steeped in both United Methodist (Wesleyan) and charismatic evangelical interpretations of the Christian message, with all the gifts and weaknesses, of each of these traditions, I find it important to clarify that my theology is, first, Christian. Second, it is a type of relational and integrative theology. Third, it is a womanist approach to theology, with attention to the diverse human contexts of social-historical experience as an aspect of its theological method.

No one writes theology in a vacuum. We are influenced by the ideas of theologians and metaphysicians past and present. Theologians have a responsibility to acknowledge their predecessors, while also understanding that God beyond our words relativizes all that has been written about God, whether in the past and present work of thinkers who have influenced our own work or our own work. We each have to do our own work,[14] offering fresh insights and calling the church accountable to whatever matters of faith it may be neglecting in any given era. At the same time, we must continually recognize that any one theology is at best adequate, not perfect, in orienting us[15] into right relationship with God. God is present in our God-talk in an integrative, relational understanding. Yet God also exists beyond our words. Giving primacy to schools of thought or the people for which they are named easily leads to idolatry rather than to a focus on the God beyond human expression. Therefore, not only is God the One who humanizes us, if we claim that humanity comes from God, but also God relativizes all our human constructions of theology and the metaphysics we humans construct in which to ground our God-talk.[16]

Theology (*theos* and *logos*) most simply means words about God. Whether we employ sign language, speech, writings, sacred dance, or varieties of nonverbal symbols to communicate our understanding of God, we are employing "words," in a broad sense, to communicate the ineffable. We are employing some type of language system, which is a symbol system.[17] While a diversity of Christian theologians and writers throughout the Christian era have made important contributions to the field of theology, none is perfect, because only God in Christ in the power of the Holy Spirit is understood as perfect in the tradition of Christian faith.

Womanists have debated the meaning of the term *womanist* almost from its inception. For some others and for me, a "womanist" is a "black feminist," as defined in Alice Walker's original 1983 definition. Many, however, insist that "womanists" should and have moved beyond Walker's definition. Some others and I share the concern that none of us are strictly tied to Walker's early definition of 1983. However, as women scholars of religion who want to emphasize connection with global feminists and, in my case, also with "White American" feminists, we continue to define "womanist" as a "Black feminist" or "feminist of color."[18] Originally, I was drawn to Walker's term because of her overall concern for interrelationship with *all* people, male and female. Like many Christian womanists, I do not share Walker's pagan spirituality, but I do share some of her insights regarding the evidence for divine presence in the intelligent and relational design of the universe. God loves entire, interrelated communities, human and nonhuman.

This book is about the courageous love, grace, and healing available to all peoples and an entire earth. It is a book about God. Specifically, it is about God's courageous, gracious, relational, Trinitarian response to the unnecessary violence that affects the entire earth. It goes beyond an appreciation of Walker's definition of "womanist." As a Christian theology, it departs from Walker's pagan spirituality even as it embraces her understanding of God's omnipresent love of an entire universe. My sense of the American and global audience is that many Americans and persons in other nations are ready to move beyond the old racialized categories. While racism is real, race itself is a false category developed in the modern period. Racism is a very real problem based on the delusional thinking that some human beings are superior to others because of their color, physiognomy, hair texture, or continent of racial origin. Likewise, sexism, classism, tribalism, ethnocentrism, and nationalism are all based on delusional understandings of what it means to be human. To be human originates in God, because we earth creatures (*adam*) are created in God's likeness. Humanity as a virtue comes from God. Historically the delusional conclusion that the diversity of forms in which humankind is created means that some bear God's likeness more than others has led to hatred and violence. Through such alienation from one another, the rest of creation, and God, we humans have failed to realize our full humanity. We have failed to experience the richness of diversity among ourselves. We have failed to learn more about God from one another, especially as Christians in the modern era. Even in the twenty-first century, Sunday morning Christian worship is still the most segregated hour in the United States. There is even reluctance to learn from one another's theologies, appreciatively referencing Christian thinkers whose Christian thought and experience emerges from a culture that is different from one's own culture.

My own understanding is similar to that of scholar of religion and pastor Howard Thurman. I find a profound teaching in Thurman's saying that ""what is true in any religion is in the religion because it is true; it is not true because it is in the religion."[19] Thurman's saying is true for Christian theology. If there is truth in a theology, then it is present simply because it is true, not because it is in the theology. Whether or not we can find truth in a school of thought or particular theological construction is most important, not the school of thought or particular theological construction. Therefore, I find events of truth to draw on from a diversity of theological writings, rather than locate my work in a particular school of thought. The truth we Christians seek, beyond all our words and all of our labels, is found through unity in diversity. It is the common ground we all long for.[20] No one theology alone is capable of revealing this common ground. We require a diversity taken together, each with its distinctive gifts. Together, these various insights into Christian truth correct and inform one another. This is the gift of ecumenism.

The church, in its striving for unity with God and with one another as the body of Christ, develops a more adequate understanding of the whole of what is true about God through unity in diversity. This does not mean that all Christians will agree. The striving itself has integrity and value as we humans, with our finite minds, remain in fellowship with one another in our spiritual striving to know and understand God better. While this theology, like Thurman's writings, emerges in part from African American Christian experience, it is in relationship and in conversation with many people of faith. It is inspired in part by Thurman's commitments to The Church for the Fellowship of All Peoples in San Francisco in its intercultural emphases.[21] It is inflamed by the deep conviction that we Christians are called to be one, holy, Catholic Church.

God in Christ in the power of the Holy Spirit is all worthy of our spiritual striving to become the church–God's body in the world. Indeed, if, as Paul suggests, the entire creation waits for our salvation so that it too may be redeemed (Rom. 8:18–23), the entire creation awaits redemption into the body of Christ. Therefore, this book examines the nature of God in relation to creation and in response to the problem of hatred. Hatred leads to division and unnecessary violence. It is a destructive, nihilistic privation of goodness, healing, and right relationship. Hatred is the negative power of evil.

Dancing With God is about the grace and courage of God. It is about God's call to the world to overcome hatred and violence. It particularly examines how some survivors have experienced hatred and violence. Moreover, it examines their faith and spirituality, the grace and courage they have found in God. Turning to the writings and life of Zora Neale Hurston, Katie Cannon, in her early work, writes about an ethic of courage that African American women have employed in quiet grace and invisible dignity to overcome evil. She describes Black women's "unshouted courage" as "a virtue evolving from the forced responsibility of Black women" and as "the unacknowledged inner conviction that keeps one's appetite whet for freedom."[22] Here, I want to focus on such courage, considering what courage means for the body of Christ in its diversity. *Dancing With God* focuses on God as the source of that courage, because God is the source of all virtuous attributes. God calls the world to overcome evil and shares power with the world to realize such overcoming.

Social-historical Intellectual, and Spiritual Influences

As for the particular social-historical beginnings of this work, one of my earliest memories from childhood is Easter season in a Methodist Episcopal Central District (Negro) church. I remember the fans from the funeral home the ladies fanned and the children played with. I remember the white gloves and patent leather "Mary Jane" style shoes, white anklets with lace, and hair in satin ribbons. I remember the smells of girls with sprinkles of their mothers' talcum powder and the entire congregation's freshly done hair, ladies' perfumes, and men's shaving cream mixed with cologne. I remember the forsythia bushes that bloomed yellow each Easter season and the new green grass, just ripe for the first mowing of the year. I remember the joy of children with fantasies of the Easter Bunny, boys in suits from tan to black, the youngest in short pants, and girls in pastel dresses.

Beneath the joy of children I recall the curiosity and the questions that did not yet have words–the wonder of why there was a sadness that seemed to be more than mourning Jesus' dying on the cross. I detected a deep twilight tone that colored the sound of grown-up voices as they sang "Were You There When They Crucified My Lord" that made me feel that somehow they had been there, although they said that Jesus died almost two thousand years before they were born–in the Bible days, in ancient times. Even children could hear the very present sadness in their voices, for something they knew, something they'd seen, something they'd experienced. This was in the early 1960s. Schools were still segregated, even in the "North," the Midwestern town where I was born and raised, though I did not know it at that young age. As I grew older and learned at home and in school about slavery, segregation, and the civil rights movement being led by Martin Luther King, Jr., I came to understand the meaning of the tone.

The tone was about more than Jesus' crucifixion. It was about historical and immediate African American experience. It was about the experience of anyone who has ever lost a loved one to unnecessary violence throughout the ages. It was about global, national, communal, familial, and personal loss. It was about lands and bodies stolen, captured. It was about the horrors of homes and businesses burned to the ground. It was about the deaths of Nat Turner and John Brown. It was about lynching. It was about the assassinations of Medgar Evers, Malcolm X, James Chaney, Michael Schwerner, and Andy Goodman. The tone was there because of the assassination of John F. Kennedy. And later, in 1968, it was about the assassinations of Martin Luther King Jr. and Robert F. Kennedy.[23]

Only after I completed the manuscript for this book did one of my paternal aunts tell me that her father, my grandfather, fled from the South, to the Midwestern city we came to call home, to escape a lynching. His story is hushed in silence, so much so that we can only ponder the scars on his back. He has never told how he got them–the escaped lynching, an accident, or some other painful event. We only know that at some point, whether as a result of or after the escape from lynching, he speaks of "hoppin' a train and hobo'in" North, later sending for his wife and children. In the midst of his ambiguous version of the common story of African American migration from South to North lies the palpable anger at suffering in a world of crucifixion and his openly shouted proclamation that "Heaven and hell are right here on this earth!" Through osmosis as a child and later through research and study, it seems I, like many, have always understood lynching as a form of crucifixion and crucifixion as a form of lynching. It is something that you learn through the tone that silences your insides in curious awe seemingly from birth if you grew up in such an environment. Some get better in a world of crucifixion, while others get bitter. Therefore, this book is about dancing with God in a world of crucifixion. It moves from unnecessary violence and suffering to healing. To dance with the divine is to dance with courage. This book is inspired by the tone that laments and overcomes, a tone still heard in the voices of those who know global, national, communal, and familial loss in many Christian churches during Easter season. What is present in the tone is real pain and the courage to overcome. It begins with the joy of creation and moves to hate crime, lynching, and crucifixion. It ends with re-creation. It celebrates God's dynamic, relational, courageous activity throughout.

Overview of Chapters

Chapter 1 presents the theological task and methods of this work, with attention to epistemology, relational and womanist emphases on experience as knowledge, liberationist attention to praxis, theological language as symbolic with metaphor as a type of symbol, and the roles of scripture, tradition, experience, and reason in theological construction. It raises questions regarding dualistic understandings of reason and experience to emphasize an integrative understanding of knowledge that embraces internal as well as external experience. It also introduces the metaphor and activity of dance for describing dynamic, integrative, relational divine activity and divine response to the world in a Trinitarian theology.

Chapter 2 emphasizes that the context for theology is God, who is omnipresent in the many particular existential contexts that are also part of creaturely life. It further considers dance as a metaphor for divine activity in the world in relation to the performance art of Vanessa Baker and a world whose identity is in a process of ongoing change. It describes this world as finding its ultimate identity in the divine context, which is everlastingly and constantly responsive to every situation, whether we name particular existential contexts postmodern, postcolonial, or by some other name. Moreover, this chapter considers the dance of divine, creative, loving, and just response to the world with the world's existential dance between the goodness of creativity found in divine love and the evil of destructive devolutions into unnecessary violence. This chapter also defines what is meant by "unnecessary violence."

Chapter 3 explores the dance of the Trinity in relation to creation. It considers God-language and introduces God as Provider/Nurturer. It begins with attention to the immanent Trinity– God's communal, creative, loving, and relational activity within the divine nature. It moves rather quickly to the economic Trinity and God's response to creation. Moreover, it considers the divine nature in relation to God's aim for creaturely entities, particularly human beings, to reflect God's communal nature, love, justice, and creativity.

Chapter 4 asks, "Why evil and suffering?" and draws on Marjorie Suchocki's understanding of "the fall to violence" in relation to the unnecessary violence found in the First Testament story of Cain and Abel. It attends to the problem of sin as violation of another creature and of God who feels with the earth, which cries out.

Chapter 5 begins to explore the praxis of sin in relation to the problem of what Korean theologians call *han* and what African Americans have called the blues, which is the experience of the sinned against. Andrew Sung Park refers to this as "the other side of the cross." It considers several different types of unnecessary violence and focuses on hate crime, particularly the dragging of James Byrd Jr. in 1998 as an illustration of cycles of sin, *han,* and the blues. This chapter finds that what author Joyce King calls hate crime is what Park calls an *aggressive form of han* in contrast to Byrd's *passive, bluesy form of han,* which Byrd expressed in his music. It focuses on the *han* or blues resolution journey of the Byrd family, who instead of responding in *aggressive han* toward King and his abettors, committed their lives to racial healing with many others from the Jasper community and nationally.

Chapter 6 is about the nature and ministry of Jesus, Mary as the mother of God, Jesus' crucifixion, a critique of the notion of "redemptive suffering," and the power of overcoming evil revealed in Christ's resurrection. This chapter examines Christ as the Word/Wisdom of God, classical conceptions of Christ's nature, and the significance of experiences of Jesus. In this chapter, we also consider what Christ contributes to our understanding of theodicy, particularly with reference to African American writers past and present who question whether or not Christianity is a viable religion. We consider what it means to live in the courage of Christ in a world of persecution, crucifixion, hatred, and evil. What does it mean to overcome evil when we are still living in a world of "crucifixion"?

Chapter 7 explores the resurrecting, encouraging Spirit of God and turns to the Holy Spirit as the divine and encouraging agent of the Trinity that empowers or strengthens the heart, making renewed life possible. It focuses on the Holy Spirit as the source of courage to find goodness in the land of the living, to renew and strengthen entire communities. It brings the understanding of divine love, creativity, and justice in this theology to some conclusions in relation to the metaphor of dance. It continues the theme of divinely inspired dance from earlier chapters as a metaphor for creative response to unnecessary violence. It focuses on the performance art of Vanessa Baker, particularly the choreopoem "Sacrificial Fruit" that she produced with Cheryl Swann. This particular dance is about Emmett Till, who was lynched while visiting relatives near Money, Mississippi, in 1955 and about his mother's defiant "No!" to modern crucifixion. It compares lynching to crucifixion, as did Mamie Till-Mobley, Vanessa Baker, and a number of poets in American religious history. This chapter begins a discussion of whether or nor suffering is redemptive or whether it is something to overcome.

PART I

Task, Method, and Context

An infant crying in the night,
An infant crying for the light,
And with no language–but a cry.

From Anna Julia Cooper (1858–1964),
"Our Raison D'être," *A Voice from the South*
(Xenia, Ohio: The Aldine Printing House, 1892)

I had fainted, unless I had believed to see the goodness of the Lord in the land of the living. Wait on the Lord: be of good courage, and [God] shall strengthen thine heart: wait, I say, on the Lord.

Psalm 27:13–14 (KJV)

CHAPTER 1

Renewing Our Minds

Theological Task, Method, and Sources

Violent death afflicts the global land, and the world is intent on perpetuating distortions of goodness. According to the sayings of Jesus, even the rocks cry out with no language other than a cry (Lk. 18:40; compare Hab. 2:11). In the midst of it we wonder about the who and where of God when the divine appears to be absent. And yet, something in the universe sustains life in the midst of evil and suffering when words and hope fail us. In 1892, Anna Julia Cooper published a brief essay entitled "Our Raison D'être" as a preface to her book, *A Voice from the South.* Eleven years later, W. E. B. DuBois would write about the cry of black folk in *The Souls of Black Folk*, quoting lyrics by Arthur Symons.[1] If the word *God* points to a truth that is real, then surely God as such relativizes all of our language about reality to naught but a cry.

The Death of Optimism

Today, we continue striving toward clearer articulation of God's activity in relation to freedom, not only in relation to humankind but also in relation to all of creation. However, we no longer live in a world in which one can assume the progress of civilization. Anna Cooper was optimistic that the world would become more civilized through the teachings of Jesus. The truth is that the world still struggles with good and evil in ways Cooper never could have imagined. Humankind has developed nuclear, biological, and chemical weaponry that could destroy the world in ways that were inconceivable during her time.

It is one thing to place hope in God who is in Jesus the Christ, quite another to place hope in "civilization's" openness to fully participate in divine love, creativity, and justice.[2] By the end of World War I, Cooper's social Darwinistic optimism began to give way to a Niebuhrian realism that responds to the problem of despair and disillusionment. Such realism flourished in the wake of World War II. More wars, poverty, assassinations, terrorism, hatred, and crime have left much of the world fighting not mere despair, but cynicism.[3] The world today is as concerned about devolution as much as evolution, patterns of nihilism as well as patterns of creativity. It is aware of the potential of destroying the earth as we know it by means of nuclear holocaust or ecocide. It is aware that freedom and wholeness have not been realized everywhere. It is a world in which racialized thinking, religious bigotry, gender oppression, child exploitation, and economic greed persist in presenting obstacles to physical, social, intellectual, and spiritual freedom.

Yet Cooper's attention to the cry of those whom Howard Thurman, in the twentieth century, called "the disinherited"[4] continues to point to a biblical truth. Where suffering, evil, hatred, unnecessary violence, and injustice exist, the entire earth "cries out" to God. As Cooper's title of her essay, *raison d'être* or "reason for being" implies, those who lament evil and suffering are not irrational. They are imbued with reason. This reason is integrated with *feeling*, which is the experience of reality. Such is the intelligence of the spirituals, the blues, jazz, and hip hop. Filled with the pathos of an infant's cry at times, it quickly moves beyond pure sound to articulate meaning in the midst of suffering and joy through its tonality, rhythms, and sometimes lyrics. Certain experiences of evil and of goodness reduce humanity to naught but a cry of lament or of joy. These cries continue to rise in the twenty-first century. Theology itself, in its discourse about the ineffable, is a cry for adequate understanding of God's response to the world, given the world's peculiar experiences of goodness and evil.

Method and Sources

Experience

A Christian integrative relational womanist theology begins with God. Christians find the God they worship in biblical and experiential revelation. More broadly, God's revelation is present in the experiences of scripture, tradition, and reason. Scripture, tradition, and reason are part of the human experience by which we come to understand divine omnipresence and transcendence through God in Christ, in the power of the Holy Spirit. Therefore, our starting point is Christian experience and the relationship of the body of Christ with God who is revealed in the Word/Wisdom of God. Scripture and the traditions within Christian tradition, are common shared sources in which the body of Christ experiences divine revelation.

Without scripture and tradition, the body of Christ, which is the church, is unable to consider and even debate (acts of reason) what we mean when we say we worship God who is revealed in Jesus or revealed in Jesus the Christ.

While some question the existence of God, theology presupposes that God exists. If God did not exist, then there would be no life–no universe of which to speak, no earth, no "sky," no atmosphere, no creatures, no weather to "shoot the breeze about." There would be no *ruach*, which means in Hebrew "breath," "wind," or "spirit." We would not be able to breathe and live without the very power of life, which is God. With each breath we take, we are experiencing the power of life. The word "God" is a symbol for the power of life, creativity, love, justice, goodness, and compassion. To speak of all these things is to speak of experiences of God, for it is God who makes lips, tongues, vocal chords, and bodies to even speak of such things. In God–the power of life and thus the power of relations–the concept and practice of courage are possible and may be realized. In finding courage for justice and life, we may hope in the concrete movement of God in every moment.

The scientific insights of Whiteheadian, Einsteinian and quantum physics contribute new analogical possibilities for understanding God's relationship to the world, while also maintaining understandings of God found in the religious experience of African American people of faith like Mamie Till-Mobley, James Cameron, the family of James Byrd Jr., Vanessa Baker, and classical Christian writers. This Christian integrative relational womanist theology highlights the experienced revelation of biblical writers, classical Christian theologians within the larger tradition, and experiences of God by writers and narrators from the recent past. Experience is key to understanding the divine-creature relationship, particularly as we understand that scripture, in its inspiration by the Holy Spirit, is also part of the religious experience of biblical writers.

We sometimes speak of tradition as if it were separate from experience. Experience, however, is a unifying relation of interlocking sources of tradition, scripture, and reason. Experience of God is found in tradition, experience, and reason. Tradition, which is part of the past, with its long history of experiences in the temporal world, involves the prehension or feeling of ongoing series of events. Tradition and the traditions within tradition are steeped in Christian historical experience. Their response to God emerges from a multiplicity of experiences, spanning not only years, but incremental moments and nanoseconds of time in physical space. Whenever we refer to past and present decisions, writings, liturgies, narratives, and theological treatises or when we refer to past and present situations of joy and suffering, healing and pain, goodness and evil, righteousness and sin, we are speaking of the experience of past and present persons.[5]

Likewise, language is steeped in experiences. Even the cry of infants is an expression of prelinguistic experience. Therefore, it is not helpful to argue that language precedes experience when language is a learned behavior for communicating experience. To do so leaves one bound to a worldview in which internal experience, as John Cobb argues, is ignored and neglected. One fails to see that creatures communicate experience of divine and existential reality not only in our words, but in sounds, moans, groans, sighs, smiles, frowns, ritual, and bodies. From birth, without words, we experience breath, earth, water, sun, earth, and air which sustain our bodily, animated lives and are part of God's beloved creation.[6]

God is omnipresent, literally inspiring each exhalation and inhalation of human experience. This is the meaning of prevenient grace, that grace which protects us not only from physical death, but also from spiritual death and the loss of our capacity to enjoy each breath we are gifted to take. God as an actual entity is distinctive from us. We are finite, created actual occasions, events, and drops of experience that live and perish with hope for everlastingness in the memory of God. God alone feels, that is, experientially knows, all entities in their entirety.[7]

Even without language, creation would continue to experience internal and external creative processes. Moreover, divine creativity continuously experiences the inner workings of creation because God, who is omnipresent in creation, responds to creation. God is present, and not far off, in our imaginative and constructive processes. There is no place where God is not present. Otherwise, incarnation is a sham, and Immanuel–God with us–a delusion. When words fail and hope falters, experience of the power of life remains because God is everlastingly responding to creation internally and externally. God is available, even when it may not seem like it, to strengthen the heart and keep it from fainting. God calls the world forward, beyond the immediacy of sheer survival into abundant life. Experiences of suffering, violence, crucifixion, and death make sense only in reference to a greater norm, which is the power that makes all life possible. In relation to the greater norm of the power of life, unnecessary violence, suffering, and death lose their claim to be normative.

Scripture reveals the experience of God as understood by the writers and by human beings that they write about. It also reveals much about biblical writers' understanding of divine revelation through creation and God's love for creation. Likewise, whether we examine classical Christian writers or traditions within "the tradition" throughout the Christian era, that tradition emerges from human experience of God, including the experience of scientific observation of the inner and outer workings of the cosmos. Therefore, when we appeal to scripture, tradition, and reason, we are appealing to experiences of God who is the ultimate knower. Moreover, we are always appealing to an integration of faith and reason. Indeed, according to New Testament literature, God renews both our minds and our hearts. Experience is the starting point for integrative relational theology. Scripture, tradition, and reason are all aspects of human experience. Reason is not separate from experience. Experience is a form of knowing. We human beings experience God through mind, body, and spirit. This is evident in scripture and tradition. God is intimately amongst us as Immanuel. Moreover, there is no hiding place from God (Ps. 139), because God is omnipresent. Yet, God is other, knowing the whole world in its fullness. God, therefore, transcends all creaturely knowing and experience. If God is omnipresent, then the world experiences God's presence prelinguistically and linguistically, preconsciously and consciously. The world consists of a multiplicity of entities, each one a society in its particular biological, atomic, subatomic makeup. No one entity or group of entities knows the fullness of the world as God knows it.

The Subject(s) of Dancing With God

General Understanding of the Subject(s) of Theology

God is not the object of our faith. God is the subject of our faith.[8] The tendency of human beings to objectify God and one another is an effect of separation, violation, conflict, and disharmony, which we human beings experience as "estrangement"[9] or sin. God is the subject of theology, because theology simply means "words about God" or "study of God." Theology also is a study of those whom God has created and those whom God–identified by Augustine as love–loves. The first among God's beloved is found in the immanent Trinity, in which we see God's love of God's own nature. As Augustine puts it, God as "Lover," loves the Son who is "Beloved." The Holy Spirit, who is love, unites these two.[10] All three love one another relationally, in the distinctiveness of their personalities. God is communitarian within God's own nature.[11] In the economic Trinity, which is God's revelation and response to the world, the world experiences and learns from God's love. The world experiences itself as beloved in Christ and in the power of the Holy Spirit. The world, then, also is a subject in theology, because not only is the Son God's own beloved, but creation, which the Trinity has created according to the laws of its own relational and integrative nature, is also beloved by God. The world, however, does not come into existence without divine creativity. Therefore, in this sense, the world is a secondary subject in relation to divine creativity. Indeed, the world as we know it is not everlasting, because it is temporal and finite. God, however, is everlasting, even as God creates a new heaven and a new earth.

The Divine Subject

The subject of our study is exploration of the dynamically, dancing Trinity in relation to divine gifts of courage and grace in the face of evil. We will examine the source of the strength to "take heart" in the midst of hatred and unnecessary violence, as Jesus en-courages or en-heartens[12] his followers prior to his arrest and crucifixion: "The hour is coming, indeed it has come, when you will be scattered, each one to his home, and you will leave me alone. Yet I am not alone because the Father is with me. I have said this to you, so that in me you may have peace. In the world you face persecution. But take courage; I have conquered [overcome] the world" (Jn. 16:32–33).

The theme of Christ's overcoming the world, specifically overcoming transgressions against divine and social justice in the world, became a key theme in the civil rights movement of 1950–1968 in the United States. Today, we still need the courage in Christ that is implied in all Christian inspired themes of overcoming. Moreover, it is important to understand the role of the Holy Spirit as the power of encouragement in Christ. Therefore, the subject of "dancing with God" is the Trinity, because if we emphasize only God in Christ, we cannot understand the full power of God to heal and transform the world. Prior to statements regarding "overcoming the world," the author of John writes that in speaking of the world's hatred of truth, Jesus promises to send his disciples an advocate, the Spirit of truth, who is the Holy Spirit (Jn. 14:16,26; 15:26; 16:7–15). A dipolar theology will not suffice, if we presuppose it is true that God in Christ promises to send God's Spirit of truth to his disciples and if we presuppose that this promise is realized according to the story of Pentecost in the book of Acts (Acts 2:1–423). A dipolar theology cannot adequately lead us into conscious, full relationship with God who is in Christ, because Christ reveals God the Father–who in a feminist or womanist view may be understood as God the Parent, –and God the Holy Spirit. When we talk about the source of the strength to "take heart" or "to be of good courage," we are talking about God, who is three dynamic relations (hypostases) in one nature.

The Creaturely Subject(s) of Theology

Not only does God love God in three hypostases (relations), but God also loves creation. Theologians examine what God loves–not only the divine community, but also the creaturely community which God has created and recreates moment by moment, day by day. Creation has many problems from the effects of sin and evil. Creation experiences divine love and joy, but creation also experiences much suffering, because of sin and evil. For this reason, Jesus the Christ promises to send an advocate and comforter in the divine relation of the Holy Spirit, which is the Spirit of truth, comfort, healing, and empowerment. If the Holy Spirit is unifying Love, then this is a very strong love indeed. Love has the ability and capacity to strengthen the human heart and advocate for the redemption of all creation. Katie Cannon, in her early groundbreaking work emphasizes an ethic of courage as she writes about womanist courage. Specifically, she turns to the life and writings of Zora Neale Hurston, a black female Harlem

Renaissance anthropologist and novelist, for an example of black women's "'unshouted courage.'" She affirms Alice Walker's observation that one "must struggle every minute of life to affirm black peoples' right to a healthy existence." Cannon observes, "This idea concurs with the understanding of courage in Paul Tillich's work...that courage is an ethical act when humans affirm their own being in spite of those elements in their existence which conflict with their essential self-affirmation." We need to take Cannon's observation seriously. In a world of crucifixion, theologians must recover the gift of God's courage in a whisper and a shout. Its presence is everlastingly available to the wounded, resurrecting the pressed down life of all who experience the other side of the cross where humankind experiences the tragic, existential reality of being sinned against. We require the courage and grace that is available to us to overcome evil, hatred, and suffering. Without courage, in an empowering whisper of the Spirit or shouted in the church, it is not possible to overcome evil.

The Task of Theology

The subject of our study is related to the task of theology. The task of theology is to understand the God of our faith. In other words, the task of theology is to seek understanding of the ultimate source of courage and grace, God. When we speak of "courage," we are speaking of matters of the heart, specifically strength of heart. If God is the source of our strength, indeed the "strength of life," then when we speak about divine courage we are speaking of the strong heart of God. According to John 16:33, Jesus told his disciples to "be of good courage, for I have overcome the world." In this Johannine account, Jesus the Christ has informed his disciples that he will soon go away, a foreshadowing of his coming crucifixion. Yet Christ has overcome the troubles of the world, a statement that suggests the promise of his resurrection and victory over death. "Be of good courage" is in some translations interpreted as "take heart" (NLT). Courage has to do with the condition of the heart. The disciples are asked to be of strong heart in times of coming trouble. Times of trouble are ripe for experiences of existential angst.

As Paul Tillich observed, however, grace makes courage possible when meaning seems lost. He wrote about courage and existential angst in response to a post-world war context. He had served as an army chaplain in World War I and had witnessed the early anti-Semitic pronouncements of Nazi socialism in Germany with its resulting death camps and holocaust. He wrote of the existential angst that emerges when evil has shattered meaning. Our world, like Tillich's, is still ridden with wars and rumors of wars. However, it is also different in certain respects. Viewing this planet as "a big blue marble" concretely relativizes our sense of earth in relation to a larger universe. The world has experienced the fall of colonialism, the rise of neo-colonialism, and the emergence of post-colonial movements. It has witnessed the nuclear disarmament movement, the fall of the Berlin Wall, and the end of the Cold War. Hate crimes, rapes, war crimes, and other crimes against humanity, however, have not ceased.

The Newtonian science that grounds Tillich's writing leaves him with a God who is not very powerful or transformative in everyday life. Tillich leaves readers dependent on a God who, as the Ground of Being, inexplicably grasps human beings from some mysterious depth. Why believe in God or freedom at all if human beings have so little freedom to respond to the divine call that it is only through being "grasped by the ground of being" that one has hope for salvation? Tillich's particular understanding of divine grace leaves little room for a relationship dynamic of call and response in the divine/human relationship. In a relational and integrative understanding of God that is more Wesleyan than Lutheran, human beings have more freedom to respond to the divine call, choosing to receive the grace of salvation. As John Cobb suggests, to be so utterly bound by estrangement–Tillich's definition of sin–leaves humankind bound by past events.[13] The past utterly determines us aside from rare moments of divine intervention. Therefore, a Christian, relational, integrative, and womanist theology borrows one of the insights of process metaphysics to observe that the freedom present in the physical world indicates selectivity or choice. Therefore, if the physical world as God's creation reveals something of God's nature, then God must share power or there can be no freedom in the universe. God, then, is not coercive, but persuasive. God shares power with the world, providing freedom to participate fully in divine creativity or not. At the same time, Tillich's attention to courage and grace is an important contribution. Tillich emphasizes the grace that empowers humankind to have courage, which makes it possible to overcome evil. We still have much to learn from this Lutheran insight.

Faith and the Task of Theology

In the twelfth century, Anselm of Canterbury (1033–1109 C.E.) defined theology as faith seeking understanding.[14] The task of theology is to seek understanding of God for our time in response to the existential questions raised in our present historical moment. On the one hand, these questions are novel in that they emerge from a context in which we have seen our planet from space and in which our more advanced technology affects others in ways that are increasingly harmful or healing. At the same time, however, our questions are perennial. Who is God?

Moreover, how can God help us overcome the existential problems of hatred and violence with love and healing? The primary task of theology as faith seeking understanding for our time is faith seeking understanding in response to the divine call to overcome hatred and violence. The task of theology, then, is an organic intellectual task.[15] As womanist and liberation theologians have emphasized, faith seeking understanding integrates practice with theory to form the praxis of mature persons of faith. It is significant for the everyday and ongoing life of the church, past, present, and to come. Moreover, it is significant for the larger societies around the world and across the centuries.

Faith seeking understanding involves *spiritual striving* toward meaning and wholeness in historical existence, in which the world everywhere and simultaneously experiences events of tragedy and joy. In its reconstructive aspect, this task involves bringing forth neglected language about God and understandings of God in scripture. Moreover, it involves recovering neglected articulations of faith from the traditions that are part of Christian tradition, including Christian symbolism for the sacred in dance, poetry, storytelling, and liturgy. Theology as faith seeking understanding includes the courage to ask questions about God. As Tillich observes, faith includes courage and doubt.[16] Faith has room for Job's questions to God about existential experiences of evil and suffering in the world. Faith, and the courage included in faith, are gifts of divine grace. To ask questions of God is to remain in relationship with God, which is faith. Faith seeking understanding might be understood as a form of "spiritual striving."[17] Asking questions in our spiritual striving is an act of courage and faith.

Tradition and the Task of Theology

Christian tradition with its canonical texts, extracanonical texts, liturgies, creeds, theological treatises, narratives, and testimonies from the time of the early church to the present is a secondary source, not a primary one. Scripture is primary. Yet, we do not interpret scripture in a vacuum. We interpret it in relation to the many centuries-old tradition of the church and to the traditions of churches within the universal body of Christ. Today, one cannot assume that all theology is Christian. The contemporary world has many theologies from a diversity of religious traditions. Therefore, we must clarify that we are talking about Christian theology and that Christian theology is, by definition, Christ-centered, grounded in Christian tradition and biblical literature. Christians are those who come to know God through Jesus the Christ, the anointed one of God and promised messiah.[18] Christians believe that God is revealed in Christ. This is what makes the Christian tradition, in all of its historical and community diversity, distinctive. "Christian tradition" contains many traditions that inform and enrich one another.

Traditions within the tradition reveal strengths and weaknesses in various forms of social-historical practices and interpretations of scripture in the global body of Christ. Traditions within the tradition correct misinterpretation and abuses of scripture to call for more holistic, healing, and liberating understandings. During the time of slavery, for example, slave masters frequently preferred lessons for their slaves that emphasized Paul's injunction that "slaves be obedient to your masters" (as in Eph. 6:5–8 and Col. 3:22–25) while failing to question whether slavery of any kind was of God. North Atlantic slavery was dehumanizing and abusive, much like the slavery the Israelites endured for four hundred years in Egypt. Much of the African American Christian tradition resisted slavery-promoting distortions of the Christian message. It found instead the God of liberation in the book of Exodus, the liberating prophet Moses, and the liberating message of Jesus in Luke 4 and Matthew 25. The Christian tradition of many slaves and their descendants, then, became a separate, very distinctive tradition from the Christian tradition of most slave masters and many of their descendants. For several centuries, now, the liberating message of scripture that the slaves discerned has worked as a corrective to those who are tempted to distort biblical literature to promote self-serving aims through oppressing their neighbors. Moreover, this liberating tradition offers prophetic clarity regarding the humanity of all peoples, emphasizing that everyone is a neighbor, beloved by God, and ought to be loved as one's own self. Such conclusions, however, do not emerge from a vacuum. They emerge from understandings of scripture and from later creedal formulations, as well as from Christian experience. Moreover, such conclusions emerge from much thought about understandings of scripture and religious experience in the traditions that are part of the holy, catholic church in which we are many members of the body of Christ in One.

Testimony and other types of narrative in many African American, Hispanic, and other folk Christian churches form part of the living tradition of faith in which stories of God's work revealed in Christ abound. Systematic theologies, poetry, novels, and sermons by Christians from every culture are part of the tradition. Scripture, the primary source, however, serves as a test for discerning the authenticity and truth of all aspects of tradition. African American Christian tradition is distinctive. It offers particular contributions to the whole in its emphasis on the Holy Spirit and what it means to be "led by the Spirit." It interacts with the traditions of eighteenth- and nineteenth-century revival religion of the First and Second Great Awakenings in North American history, synthesizing African understandings of spiritual life with New World frontier Christian understandings.[19] The scope of this book is to consider the work of God in a world of crucifixion in general, with attention to the activity of the three relations or "persons" of the Trinity with emphasis on the Holy Spirit as "Encouraging Spirit" who empowers the liberating activity of dancing with God.

Tradition and Trinity

One aspect of tradition that postmodern, particularly process theist, thinkers debate is the Trinity. Some Whiteheadian process theologians like David Ray Griffin, Marjorie Hewitt Suchocki, Bernard J. Lee, and Joseph A. Bracken have developed Trinitarian arguments. Marjorie Suchocki, as a modified Whiteheadian, develops a relational doctrine of the Trinity in which the Holy Spirit is revealed in the consequent nature of God.[20] However, such revisions tend to leave us with an economic Trinity almost exclusively–God's response to the world–with insufficient understanding of who God is in response to God's internal relations. Many argue that the Trinity is not a biblical doctrine, but the author of Matthew indicates that Jesus implies a Trinitarian understanding of God. In his last instruction, Jesus commissions the apostles to practice a liturgy for baptism "in the name of the Father, the Son, and the Holy Spirit" (Mt. 28:19–20).

Like open theists, in contrast to orthodox process theism, our particular type of relational integrative theology is strongly Trinitarian. In orthodox Whiteheadian process theism, the argument is that God is more than three, because God is many. In orthodox Hartshornian process theism, God is the one who includes the many–"the all-inclusive one." At this point, the relational integrative theology I propose departs most sharply from orthodox process theism. Orthodox process theism has made tremendous contributions in demonstrating connections between science and religion as well as certain key connections between postmodern physics and biblical Christian faith. They have reminded the world that the God of Christian scripture, as well as the God of scripture in many religions around the world, is a relational God and that postmodern physics indicates that this must be true. When, however, orthodox process theism in effect dismisses matters of faith like bodily resurrection and the Trinity, I and many other Christians experience a parting of the ways. Modified Whiteheadians such as Marjorie Suchocki, who carefully define bodily resurrection in relation to Pauline biblical understandings in the New Testament and who make room for Trinitarian understandings, are more appealing. It is necessary to revise process theism's understanding of examining internal experience to include the internal experience of Christian writers and people of faith throughout the ages. If process metaphysics values internal experience, then who are we human beings to question the internal experience in the life of the ancient and contemporary church? Relational theology need not, indeed ought not, devalue the diversity of internal experiences of God as Father/Parent, Christ, and Holy Spirit throughout the ages.

Our more conservative integrative relational theology presupposes God as three relations or modes of being in one nature. It respects this Christian tradition, based on the liturgical last commission New Testament scripture attributes to Jesus the Christ. While it makes sense to argue that such scripture does not develop the full-blown doctrine of Trinity, which the tradition has developed, this book claims that we have no reason not to think of God in at least three relations to name three primary experiences of God's relationship to the world. Therefore, it fleshes out the meaning of the traditional names "Father, Son, and Holy Spirit" or "Holy Ghost." Historically, the Greek Eastern Orthodox tradition speaks of "the dance of the Trinity" or *perichoresis*–the way in which God relates dynamically within

God's self as the immanent Trinity. "Dance" names this divine, creative, compassionate "whirlwind." Our theology considers the dance of the Trinity metaphorically as a way of describing the dynamic relational nature of divine creativity. It also reflects on sacred dance as a concrete tool for healing. It examines this dynamic movement in the lives of literal artists, dancers, and poets.

Scripture and Tradition

Christians learn of Christ through the hearing and reading of the gospel. Scripture, like tradition, is a source to which Christians turn for wisdom regarding praxis. In fact, scripture is the primary source for Christian theology. As Karl Barth reminded the false church of Hitler in response to Nazism in Germany in the early and mid-twentieth century, the church is not the church if it is not grounded in Christ as revealed in scripture.[21] Christian faith and its theology are centered in the concept and reality of Christ. Barth's most important contribution to the understanding of Christian theology is that this Word, who is Jesus the Christ and the Son of God according to the Fourth Gospel, is revealed in the words of scripture.[22] Barth's Word-centeredness or Logo-centrism as the distinctive marker of Christian faith provides one of the strongest definitions of Christian theology and its task that is available. He provides a clear definition of what makes a body of believers in God Christian and what makes the theology that responds to the witness of those believers and its scriptural moorings Christian.[23]

Christian theology is centered in an understanding of God revealed in Jesus the Christ, the Word or divine Logos. Christians believe that the truth of the nature of God in Christ and what it means to follow God in Christ are revealed in scripture. The New Testament part of the Christian canon includes the synoptic gospels[24] (Matthew, Mark, and Luke) as well as the Fourth Gospel–the gospel of John–and the letters attributed to Paul and other followers of Christ. Luke 4 portrays Jesus as proclaiming that he has been sent to preach the good news to the poor, to release the captives, to heal the sick, and "to proclaim the acceptable year of the Lord." These four gospels present the story of Jesus, variously portraying Jesus as preaching good news to the poor (Luke), healing and performing miracles (all four gospels), and as the living Word or *Logos* of God (John).

It is important to emphasize that biblical literature is not subordinate to philosophy in Christian theology. For Christians, God is revealed in the scriptures of the First and New Testament. These scriptures are a collection of texts that offer accounts of human experiences of God. Such writings provide information of past experiences and understandings of God's revelation of God's self to human understanding.

Is scripture a primary source of authority?[25] Is it written by humans or inspired by God? Yes, scripture is a primary source of authority inspired by God. As Donald Dayton suggests, scripture is the "norming norm" of Christian faith, but it is also written by human beings in particular cultural contexts.[26] These human writers were inspired by the Holy Spirit to relate their understandings of divine revelation. The Holy Spirit continues to guide and teach human beings in the interpretation of scripture. Human beings, past and present, are also influenced by their culture. God is God, transcending scripture, yet inspiring it. Augustine, in his discussion of scripture, speaks of literal and figurative interpretations of scripture. He understood it to be inspired by God and written by men in literal and figurative language to describe the ineffable.[27] This work represents a classical view, then, and not a new one at all.

Scripture is authoritative and inerrant in the sense that it is a witness to the infinite and inerrant nature of God and to the finite and fallible nature of human beings. Scripture witnesses to God who is Truth. The culture of the biblical writers influenced their understanding of what they were inspired by God's omnipresence in their lives to write. Even biblical literalists of the present era must admit that only in the most strict Holiness, Catholic, and Orthodox churches, for example, do church leaders require women to cover their heads. Both testaments are inerrant in their intent, as witnesses to divine Truth. Scripture is also a witness to human sin, hatred, and violence. We who interpret scripture are fallible. Many have used biblical texts to rationalize their own errant desires and lust for power, sometimes fully convinced they were following God. Yet, others have more rightly interpreted its authoritative guidance for authentic participation in divine goodness. Biblical literature is as much about human imperfection, sin, and preferred *cultural practices* as it is about divine power, goodness, righteousness, love, relationship, and justice.[28]

The revisionist theologian Schubert Ogden considered the meaning of the gospel for a scientific age, correlating the apostolic witness of Paul on freedom with the words about love attributed to "Jesus who is said to be Christ."[29] That human beings write scripture does not mean that it is so utterly relativized by God or diminished by cultural contexts that it is an inadequate starting point for theology. God is not so utterly transcendent that biblical literature is strictly a human activity. God, who is omnipresent, is present in that activity and, therefore, logically revealed in it. The apostolic witness, then, becomes central to understandings of the nature of God who is said to be Christ among those who claim to represent Christ.

Without scripture, communities of faith have no common understanding of God's revelation in the world. Without the New Testament with its account of Jesus the Christ, it is impossible for "Christian" communities of faith to discern what it means to follow God revealed in Christ. There is no common text for comprehending what one means by "God who is revealed in Jesus the Christ." Without Christ, there is no church, no body of Christ. Human beings write scripture, yes, but the breath of God, which lives and breathes consciously in those who love God, inspires it. This breath of

God also lives consciously and unconsciously in those who do not know how to love God. Other forms of God-talk (the creeds, texts by Christian writers) reveal the divine presence when they are consistent with the divine initial aim revealed in the gospel of Jesus Christ. The criteria of discernment, is, as Karl Barth suggested, not only a matter of proclamation but of witness. Does the community of faith witness to the Word of God revealed in scripture, which is the word of love, faith, and freedom?

Reason and Science and the Task of Theology

Reason is another authoritative source for an adequate theological construction. Reason is necessary for reflection on scripture, tradition, and experience. Without reason we fail to adequately communicate experience of God to one another, and we cannot adequately interpret scripture. Theology is not *merely* a human imaginative constructive task. God is not absent in our symbolizing activity. Nor can we understand Christian tradition and the traditions within that tradition without reason. "Faith seeking understanding" inherently involves the use of reason. What, however, do we mean by reason?

Reason and Feeling

Reason is not separate from feeling, which is experiential knowledge or knowing. Without reason, we cannot claim to understand God. Indeed, without reason we cannot speak of understanding knowledge itself. Ultimate knowledge is found in God. If God exists, and we are presupposing that God exists, then our ability to know anything comes from God. Moreover, in integrative relational theology divine reason is not separate from divine feeling and experience. To know is to experience. God experiences God's own nature, and God experiences the world. In this sense God knows, "prehends," or "feels" God's own nature as well as the suffering and joy in the world.[30] Some would argue that this understanding would violate the orthodox position that God is *impassible*–that we humans cannot affect God in our sin or in our processes of sanctification. Yet, classical thinkers merely wanted to emphasize that creatures cannot control God, who is their creator. They were not saying that God is insensitive. Indeed, in biblical literature and in early Christian writings, God is compassionate, meaning that God is passionate with God's creatures. God, then, is empathetic,[31] which means it is possible for God to be merciful, forgiving, to hear the cries of the earth, and to be grieved in God's Holy Spirit when we commit sin through violating God's intention for right relationship with God, one another, and the rest of creation.

Omniscience and Freedom

In classical theism, God is "omnipotent, omniscient, impassible, and immutable." In other words, classical theists understand God as "all powerful, all knowing, unaffected by the world, and unchangeable." In understanding that God is omniscient, classical theists presuppose God's omnipotence, impassibility, and immutability. As all powerful, God knows all things and predestines some for salvation if we turn to Augustine, for example.[32] The early church theologians, particularly Augustine, were not clear as to whether or not God predestines some for damnation. Calvin's doctrine of double predestination develops such an understanding, whereas Wesley a century later is open-ended in his understanding of divine omnipotence, omniscience, and human freedom to choose salvation or not. A perennial question for Christian theologians throughout the centuries is, "If God is omnipotent and omniscient, then what does this mean for human salvation and freedom?"

For process theists who strictly adhere to Whiteheadian physics and metaphysics, God knows all possibilities but not the final decisions of and outcome for each individual. Otherwise, it does not make sense to speak of the freedom of human creatures, and evangelism does not make sense, because humans have no freedom to choose God or evil. God has made the decision for us in advance. In orthodox process theism, God does not know which possibilities entities will choose or reject in their free becoming. God does not predetermine who will receive salvation and who will choose evil and damnation. In this view, God knows all possible outcomes of all possible choices but not the choices we will make. Therefore, God does not know the final outcome in advance. This makes some sense, but it is not adequate for an integrative relational theology that conserves the contributions of early orthodox Christians whose liturgical understanding, religious experience, and reasoning suggest otherwise. If God experiences the world, then God has awareness not only of all possibilities but has experiential knowledge of all probabilities as well.

Freedom does not exist if God decides for us whether or not we receive salvation, healing, and wholeness. Yet, in the sense that God knows all possibilities and probabilities, then God knows the final outcome of each possibility and probability. In this sense, one can argue that God is omniscient. God is all knowing, because God knows that which we cannot foresee even as we make discreet decisions about our becoming. God knows all possible outcomes of each discreet decision, in each moment and micro-second of time. This is more than process theism generally grants. One might also conserve the classical claim that God is omniscient and omnipotent, because all probabilities are in God.

Omniscience and Mutability

Does God change? Specifically, does God "change God's mind"? Some conservative Christians argue against process-relational theology that "God does not change." In process-relational theology, God changes. Critics mistakenly associate this understanding exclusively with Heraclitus, insisting that it is not a biblical concept. Actually, it is a biblical concept. With other evangelicals, I often praise God for God's increasing glory. Divine glory cannot increase unless God's glory is always growing. I have often wished that process theologians would simply clarify that "change" is a synonym for growth. In the economic Trinity, individuals in community experience the increasing glory of God's reign through Christ. One might understand this as creaturely perception of change in God, because creatures experience God's glory as expanding. Perhaps it does increase or expand, but in the end God alone can know whether or not this is true. Human beings can only say that this is true of our experience. For example, in John 3:30, Jesus says of God that "God must increase, but I must decrease." Isaiah 9:7 says of the messiah's government that of its increase "there shall be no end" (KJV). This suggests the glory of God's reign increases, or grows, eternally. The term "increase" means to multiply or enlarge. God's reign or realm is always multiplying and enlarging, because God is always creating. This increases the glory of God. In this sense, God changes and is worthy of praise. To the extent that God responds to each situation, creating each moment and day anew, God changes, because with each divine act the glory of God increases. Yet, that God creates, loves, encourages, and persuades creatures to participate in rigorous divine love is a constant. In this respect, God is constant and does not change.

John Cobb points to scriptures that portray God as "repenting" or changing God's mind in Genesis 6:6; Exodus 32:14; Amos 7:3, 6; and Isaiah 43–45. In these texts, God repents of making human beings, repents of the evil "which he thought to do unto his people" (KJV), repents as a result of Amos's pleading that God not destroy Israel, and "repented according to the multitude of his mercies" (Ps. 106:45, KJV).[33] Repentance means to turn around, to change. This is helpful. In our human experience of the economic Trinity, it does appear that when we pray, God does change God's mind. We affect God and one another through prayer. Yet, that God hears and responds to prayer is changeless. God is perfectly virtuous, and divine virtue is everlastingly responsive. That God is relational, responsive, compassionate, discerning, judging, forgiving, and merciful is an unchanging truth. God does not change in God's own nature. God changes in creaturely experience of God only in the sense that God may change God's response to particular events and situations as God changes others and us through our prayers. This makes sense in what process theists call "the consequent nature of God" and what classical theists call "the economic Trinity."

A Conserving, Integrative, and Relational Proposal

We can agree with process theists that God does share power and knowledge with the creatures who inhabit the world. Our theology is different, however, in that it is all God's power and knowledge to share. All power and knowledge come from God. Whiteheadians are helpful in their understanding that human beings are creatures and know only in part, that

God knows all of creation as each creature cannot know creation. Creatures are finite. They are not the power of creativity itself. They do not know all possibilities for their individual or for the world's becoming. As finite, temporal *enteritis*, we know in part. We do not know the whole. God alone as the source and power of life knows the world in its entirety. Therefore, some things remain mystery–an unsatisfactory term for some philosophers, but existentially true. Such is creaturely life.

Our integrative relational theology does not participate in the process theist argument for a "natural theology" over and against theologies that maintain the concept of a "supernatural, interventionist God." This theology finds that it suffices to say that what appears to be "supernatural" for human beings is "natural to God." It is open to and conserves classical Christian understanding of divine revelation. Drawing from womanist methodology regarding both/and thinking in contrast to either/or thinking, which is predominant in Western culture, the type of theology we are constructing here sees that a language barrier divides process and evangelical theists. All of God's actions are natural to God. Our theology, however, does not employ either the term "natural" or "supernatural" to describe God or the theology at hand. Both words are metaphors, which of late, in this theologian's view, contribute more confusion than clarity, closing off conversation rather than opening it.

A conserving integrative relational theology shares the idea of "thinking" as a creaturely experience with process theism and open relational theology. We feel whether or not the synapses in our brains are firing to make sense of the world and of God. Theologians and scientists alike are human. We are not able to engage in disembodied knowing. Our brains, our logic, our intuitions, and our feelings are all human ways of knowing. Thinking is *not* separate from feeling. Moreover, feeling is experiential knowing. Yet, how do we know that we understand well? How do we know that we have adequate knowledge of God and the world so that we might engage in right praxis? Here, we enter into a discussion of *epistemology*.

Epistemology and Science

Epistemology is the study of knowledge and what it means to "know." How do we know that it is God we are talking about, when we say that that we are talking about God? For Tillich, human beings come to know God through divine revelation in the experience of being "grasped by the ground of being." Tillich was also aware, however, that the language we humans use to speak of such experience is symbolic of that to which it points. On the one hand, it participates in the sacred. On the other hand, it is not the sacred itself but only points to it. The word "God," for example, is a symbol–a word–that points to the actual God beyond all of our words. In other words, God who transcends all of our cultural efforts to describe God in words, pictures, and descriptive ritual movement gives meaning to all of our language *about* God. Tillich's sense of "the Eternal Now" assured audiences of the ongoing presence of God in the world–Being Itself or the Ground of Being, which is the very content of what Tillich called "the dynamics of faith."[34] Tillich's lack of clarity regarding criteria for discerning authentic religious experience is problematic. Religious experience, being "grasped by the ground of Being,"[35] as he understood God, reveals the theological answers that existential philosophy asks. It is unclear, however, *why* religious experience is imbued with credible authority.

Science is a form of epistemology. Indeed, the word "science" simply means knowledge. A scientist is a "knower." Generally, when we employ the term "science" we have in mind empirical knowledge, based on evidence. When postmodern scientists examine the relationship between energy and matter, it is evident that reality is not static but dynamic, processive, and ongoing.[36] We have yet to discover all there is to know of time, space, energy, and matter. Scientists, for example, have already published studies documenting that when people pray for those who are sick, these sick individuals heal better and more quickly than those who do not receive intercessory prayer. Moreover, scientists have observed that this is the case even when the sick do not know that others are praying for them. Why? Perhaps one day a professional scientist will find conclusive proof as to why prayer works. Until then, we do know that in the design of the universe, human beings are wired in such a way that our prayers work. If there is intelligent design in the universe, then the very power of this intelligent design must exist. God is the ultimate scientist or "knower." Perhaps the most important insight of process theism is its understanding that this finding suggests something important about God and the world. Specifically, just as matter and energy exist in dynamic, integrative relationship in the world, so also God or Spirit exists in dynamic, integrative relationship with the world, which is itself matter and energy. Moreover, it is empirically true and has been proven that there are universes beyond the one we humans live in and that creativity transcends the universe we humans have come to know. Further, empirical scientific evidence demonstrates the integration of matter and energy, which theologians might call matter and spirit.

Finally, findings regarding the dynamic relationship between God and creation in process physics and metaphysics are consistent with biblical understandings of reality, according to which an entire creation awaits for human redemption so that it, too, may be freed and redeemed from decay (Rom. 8:22). When scientists find that the earth and its creatures evolved over a period of millions of years, this does not contradict the account of creation in Genesis 1 and 2. When read together, various biblical texts suggest God's time is not our time. Elsewhere, there is understanding that "with the Lord one day is as a thousand years" (2 Pet. 3:8). The numeric unit of "thousands" was the greatest number ancient writers could imagine.

The word "thousand" is a metaphor for a "long time." Therefore, evolutionary science does not contradict the biblical witness. This book, however, is not about creation science versus evolutionary science. It is about the presence of divine relational grace and courage in the midst of all our human disagreements, sin, and harm of one another.

Theologians must employ science in a way that does not reify (exalt) the science of this era by drawing too literal connections between God and the world, given that in each era we know only in part. Yet, process theism makes a very important contribution for our time in finding that it is literally true that God is relational, because the matter and energy of which our world is made reflect the relationality of God's own nature in creating the world. An integrative relational theology that employs the analogy of matter and energy to better understand divine relationship to creation (spirit and matter), while also maintaining certain orthodox claims, is inherently more conservative than orthodox process theology. It conserves key past influences from the orthodox traditions of the early church, making sense of them in relation to new scientific understandings.

Experience

If process theology has a method, then, it is precisely in its starting point–experience as understood through the contributions of Whiteheadian and Hartshornian metaphysics. An integrative relational theology considers the criterion of God's initial aim or goal for the world in relational experience. Process metaphysics examines the relationship between God and the world. It examines the internal dynamics and experience of complex entities. Whiteheadian metaphysics literally explores what is invisible to the naked eye, the subquantum particles of energy that make up the universe. Whiteheadian theologian John Cobb, argues that he does not prove the existence of God. This is not his goal. Rather, he makes sense of what one might call God in a scientific, philosophical-theological analysis of the actual presence of ongoing activities of freedom and creativity in the universe. The strength of Cobb's Whiteheadian approach is his emphasis on the reality of the unseen and its integral relationship to external reality, which creatures perceive as visible or sensible matter.[37]

Whiteheadian, process physics is not the first system of relational philosophy that has observed ongoing, dynamic movements of creativity and freedom in the cosmos. Peter Rukungah has found parallels between process thought and African Ntu or Muntu philosophy with its emphasis on creation as community and the interrelatedness of all life.[38] Whether we turn to process physics and metaphysics, to Muntu philosophy, or relational understandings of the universe based in the Christian biblical canon, such worldviews must always be tested in continuing self-critical iconoclastic activity in the battle between God and the idols. The theologian must recognize that each theology is incomplete, at best adequate, and always subject to the relativizing and humanizing judgment of God. God, "the all-inclusive one," as Hartshornian Theodore Walker Jr. emphasizes, experiences the many.[39] Or, as Whiteheadians observe, God is the only one who experiences the world in its entirety. All analogies of God's response to the world come to a point where they are not helpful. At some point the faith of Christianity and the faith of science determine truth on different grounds, although ultimately they are far more intertwined than any particular age can know. To separate faith, which seeks understanding, from knowledge is ultimately a human artifice. In the words of 1 Corinthians 13:12, "For now we see through a glass, darkly; but then face to face: now I know in part; but then shall I know even as also I am known" (KJV). The time of full knowing is at hand, but that time is not yet.

Praxis

Theology is more than an abstract exercise. We construct theology to better understand what it means to live in right relationship with God and the world. An adequate theology never concerns itself merely with theory but integrates theory with practice. This integration is called "praxis." Womanist theologians engage in praxis by turning to "real-lived experience"[40] as a resource for theological construction to draw on tried and proven events of faith seeking understanding. Here, we turn to case studies drawn from late twentieth- and early twenty-first-century events to provide illustrations of those who have practiced Jesus' message of empathy, love, courage, and justice in response to situations of unnecessary violence.

The sacred dance productions of artist Vanessa Baker provide a type of healing theological praxis. We will look at Baker's work as a form of liturgy that provides healing for those wounded by the social-historical experience of unnecessary violence. Baker's work is important, because she and the artists who participate in her work literally embody *orthopraxis* or right practice, the integration of theory and practice. Baker explains that through the inspiration of the Holy Spirit, she creates sacred dance and poetry that serve as instruments of healing. God in Christ, through the power of the Holy Spirit, literally inspires the sacred dance of life, which laments evil and suffering while praising the ever increasing glory of omnipresent divine love, creativity, and justice.

Theological analysis of events and practices like those above provides heuristic (experimental) insight into effective responses to God and to evil in the contemporary world. It considers the strengths and weaknesses of various responses to evil, turning to an analysis of the effects or fruits of various responses to evil.[41] Does the response break cycles of hatred and unnecessary violence, leading communities to experience healing? Or does the response perpetuate cycles of hatred and unnecessary violence? We search for sound theological *praxis.* Paolo Freire coined the term *praxis* in his construction of liberating pedagogy–liberating teaching/learning.[42]

Praxis integrates faith seeking understanding with the practice of faith. Much understanding about the Christian message comes not only through reading and hearing the Christian message, but also through living it. Living the Christian message cannot be separated from hearing and reading it. Some refer to this as *orthopraxis,* because it integrates right doctrine with right practice. The term *orthopraxis* is a helpful and adequate term, however, only when those who employ it do not practice the unfortunate habit of separating it from *orthodoxy.* There is no such thing, in other words, as suggesting that a theology is "orthopraxis, but not orthodox." Theologians who engage in *orthopraxis* are, by definition, engaged in constructing theologies that claim to provide *orthodoxy* (right doctrine), given that *orthopraxis* integrates doctrine with practice.

Language

When the wounded cry out in suffering, they are imbued with reason as we saw in Cooper.[43] When hope seems empty, when faith's resources are exhausted, the earth cries out. This cry has many different tones and meanings. The cry may be a shout of praise and rejoicing. The cry may be a lament of evil and suffering. Theology itself is a cry for adequate words about God. Theologians emphasize linguistic clarity in articulation of the nature of God. Yet, theologians ultimately engage in talk about the ineffable. To find words that adequately name God requires courageous striving toward meaning.

Courage makes it possible to consider the nature of our words and images for God and creation. God, in the words of Anselm of Canterbury, is "that than which nothing greater can be conceived."[44] How do we know, then, that our words for God are adequate and that it is really God we are talking about when we claim to talk about God? What do we mean when we refer to God and creation with the language of "courage, dust, spirit, breath, pulse, touch, heart, Parent, Father, Son, Word, Wisdom, or Holy Spirit?" How do we know these words and images adequately represent God and creation?

Part of our spiritual striving is to understand how we arrive at meaning. Human beings employ a diversity of languages and images to orient themselves in relation to God and creation. Words and images may be freeing and imprisoning, particularly when one idolizes the words or images themselves instead of worshiping the God to which they point.[45] Words that point to God participate in the divine life and may be said to incarnate divine reality to the extent that God is present in their meaning, yet they are not God. God transcends language. No word adequately describes God, except the one Word or Logos incarnate–the true and living Christ. Therefore, in the finite world of language where we humans exist, words and images meant to enliven understandings of who we are in relation to God can become labels that function as categorizing, commodifying signifiers in the marketplace of ideas or the worship of tradition. Failing to explore the depths of the words and images we employ to communicate experiences of God and creation, we fail to see or hear one another. Through miseducation and misinterpretation, our theological conversations about personal, social, and ecological transformation turn into a downward spiral staircase toward a basement of discarded hopes, broken dreams, and misplaced commitments.

This particular relational and integrative theology is *one* novel creative product among multiple possibilities. It potentially leads to new possibilities beyond this specific writing or author. It is novel not in the sense that it is original in a world in which "There is nothing new under the sun" (Eccl. 1:9). Rather it is novel in the Whiteheadian[46] sense of a novelty by which each entity, including this theologian, participates in an ongoing process of becoming, called forward toward positive, creative possibilities by the divine initial aim. The divine initial aim, God's vision and desire for the well being of all that God created, is omnipresent in creation, including in scripture, classical Christian literature, the living testimonies of people of faith, and the contemporary thought of a diversity of Christian writers.

"God" is a symbol for God beyond all of our words. Theologians throughout the ages have contemplated and debated the meaning of the word "God." If God inspires even our God-language, as scripture suggests, then the various words we employ to describe or name God, must participate in God's own nature, particularly if God is omnipresent. A relational and integrative theology understands our words for and about God in this way. This understanding is in contrast with that of Gordon Kaufman, a contemporary revisionist and historicist theologian,[47] who argues that theology is a constructive, imaginative activity. Kaufman by "imagination" does not mean fancy, but reason. To a point, Kaufman's claim is true. Theology, if it is good theology, however, is not "merely" a human constructive and imaginative activity. Kaufman borrows Tillich's understanding that the word "God" is a symbol of that which ultimately concerns us, while rejecting Tillich's appeals to religious experience as a starting point for theology.

For Kaufman, "God" is the most basic symbol for referring to "mystery" as "serendipitous creativity," which provides human beings with adequate orientation for life. Words, symbols, and images that do not adequately orient human beings toward life do not adequately name "God" as God. Kaufman, however, does not carry over Tillich's understanding of God-talk participating in the sacred to which it points. His theological method is not sufficiently integrative and relational in its approach to reason and experience, sacred language and the sacred, God-talk and God. Just as a symbol of the sacred for Tillich is never a "mere symbol," neither does it make sense to say that an entire symbol system about God (scripture, creeds, religious narratives, sermons, various types of theology) are "mere" imaginative constructions of reality. If we employ scripture as a "norming norm" for a relational integrative theology, then we are turning to texts with words about God that are inspired by God who is omnipresent, revealed in human experience. The testimony of Christians throughout the ages, from the time of the first Christians in Acts and in the writings attributed to Paul in the New Testament to the present offer evidence of being true when evidence of authetic healing is present in praxis.

CHAPTER 2

Our Spiritual Striving

The Context of Theology

Be still before the Lord, *and* ***wait*** *patiently for him;*
do not fret over those who prosper in their way,
over those who carry out evil devices.

Psalm 37:7

God's Call to Life

We live in a world of hatred and unnecessary violence. God calls the world to wrestle with the consequences of this existential reality, even as God calls the world forward into the land of the living. Entering the land of the living is a process of spiritual striving in a world plagued by unnecessary violence. What does the phrase "unnecessary violence" mean? Most people in speaking of "violence" have in mind traumatically destructive activity. To the extent that creatures eat other creatures, whether plant, animal, insects in some parts of the globe, or other organisms, we all participate in levels of necessary violence to feed and sustain our physical lives. A certain degree of destruction is part of the cycle of life.

Unnecessary violence, in contrast to necessary violence, takes life from another individual or group of individuals out of sheer hatred, morbid or sociopathic curiosity, or because either individuals or governing authoritative powers can see no other way out of threatening situations, real or imagined. In the latter case, sometimes human beings and other creatures have difficulty discerning whether or not violence is necessary. For example, when lives are threatened, self-defense is necessary. Survival instinct kicks in. While most of us prefer to simply stop our attackers so that we can get away to safety, self-defense may result in the death of one's attacker(s). In personal situations such as attempted rape or attempted murder, the need for the degree of self-defense is generally clear and evident. Decisions regarding war or other more complex situations require more deliberation and debate.

Sometimes whether or not violence is actually necessary becomes a matter of painful debate, and debate results in oppressive silencing by obdurate structures of political and economic power. When debate moves to silencing, people feel a loss of freedom to engage in creative alternatives for solving personal, corporate, national, and global problems. They experience silencing as oppression and as a form of violence that perpetuates their distress. Those who have lost loved ones to unnecessary violence sometimes feel vengeful. They want to retaliate in kind, seeking not justice but vengeance. Still others doubt the existence of God in a world plagued by unnecessary violence and grave injustices. Sometimes such doubt leads to cynicism and faintness of courage. Sometimes cynicism and faintness of courage lead to despair. Finally, sometimes despair leads to nihilism with its desperate destructive actions toward self and others.

Yet others find hope and release in their faith, moving beyond cycles of hatred and unnecessary violence to experience healing. Some among this latter group have gone on to heal others, making firm commitments to help reduce the influence of cycles of hatred and unnecessary violence by volunteering in their communities and, in some cases, by setting up centers or foundations. Still others, who experience a call to ministry, make this part of their ministry in the work of the church. It takes grace and courage to commit one's life to the healing and justice-producing activity of God in the world.

The context of theological praxis is not evil, death, and violence but the goodness of God in the land of the living. The goodness of God in the land of the living is present even in the depths of earthly and cosmic hell. Evil cannot overcome it. The context of God is present in the midst of this war-ridden, crime-ridden, hate-filled world, forever calling us to "the more" of rigorous love and healing. To focus on evil, as if that were the primary existential context, spirals heart, mind, and God-given gifts for ministry down into a pit of hopelessness in which one disremembers[1] reality–God's context. God is present in the temporal, existential lives of all creatures. It is to this divine context, omnipresent in the midst of this existential context with its mixture of good and evil, that this theology turns. Who is this God on whom those who find grace and courage to commit their lives to healing and justice draw?

God as Norm and Ultimate Concern

The God of life is the norm and ultimate concern of theology. In a world of crucifixion, theologians seek ultimate answers regarding the God of life in relation to the problem of evil and suffering. To engage in theological questions about the nature of God in relation to the problem of evil and suffering is implicitly an act of thanksgiving for life. Without the power of life, there is no breath for God-talk. Nor is there ability to reflect on the problem of evil and suffering. God is the only appropriate first love of theology. Second is love of neighbor, made possible by love of God from whom the life and power of love comes. Theology engages in a relational dance between love of God and love of neighbor, seeking greater understanding of the nature of the power of love and life which is God. Theologians consider the earth's cries to God in a world of crucifixion, giving attention to the dynamic relationship between God–Creator and source of all life–and creation. Theology begins by presupposing that the last word in the struggle of good and evil, life and death, is the Word of Life, which is God. It then considers the response of the Word of Life to an earth that cries out for answers to the problem of evil and suffering.

The context of theology in a world of crucifixion is life. Life is primary and precedes conversation about the problem of crucifixion, suffering, and death. One cannot speak of death without presupposing the existence of life and the power that makes life possible. Ultimately then, the context of theology is God who is the source and power of life. This is the essential context of theology that is omnipresent in existential reality. There is no talk of existence without the concept of life and the ground of life, which is God. Theologians seek answers to existential questions about life and death from the ultimate, divine context of life. In existence, human beings are confronted by pain, suffering, and death. Death as the result of unnecessary and unjust violent causes in human societies is a problem that requires divine response. What does the power of life, God, whose context is everlasting life, have to say to the problem of violent death and destruction? This problem is perennial in human history.

Regardless of what one names a particular historical period, the ultimate context is always life; for it is the living who raise questions about pain, suffering, crucifixion, and death. The living ask questions about God, life, violence, and death. Without the context of life, it is impossible, like Job, to question God. The ultimate context, then, with which theology is concerned is the context of life, which is the context of God The task of theology is to focus on the dance of the Spirit of life, our ultimate context, in relation to historical existence. The dance of life, found in God who creates, incarnates, and passionately loves creation precedes all other contexts. Without this context of life, in which the power of life is revealed, historical creaturely existence is not possible. There is an expression, "the vicissitudes of life," that refers to the tragic nature of historical existence. Theologians respond to the tragic nature of historical existence by seeking understanding of God, who is the power of life. That there is life indicates that there is power of life. This power of life is God.

Historical Context

To refer to the "historical context" of human creatures is to refer to the context of life in the world. This context is temporal and limited. It is characterized by cycles of life and death, by goodness, righteousness, sin, and evil. All of these are present in the world. Moreover, this context is characterized by finitude. It stands in contrast to the context of God, characterized by everlasting life. Yet, God infuses the temporal created world with the life and power of the Spirit. Much debate continues about how to name the present historical context with its struggles between good and evil. Thinkers variously refer to the present context as postmodern, postcolonial, or "the end of modernity."[2]

Theologians contemplate whether their theology is postmodern, postcolonial, twenty-first-century, stubbornly still "modern," or whether some other term would capture the historical context in which they construct theology. This sometimes distracts the theologians from the ultimate context, which is the life found in God. It is not desirable to be distracted from the ultimate context, the life found in God, because then one is easily distracted from the task of theology. The task of theology is not to focus on the existential context alone, but rather to clarify the relationship between God and the world. God is involved in the existential contexts of this world, while also transcending them. God is involved in the life of all possible universes, not just this one. The task of theology, then, is to understand the divine creativity that makes existence possible and to understand divine response to creaturely existence.

Yet, how might one name the present historical context? Womanist and other theological scholars from historically colonized contexts have been reluctant to name their work "postmodern," although other scholars sometimes refer to it as such because of the influence of such work in shifting understandings of Western culture and hegemonic social structures. Cornel West sees postmodernity as the continued fragmenting of modernity that begins with its inception in false premises about who is human.[3] I agree with West that postmodern literature as developed by predominantly white scholars easily falls into certain racialized tropes from modernity. Yet, it is important to consider that participation in postmodernity is probably as inevitable and inescapable as participation in modernity. Therefore, it would be best to engage in constructive intellectual activity that (1) makes sense to communities that find the ideas of racialized postmodern presuppositions simply unviable and therefore refuse to incorporate them into thought and practice, and (2) offers some correctives to the already developing postmodern Western consciousness. Responses to postmodernity are navigational as one dances a dance of life through the death dance of the fragmenting false constructions of self produced by modern Western consciousness.

Definitions of postmodernity are so diverse that we must consider which understandings of postmodernity are being referenced. For example, one may refer to poststructuralist thought in philosophy, psychology, and literature as postmodern. Other postmodernists participate extensively in the deconstructive methods such as those found in the writings of Jacques Derrida.[4] Yet others argue that in fact we see elements of such a hermeneutic in Friedrich Nietzsche's writings.[5] For some, like West, this indicates that much of what is understood as postmodern is actually deeply modern, including perspectival understandings of truth, which in the United States have a long-standing basis in nineteenth- and twentieth-century American philosophical pragmatism. In another view, process theist David Griffin more readily places postmodernity within the emergence of Whiteheadian physics and Whitehead's later attention to Einsteinian quantum physics.[6]

Feminist scholar Susan Dolan-Henderson defines postmodernity by identifying three moments. The first moment is "*critique of modernity,*" in a way that unmasks "modernity's contradictory impulses and results," particularly as regards "freedom, equality and unlimited progress."[7] Second, are concerns about the autonomous self and postmodernism's seeking of "the 'disappearance of the subject.'"[8] Dolan-Henderson puts it this way: "The autonomous self of the Enlightenment centered meaning in itself and its belief in its unlimited power and freedom. Since this power and freedom have proven illusory, the shift has been away from the subject to communal forms of meaning."[9] The third moment, she argues "concerns the *end to universal and hegemonic definitions,* discourses, and worldviews" [emphasis Dolan-Henderson's].[10]

The places in which African American intellectual discourses and womanist theologies find themselves in relation to such definitions of postmodernism are complicated. Historically, African American intellectuals have approached questions of freedom, self, and community from the underside. The perspectival approach to truth from this underside is part of both modern and postmodern African American experience. It leads black intellectuals to question what exactly has changed in the so-called paradigmatic shift from modernity to postmodernity? In short, more has changed for those who believed enlightenment understandings of truth to be real and absolute than for those who have questioned it all along. Therefore, examining postmodern claims from the underside one asks, "But what is new about this?"

Even as we look at intellectual thought produced by white *and* African American intellectuals alike in the late nineteenth century in Europe and in the United States, controversy rages as to whether their ideas are modern or postmodern. How should black intellectuals and other intellectuals of color who produce work that is critical and constructive of the assumptions of the Enlightenment and modernity as described above refer to their work? Is it appropriate for those from the underside, for whom the critical analysis of such assumptions is long-standing, to refer to their intellectual productions as postmodern? This has prompted a number of intellectuals of color to refer to their work as "postcolonial."

Joerg Rieger, a liberation theologian who engages postmodernity, cautions against tendencies either to celebrate or reject postmodernism, arguing that it does not make sense to do so.[11] For Rieger, postmodernity cannot easily be rejected because it is deeply North American. It makes little sense to reject it because that would be to deny its very concrete impact on the globe, particularly the spread of consumerism with its dire effects on the poor. For Rieger, celebrations of postmodernity make little sense because of postmodern culture's impact on the poor. Quoting Jean Baudrillard's analysis of postmodernity in the United States, he agrees that the fault lines and struggles of American history are forgotten in U.S. postmodernity.[12] Postmodernity, Rieger argues, is no less exclusive than modernity in this respect. Turning to Disneyland as an apt initial symbol of U.S. postmodernity, Rieger, quoting Baudrillard, criticizes the "enchantment" of postmodern American culture.[13]

This book does not reject postmodernity, because its social-historical impact is concrete and cannot be understood as existing only within the abstract realm of intellectual discourse. This book does not embrace postmodernity for reasons similar to those Rieger describes. In a kind of middle way, it recognizes postmodernity as a social, historical, cultural, and economic force with which to contend.

Is the work of this book postmodern? In certain respects, it fits current definitions of postmodern thought. Womanist theory engages in critical analysis of racial and gender assumptions in modern notions of freedom and equality, for example. Such criticisms of modernity's notions of freedom and equality belong to a continuity of wisdom from African American ancestors in modernity who engaged in criticism of racism and sexism. Such critical analysis, then, is not peculiar to postmodern texts. David Griffin's process understanding of postmodernity emphasizes the impact of Einstein's quantum physics on human consciousness and offers a more scientific starting point for the transition from modernity to postmodernity.[14] A shift in consciousness about speed, space, time, and energy emerged with Einstein's theory of relativity, impacting popular culture through technology (from the aerodynamics of cars to footwear, nuclear power plants, microwave ovens, and atomic bombs) and science fiction as well as the elitist culture of academics.

The postmodern worldview includes a host of constructed subjects and "others" whose essence, if it exists, cannot be named. This makes sense as an important step for Western thought which, since the Enlightenment, has expended much energy categorizing self and other as a means of power. Such categorizing, in the name of order, is a means of control when confronted with fearfully, negatively perceived difference. There is a time to question whether the constructs of this categorizing tendency have any real essence behind them. In contrast, the postcolonial worldview includes a world of subjects that have been perceived as negative, feared objects by modern, colonizing exploiters of others. Those who have been the "others," who are objects of systemic categorization and definition, define themselves. The emphasis is on claiming the subjectivity of all persons in a world where "otherness" has been employed as a rationale for colonization of lands, bodies, and minds. Subjects emphasize agency to define themselves, their religion, their language and its meaning, their symbol systems, and their methods for discerning truth.

Much of postmodern discourse wears the same hegemonic face as modernity–newly masked. The emperor is still the emperor, whether the emperor of modernity or postmodernity. The emperor claims the power of naming the new age, the new world, the new non-self that keeps asserting itself, the new questions, the new deconstructions, and the new, fragile, relative reconstructions.

In part, this strategy functions to keep those who have traditionally been viewed as nonpersons at bay, for if the emperor strips all persons of personhood in the spirit of equality, then ongoing challenges to the oppressive self need not be met, since the emperor has no self to challenge. As in the past, the dispossessed are told, "But you don't have a self." The dispossessed, in response, shift the rhythms of an age-old dance a few steps ahead of the slow-drag of the emperor, changing the rhythms as soon as the emperor catches on, all the while wishing the emperor would stop being emperor so the vulgar, garish interplay would cease.

The non-self is as much an illusion as the autonomous self. It is the hegemonic self that dies so that freedom of becoming can emerge. Liberative selves continue becoming *if* they embrace the fullest possibilities of becoming in the divine initial aim. If the hegemonic self is unwilling to give way to new possibilities, it dances the dance of the living dead, maintaining hegemonic power by glorifying its dance of death instead of moving into the dance of life. It remains embedded in a past from which it seeks freedom, because it fails to consciously yield to God's consequent, transforming nature.

A Dance of the Spirit

Producer, dancer, poet, and choreographer Vanessa Baker believes in a dance of God that is inspired by the Holy Spirit and is present in the body of the people of God. She believes in the dance of the Spirit. She creates poetry and dance that commemorate those lost through hatred and violence, while simultaneously celebrating survival, the power of healing, and resurrection hope. In 2002, Baker and Cheryl Swann created a production on Emmett Till and his mother, Mamie Till-Mobley, to commemorate his 1955 lynching, to honor his mother, to celebrate his mother's protest against racial violence, and to glorify God's healing and resurrection power. Baker explains that, "Emmett's voice surfaced throughout my life. I've always desired to know more. When the request came to create a piece for the youth sacred dance group at church, Emmett's voice once again spoke–spoke through a poem to his mother–***SACRIFICIAL FOOD***. It naturally flowed, as if it had always been a part of me. In some way, I found myself wanting to comfort Mamie Till-Mobley. I worked with the dramatic aspect of the production, and Cheryl created a most compelling choreography."[15]

When asked why sacred dance is important, Baker explains that for her, as for many, it is an innate gift passed down from her African and Native American ancestors: "Sacred movement is innate. My lineage is that of two strong cultures–African American and Native American. Both are grounded in histories that used CELEBRATION movements to first worship our Supreme Creator, and secondly to give honor to the people and things that our Supreme Creator created for coexistence." Sacred dance for Baker thanks God and the ancestors and is thankful to all of creation for contributing to and enhancing the gift of life. "As we thank our ancestors, nature, lower life forms, and all things for contributing and enhancing our lives, we recognize that we are truly giving thanks to God," she writes. "All things, including ourselves, exist to serve each other–in service to God. When my focus remains on God, in the Name of Jesus my Savior, PRAISE MOVEMENT done to music, spoken word, sounds of nature, or in complete silence are inevitable."[16]

Baker views the dance and poetry performances she produces as a ministry. In her words, "Being a **Christian** artist, dancer, and poet is an appointment from God carrying the same responsibilities as those of a minister of God's Word. I believe that God blesses each of us with talents and gifts as God sees fit. These blessings are never wholly our possessions, and are strategically designed to be shared, taught, and passed on–all for the glory of God." Moreover, she finds, "If I were to clutch on to my gifts and not use them as instruments for God's glory, if I were to place them in a hypothetical box only for my enjoyment, or use them in a worldly sense to bring glory to myself, they would cease to be gifts. My soul would die. Sharing in the Name of God allows my meager seed to bud and bloom in each spirit it touches." Her goal, like Swann's, is not fame and fortune, but to share in God's grace toward the world, to let the spiritual seeds she plants through her art touch the spirits of others to promote understanding and healing.

God inspires many gifts, including dance. Moreover, God, who is a spirit, moves in the world in *perichoresis*–a type of sacred dance, within

God's own nature. God is a Spirit who moves in and through creation in at least three movements, with three distinctive personalities and functions. One might say that God is one community of at least three movements. This community, traditionally called God, is one Spirit in three movements.

The dance of the Trinity is a dance of the Spirit. The word *dance* in reference to God is a metaphor, a type of symbol. A metaphor, as Sallie McFague puts it, includes an "is and is not."[17] It says something true about reality, but it can only be carried so far. God, who is a spirit, for example, does not literally dance in the way we human beings think of dancing. The word *dance* in this text refers to the dynamic, ongoing movement of God in creation as God continuously creates and recreates, making all things new. God, who is a spirit, moves creation to literally and metaphorically dance. Even the dense, subquantum particles of energy that make up rocks, which appear to be static, are dynamically moving in relation to one another. The word "dance" and the phrase "dance of life" are metaphors that refer to this movement. God, Jesus and his followers have often said, is "like the wind." One cannot see the wind, but one experiences its movement in the world. Similarly, one cannot see God, but one experiences God's movement in the universe.

In churches and celebrations led by people of color and Christians influenced by Pentecostal or charismatic renewal movements, one not only sings in the Spirit but dances in the Spirit. Something in the dance always changes, because the dance is a response to God and to the world, an ongoing, dynamic relationship. The dance of the Spirit finds postmodern claims about the self as essentialist as modernist claims about the autonomous, noncommunal self. What is this postmodernity I converse with, so reluctantly, as I seek a uniquely womanist dance-possible response, a dance that slices through the essentialist deconstruction methods of a hegemonic intellectual majority?

Generations have participated in worldviews that have engaged in critical questioning of Enlightenment ideals of freedom, equality, self, and power. "Postmodernity" for the historically colonized, then, frequently refers to a kind of awakening among those who have most benefited from Enlightenment and modern presuppositions of hegemonic cultural and economic identity. Those who belong to generations who have been sounding the wake up alarm for a few hundred years are unimpressed. The constructive work of the dispossessed continues. The alarm still sounds. Let us move to the next step. Let us not engage in nihilistic cynicism and despair about whether or not we can say anything about God and the Spirit of Truth.

While it is important to be aware of the dangers of essentialism, the claim to be able adequately to name the essence of a person, a group or God, it is equally important to acknowledge than in spite of the difficulties in naming essence, something does exists. The subjectivity of the colonized has been torn down, marginalized, ignored, and rejected. It must be recovered and reconstructed before it can be deconstructed and reconstructed again. *Recovery* and *reconstruction* of selves and communities are as important as deconstruction of false constructs of self and community. There is a type of essentialism in the anti-essentialist thinking. It is *essentially* anti-essentialist; that is, there is an identifiable essence to anti-essentialist arguments.

The objective of deconstruction and much of postmodern theory is to be self-critical. In the end, its goal is to emphasize that something changes, that the self is not static. Our words are adequate for a moment and no more. The deconstructionist Jacques Derrida moves toward a study of religion in his later work and the possibilities of a kind of grace in history. On the one hand, he considers the truth of the tower of Babel myth in which the languages of humankind are scattered and the divine essence is simply "Ha Shem" or "The Name." It is not that there is no reality, human or divine, but that human language is insufficient to name it. Divine language alone, as in the language of the prophets, says what it actually means for Derrida.[18] Once we discuss and interpret it we risk idolatry.

The Dance of the Spirit in the Existential Context

The struggle toward freedom is ongoing and processive. Ada Maria Isasi Díaz has written, "*La vida es la lucha*–life is struggle."[19] Our spiritual striving, as DuBois suggests, makes us human.[20] What is the meaning of "spiritual striving" in the theology proposed here? Spiritual striving in this context integrates what Howard Thurman called "head and heart" to make real-lived sense of the Christian faith in a world of crucifixion.[21] Martin Luther King Jr. borrowed from Thurman's teachings to develop an understanding and practice of tough-mindedness and tender-heartedness during the civil and human rights struggle for freedom and equality in the 1950s and 1960s. At the center of such spiritual striving is an *agape* form of love, disinterested love that works toward the well-being of all. Moreover, the effort to find words adequate for such movements requires serious reflection grounded in this same *agape* love, which, for King, served to move peoples into beloved community, a kind of household of God, or *oikos*. Such reflection is grounded in spiritual striving. Such spiritual striving is necessary for theological construction.

Spiritual striving is the dance of life, encouraged by the dance of the Spirit. It slices the stultifying air of oppression to generate survival, freedom, and abundant life. It defies the gravity of despair. It manifests as courage, through the power of encouraging Spirit. Is such a dance a *liberative postmodern* dance in contrast to *non-liberative postmodern* dances? Is it a *postcolonial* dance that ever celebrates and fights for freedom?

This present era is postmodern and postcolonial, but the struggle for freedom is more ancient than modernity or colonialism. Words that begin with "post" suggest an ongoing embeddedness in the past, but life moves ever forward toward novel becomings. It is important to keep an eye to the past without being embedded in it. To be embedded in the past is idolatrous. It credits more power to the past than to God's ongoing activities of creating. It is a form of bondage in which one is more determined by the past than by the dynamic movement of God. There is a need for terms that honor the influence of the past while also clarifying long-term objectives and visions. It is not a matter of choosing between established descriptive categories, but of looking to something new in the midst of present dreaming for the future. The dance of the Spirit responds to what Whitehead called "the lure" of God. The lure of God is found in the subjective aim of an individual or society who experiences God's initial aim as one's own through the mediating activity of God's response to the subject.[22]

The dance of the Spirit is a creative, renewing, and liberative dance.[23] It rejoices in the creativity of God and steps in and out of the interstices of time and space where time and space collapse to respond liberatively to each concrete, changing moment. In its movement between the interstices of time and space, it is a liminal dance–a dance in the present that creatively, dynamically transforms past experiences into new becomings. In the realm of infinite possibilities we are not bound by or determined by the past, even though we learn from and conserve the best of it in our becoming.[24] Human creatures' understanding of the universe has expanded. That our place in it is infinitesimal is inescapable. Theology of the present day is an intellectual movement living in new awareness that no one global region is the center of the world. Rather than emphasize the problem of fragmentation, which is primarily recognition of the diversity in creation that has always existed, the theological task presented here is to consider relationality in the midst of diversity. Creation is inescapably interconnected in its rich diversity, which, in the beginning, God declared good (Gen. 1).

Even without language, creation would continue to experience internal and external creative processes. The dance of life would proceed, because the context of the dance of life is God who is everlastingly creative. Divine creativity continuously experiences the inner workings of creation, because God, who is omnipresent in creation, responds to creation. God is a community of *hypostases*, a community of relations in which creation finds its life and meaning. There is a call for humanity to participate in God's relating activity. Divine relational *movements of grace* are an eternal process and the ground of all possibilities for creation's becoming. The movement of divine creativity and grace includes, but also transcends, all of our languages and words about God. It includes, but transcends, particular experiences of God.

The improvisational language and translinguistic movement of the Spirit of Life[25] that human beings are called to participate in responds in dynamic faith to the struggle between good and evil. As evil changes its face, the dance of life changes its movement in response to ongoing events. With each generation and moment, the steps are slower or faster, simpler or more complicated, but always fluid. As quickly as exploitative power structures appropriate the styles of the dance for nonliberative ends, new namings and styles emerge. Ultimately, the dance resists easy, static naming. The divine call we experience does not ask us to learn the dance completely, because God is continuously creating each step and movement, moment by moment, drawing creation and its creatures into right relationship. God calls us to live the dance in all its dynamic, responsive, loving, just, and liberating power. Those who desire to learn it without attention to its responsive, improvisational, and creative core fail to fully live it.

It is important to listen to how the music of folk spiritual and intellectual production responds to God and the world. We can hear its wisdom in activist communities, respect its challenges to our minds, and join a particular spiritual dance responsiveness with its communal, intellectual, spiritual striving. Theology must look to the present, as well as to the past, to consider steps for realizing abundant life. Before we know it, present styles of dance will perish and be replaced, although the content is enduring. In the end, the dance requires grace, sensitivity to the unexplained, respect for the unseen, and faith that, in the interplay between nothingness and becoming, life pervades. Name the dance whatever you will, the spirit of freedom that breathes through it is ancient, perennial, unnamable, ineffable, making it possible to master the steps without ever learning to dance, possible to master the dance beyond rules for the steps. Look at the ground or your feet, and the dance fails. Describe the steps, and they change in the spirit of the dancer.

The particular dance of faith seeking understanding presented here is a *liberative* dance in a world of crucifixion. It is intertwined with dances of survival and transcendence, slicing through the lies of evil, stepping from nothingness to the rock-hard places of solid ground in the energy of faith. In the holistic, holiness dance of the Spirit, one step leads to another, with the dynamic, internal, shared energies of the dancer and with the Spirit determining what the next step will be as the dance becomes what it must to survive and transcend the moments at hand. To this type of dance of the Spirit I turn in the following pages. It courageously changes its movement and style in liberative response to ever-shifting challenges of oppression. It is a dance of life. It defies the dance of the walking dead.

Before the dance of the Spirit can even begin, those who participate in the rhythms of survival and liberating movement ask: "From whence cometh our help? Is God in the house?!"[26] A dance without the Spirit is no dance at all. Moreover, the dance lacks courage. The dance of survivors with faith in God revealed in Christ is a dance of courage in a house where we are often strangers. In the words of W. E. B. DuBois, "Why did God make me a stranger in mine own house?[27] Only the Spirit can overcome the divide that keeps human beings estranged from God, one another, and the rest of creation. Only the Spirit can overcome the dance of death that manifests itself in war, hate crimes, rape, and violation of the planet.

Is this dance a dance of the Spirit and life, because it emerges with particularly novel grace from the wounded, the suffering, and the dispossessed? No. The dance of the Spirit belongs to none. We all belong to it. It has many rhythms and diverse forms. All those who love God belong to the dance. What makes a dance holy is whether or not it glorifies God and God's initial aim for the well-being of creation. The dance called the Dance of the Spirit is grounded in the Spirit of Life. Only the Spirit of God can make it holy. It is visible in evangelical programs that reach out to the poor, in holiness churches that feed the hungry, charismatic and Pentecostal churches that claim power over evil and sickness in the name of Jesus, in liberal white churches that welcome all to join them in worship and leadership, in Korean churches that resolve *han* through faith in God who suffers and rises again, in megachurches that find shelter for the homeless, as well as in African American churches that have a shared love for this dance in the Spirit. Each community finds its own pace, rhythm, and steps. The reader is encouraged to look for such movement in his or her own daily life.

The wounded of any race, gender, or culture are *not* by the nature of being wounded on a higher road or path of holier-than-thou spiritual movement. To the contrary, all must ask, "What are we hiding from ourselves?" While we resist the misdirected desires of others, are we also deluded in our understanding of what Tillich called "the really real?"[28] No one in the age-old dance of sin and righteousness, good and evil, is exempt from the judgment of truth. This age-old dance is the one that all Christian communities strive to replace, by grace, with the dance of God's new creation. Calls to accountability must continue. Games of blame run a predictable, stultifying, dead-end course. If liberation does not begin with a willingness to attend to internal creative possibilities as well as to external creative possibilities, then there is no hope.

It is necessary for Christians from all walks of life to ask, "Who and where is God in the midst of the crucifixion that afflicts the world?" There can be no holy dance without faith that seeks understanding of God. Modernity, postmodernity, and eras to come are all relativized by that which transcends past, present, and future time. God always, persuasively draws humankind toward positive possibilities and a realization of true creative potential.[29] God is present in every movement, breath, thought, deed, and word, calling the world into more profound understanding of God's initial aim for creation. When we reject God, God is still present, persuading us to receive divine grace and love, to participate fully in it. When we consciously choose to receive God, God empowers us to participate in God's activity of creativity, justice, and rigorous love.

PART II

The Courage of God in a World of Crucifixion

CHAPTER 3

The Breath of God

Providing/Nurturing Spirit

Ha Shem

Hurricane
Why
Hurricane
Sigh
A touch on
Our shoulders
In early
July
At first
So dry
Then so humid
Weather awry
The birds all timid
In shade of trees
Then diving like turtles
Without grace or ease
Dipping low
For dark and cool
Seeking oasis
In tepid pool

Past breeding
And nesting
Just wrestling
With heat
Past season
To Season
Black and
Orange
Webbed feet
Sense
Adam's empire is
The reason
For warnings
And warmings
In morning's
First "Hi"
Such sorrow
Little regret
For ignoring
Heaven's eye
Before emperors
In ties
Butt naked with lies
Muted earth's cries
In ascent to hell's throne
Deep in the bog of
Imperialist dung
Plaguing
Peasant
Pietas'
Hearts
All flung and wrung
By the tragic folly
of empire's feast
With blasphemous prayers
Mocking the least
Hailing techno whizzer's of Oz
Flaccid grey-skinned priests
Passing numbers for gods
While laboring serfs grieve
The debris on God's altars
While creation groans
With constant plea

From bayou to bay
And from bay to the sea
And the winds prophesy:
What a meager repentance
Such blasphemous offerings
What mocking remembrance
Of secret waters rippling with mirth
Spirit hovering over depths meeting earth
Swirling wind and love
Coursing down from above
Panting, then pulsing, then hearing
Sophia's hymn
At the first cry of birth
I Am
Alpha
And
Omega
Thus breathes
Ha Shem

In the beginning God created the heaven and the earth. And the earth was without form, and void; and darkness was upon the face of the deep. And the Spirit of God moved upon the face of the waters.

GENESIS 1:1–2 (KJV)

In Christian understanding, God is a divine community, consisting of three distinctive, interrelated agents or actions.[1] The Spirit of God hovers or moves over the face of the waters. The Word/Wisdom of God initiates the becoming of light, structure of sky and earth, waters and land, vegetation and creeping things, water creatures and birds, beasts and human beings. Word/Wisdom does not create without the movement of the Spirit–in Hebrew, the *ruach* or breath of God. The Spirit of God is with God the Author and Parent of all life. The Spirit of God is with God the Word/Wisdom of Life. Together, God the Author/Parent of life, God the Word/Wisdom of life, and the Spirit of God create the heaven and the earth. The Spirit of God, who for Christians is the Holy Spirit, unites and empowers Word/Wisdom and Author/Parent in the activity of divine creativity.

In the movement of the Holy Spirit, God in Genesis is revealed as breath and life itself. In the free verse above, as in the first verse of Genesis, God is genderless. The salt waters are God's tears. The breath of God swirls dust and salt waters into oases. God kisses life and truth into lips formed from clay, a fine product of dust and water.

The Creative Dance of the Trinity

Van A. Harvey writes that Western Christendom of the third century "rightly or wrongly chose to translate the Greek word *ousia,"* employed by Plato (428–348 B.C.E.) and Aristotle (384–322 B.C.E.), as "substance." In their understanding, *ousia,* referred to "the defining characteristics of a thing, the pattern or form that persists throughout its career." Later, the term came to signify "the permanent, unified, causal reality of a thing." This is particularly apparent in the theology of Saint Thomas of Aquinas, who imagines a world of "existing, enduring, concrete entities."[2] By the modern period, substantialist understandings of God came to portray God as static, changing, unmoved mover.

From the beginning, a problem arose in Western translations of *ousia* and *hypostasis.* The Cappadocian view is included in the creed of Nicea, 325 C.E. Unfortunately, the Western translators mistranslated Greek terms they understood in an entirely different way than the Cappadocians. The Nicene Creed has thus implanted part of Eastern orthodoxy within Western orthodoxy but in a way that historically has been misunderstood. The Eastern understanding works as a corrective to Western mistranslation. God is dynamically relational, a community of three distinctive actions or movements, the divine whirlwind that overcomes the existential storms of life.

Western Christianity understands the Trinity not simply as three persons in one nature, but three persons *in one substance.* Both traditions, East and West, can share the word "nature," but "substance" is a Western translation. The Western writers of the Nicene Creed in 325 C.E. assumed that the Cappadocians[3] meant the same thing in their understanding of the Greek term *ousia* that Tertullian (160–220) had meant by *substance.* Scholars believe Tertullian coined the term "Trinity." The Cappadocians had understood God as three relations (*hypostases*) in one being (*ousia*). As William Rusch puts it, they understood the Trinity as "three modes of being" or, as he translates Gregory of Nazianzus, "three actions."[4] This is the Eastern Orthodox Christian understanding. It is different from the Western translation of *ousia* and *hypostasis* into Latin. It is also very different from modalism, also called Modalistic Monarchialism, in which God is understood as one essence of three interchangeable names. In that view, God is one person or *ousia* with three different roles.

The Cappadocians understood God as three *hypostases* in one *ousia,* as did early Western Christians. They understood these three modes of being, actions, or relations as distinctive and noninterchangeable. They provide a more dynamic understanding of God as relational that is much clearer than is Augustine's later, Western interpretation with its more substantialist view. Whether we turn to early classical Christian theology in the East or in the West, or to our own contemporary theologies, however, we find some agreement that God is relational and that God is a community. Finally, we find agreement among Trinitarians that the power of the Holy Spirit inspires community within God's own nature and in the world.

The three *hypostases* of God indwell one another in one divine nature, the Greek *perichoresis,* "to dance around," or as it is often translated, "indwelling" or "to envelope." The three hypostases dynamically, relationally dance around and within one another. Each dynamically and interrelationally participates in the one work of divine love, creativity, justice, and righteousness through distinctive actions. Drawing from the understanding of *perichoresis,* integrative relational theologians today might say that the Holy Spirit empowers and encourages the dance, which is the dance of life.

God is a Spirit whom the entire earth is called to worship in spirit and in truth (Jn. 4:23–24). When we speak of the breath and word of God at creation, we are speaking of a Spirit who is one God in three relations or hypostases. The breath or Spirit of God refers to the third hypostasis of God who is a Spirit. The distinctive action of the Holy Spirit is to comfort or console, to heal, encourage, and empower. The "Word" of God refers to the second of three *hypostases* or *relations* that make up the one communal relational nature of God. The breath and word of God belong to one God who is three *hypostases, relations,* or *persons,* in many translations of early Christian literature, in one nature.

Often, theologians first discuss the *immanent* Trinity, God's internal Trinitarian relation to God's own being and increasing becoming in glory. In a second step, they discuss the *economic* Trinity–the relation of the Trinity to the world. God creates through the power of the Spirit. God, who is relational, always creates. God, the Creator in three actions or hypostases, relates lovingly to creation. God would continue to be a relational, creating God in relation to God's own being and becoming in the increase of God's own glory, however, even if creation as we humans have come to know it were to cease to exist. God, who is three relational actions or *hypostases* in one nature, is not dependent on creation. Creation is dependent on God. Therefore, one cannot speak of the economic Trinity, the relationship of God to the world, without an understanding of the immanent Trinity, which is who God is in relation to God's self. Discussion of the *economic* and *immanent* Trinity are intertwined in an integrated relational approach.

There is, in the end, one God, one Trinity that is both *immanent* and *economic.* It is important to keep in mind, however, that the Trinity is everlasting while the world to which the Trinity relates is limited by its finitude characterized by cycles of life, death, and recreation. The Trinity in its *immanent* nature, then, is primary. It is the power that makes any discussion of the economic Trinity, the dance-like relationship of the Trinity to the world, possible. God, who is three *hypostases* or *relations* in one nature, is like three distinct dancers who make up one dynamic dance. Each *hypostasis* or *relation,* often translated as *person,* participates in the life of the other, a life of mutual relationship grounded in the understanding of God as a relational community.

The First Relation of the Divine Dance

Religious metaphors, a type of verbal and written symbol that evokes an image of God, do not define God, but for McFague they describe "how we relate to God."[5] There are multiple metaphors for God. This understanding of Christian language for God as metaphorical is somewhat helpful. Today, however, many Christians and people attracted to Christianity want to know the biblical warrant for such thought. Unfortunately, McFague's turn to a revisionist task in her understanding of theology renders her insights only minimally helpful for such persons of faith. She is more interested in "the form" of scripture than in "the content of scripture."[6]

One can explore metaphors for God in the content of scripture for a lifetime without exhausting their meaning. The Psalms, for example, refer to God as provider, shelter, my peace, hiding place, as moving like a pillar of cloud, shepherd, maker, and rock of salvation. The book of Job employs the metaphor of "whirlwind" for God's dynamic presence in the world (38:1; 40:6). The book of John describes Jesus as "the true vine" (15:1). In Western Christian tradition, the second agent proceeds from the first; and the third agent proceeds from the first through the second. In Eastern Christian tradition, the second and third agents each proceed from the first. The difference between the two is known as the *filioque* controversy, whether or not the Holy Spirit proceeds from the Father and the Son (West) or whether the Son and Holy Spirit proceed from the Father.[7] In both cases, however, they are not "made" or "created." In relation to creation, however, "maker" is appropriate as a metaphor for describing the entire Trinity as divine author, artist, or poet. It is synonymous with "Creator."

During the last decades of the twentieth century with the emergence of feminist theology, scholars began to ask, "Is God male?" and "Is God literally and only Father?" As we have seen, biblical literature employs many metaphors for God. Delores Williams observes that Hagar, the only woman in the Bible who names God, called God "El Roi" which means "God of seeing."[8] It is important to remember that other metaphors are adequate referents to the God of Jesus. Reifying metaphors for God risks the sin of idolatry. As one Master of Divinity student at Perkins School of Theology wryly commented, "Nowhere in the Bible does it say, 'Thou shalt only call God, Father.'" At the same time, she observed, this does not mean that we should never call God, Father. McFague, for example, employs the metaphor of "Mother" to describe God's relational nature, particularly in relation to the world. "Mother" for McFague, does not replace "Father." Indeed, she is open to understanding God as "like a father and a mother."[9]

The gift of feminist biblical and theological scholarship is that it calls communities of faith back to the multiplicity of biblical metaphors for God. No one word describes the fullness of God's nature. This does not mean, however, that the term "Father" needs to be erased from the Christian lexicon. To the contrary, God as Father is still infused with relational meaning. Along with many other biblical metaphors, it helps us describe God's relationship to God's own being and the world and thus is helpful for understanding the nature of God.

The term "Father" or "Abba"–meaning "Daddy" in Jesus' original language (Mk. 14:36; Rom. 8:15; Gal. 4:6)–is the classical term for designating the intimacy of God with Jesus the Christ, "the Son," and with the world. Jesus the Christ is the Word and only Son of God. For many Orthodox Christians, Eastern and Western, Father is "God's name."

The term *Father* designates the first agent of the Trinity as the generator of the Son or Word/Wisdom, who proceeds from the first agent of the Trinity.[10] This is important to Orthodox Trinitarians, because it emphasizes that Jesus as Son of God is of the same substance (*homoousios*) with the first person of the Trinity. Jesus the Christ, the Word and only Son of God, is intimately related to and of one nature with God as a child is to a parent. God is not Jesus' Creator, but Jesus' "Father" in relation to Mary who is Jesus' mother (Mt. 1:16–25). The Son, who is the Word made flesh (Jn. 1:14), is conceived by the Holy Spirit of God and born of a woman, fully divine and fully human.

The terms "Father" and "Mother" describe relationships of parenthood. In relationship to Jesus' human mother, Mary, it makes sense to refer to God as Father, because God "conceived" rather than created Jesus the Christ in the power of the Holy Spirit. God is not literally a father, however, in the anthropomorphic sense of the term. God did not conceive the Son through the Holy Spirit in the literal fashion that a human father conceives a child. God is *like* what we humans call a "father" in God's relationship to the Son, Jesus the Christ who is the Word.

God in relation to creation is Father and more than Father. Mother metaphors and metaphors for God drawn from nature are present in several passages of Hebrew and Christian scripture, only a few of which we have space to name here. God is like a mother eagle who catches and bears its young on her large, strong wings until they learn to fly freely on their own (Ex. 19:4; Deut. 32:11). God labors like a woman in childbirth in God's love for creation (Isa. 42:14). In Isaiah 49:15, God is like a mother who cannot forget her children, thus functioning as a model for human motherhood and parenting.[11] Similarly, in Jesus' model prayer (Mt. 6:9–13; Lk. 11:2–4) and in the Johannine literature, God as father functions as a model for human fathers and parenting. God is like a Mother and a Father. God is like a Parent. A parent, male or female, nurtures and provides. Neither term refers to one gender or another here. Nor is provider/nurturer strictly anthropomorphic. God created the earth and the heavens to be a provider and nurturer of a diversity of creatures. In their reflection of divine creativity, provision, and nurture, the earth and the heavens are like God. "Provider/Nurturer" is a metaphor, a term drawn from concrete experience to describe the literal activity of the first relational agent of the Trinity in its *economic* nature. God is like a Provider/Nurturer.

In the book of Exodus and elsewhere, God is *El Shaddai,* God of the mountain or God Almighty (Gen. 17:1; 28:3; 35:11; 43:14; 48:3; Ex. 6:3; Ezek. 10:5; Job 8:5; 13:3; 15:25). As John Cobb observes, "God almighty" is not a very accurate translation. In the original Hebrew, the phrase simply reads "God of the mountain."[12] In Hebrew, the word *shaddai* has more than one meaning. It is also the word for "breast," because mountains look like breasts. There is a hidden meaning in the phrase *El Shaddai.* This meaning was not as troublesome to ancient peoples as it is for some readers today who are far more squeamish regarding such thinking in relation to the sacred. Squeamishness about meanings that readers with a modern mindset find embarrassing can hamper our spiritual growth, particularly our understanding of God's profound love. The "hidden" meaning of *El Shaddai,* hidden to readers with a modern mindset at least, is God's nurture. Therefore, *El Shaddai* is not only as mighty, grand, and awesome as a mountain but as powerfully nurturing, gentle, and loving as a mother's gift, shared from her bosom.[13] Behind her bosom, lie her heart and lungs–the power of life and breath. God is like a mother. *El Shaddai* is God of the mountain and God who is like a mother's bosom, mighty and intimately nurturing at once, without division or separation of nature and meaning.[14] *El Shaddai* is simultaneously an analogy for God's transcendence and intimate omnipresence.

Rather than wrestle with gendered language, this theology refers to the first relational agent of the Trinity as Parent, or more precisely, like a parent. This retains the traditional understanding of each agent of the Trinity being of the same nature as the first person of the Trinity. Jesus remains the Son or offspring of God, proceeding from the first agent or relational action of the Trinity. It is important to recognize, however, that Jesus as the Word/Wisdom of God may be understood either in the language of Word/*Hokmah,* Word/*Sophia,* or *Logos.*[15] As Elizabeth Johnson's rich and accurate theological exegesis and construction recognizes, the depictions of *Hokmah* in Proverbs 1–8 and Job 28 and of Sophia in intertestamental Jewish Hellenistic scripture such as Sirach and the Wisdom of Solomon are carried forward into the New Testament understandings of Jesus the Christ's nature and teachings as Word and Wisdom in the books of Matthew, John, and in Pauline literature.[16]

One may also employ extrabiblical metaphors for God. In sermons, preachers engage in this practice on a regular basis. Jeremiah Wright, for example, said in a sermon that God is like a navigational system in some cars. This recalls Proverbs 1–8, with its consistent call to follow Wisdom and to let God be one's guide in life. Such metaphors are appreciated in church contexts that value the larger Christian tradition when related to both the content and form of scripture. This is one of the keys to Wright's success as a preacher who is in great demand.

God the Parent is divine author or artist. This first, dynamic relation of God is also Provider/Nurturer. In liturgical practice, one might refer to God, then, as "our provider and nurturer." In private prayer, one might say, "my provider and my nurturer."[17] Traditionally, this divine action or relation is referred to as God the Father. In the sayings attributed to Jesus in the gospel of John, Jesus consistently refers to God as his father (for selections, see Jn. 4:21; 6:37; 8:19,54; 16:15; and 17:25). In contemporary Christian services, some refer to this particular action or relation as God the Creator. It is the first person of the Trinity. Jesus teaches the disciples to pray, "Our Father who art in heaven, hallowed be thy name" (Mt. 6:9; Lk. 11:2, KJV).

The Second Relation of the Divine Dance

The "Word" or "Logos," which is the second person of the Trinity in Christian tradition, is present at creation in Christian traditional understanding that draws on John 1:1–14. From this Johannine context, Christians understand God's *uttering* forth of light, land, creatures of the sea, beasts, and creeping things as the presence of the Word. In Genesis 1, the Word is suggested in the phrase, "Let there be…" In Hebrew scriptures, "word" is *dabhar. Dabhar* is multidimensional and multivalent.

God's Word and utterance are not like human speech or writing, requiring mouth, tongue, teeth, hands, and fingers. The divine Word is a living power. It is a movement or action. In the Johannine understanding of God, "In the beginning was the Word, and the Word was with God, and the Word was God" (Jn. 1:1). It is more than written words; it is dynamic and living. Filled with the light or power of God, it is wisdom and knowledge to the soul. The Greek term for Word in John is *logos. Logos* means word, knowledge, and wisdom. In John, the Son, the Word of God, proceeds from God's own nature and is one with God. This Word/Wisdom was with God and is God. In Christian tradition, the First Testament and New Testament writings are a collection of dynamic, multivalent, living words about the living Word of God.

We humans are created. We are creatures. The Son as Word of God is not created, but is of God's own nature. We humans are like sons and daughters of God by adoption through life that is found in the Son and Word of God (Rom. 8:15, 23; Gal. 4:5; Eph. 1:5). Athanasius (296–373) referred to the Son of God as Word/Wisdom, keeping alive the Greek understanding of *Sophia* (Wisdom) and *Logos* (Word), and however intentionally or unintentionally the Hebrew understanding of *Hokmah*

(Wisdom) and *Dabhar* (Word) who is with God in the beginning (Prov. 8:12–30).[18] This view integrates divine wisdom found in Jesus the Christ with the Greek understanding of divine *Logos* (Word, Knowledge, or Wisdom).[19]

Athanasius's understanding of the Son as the Word and Wisdom of God, however, also makes good biblical sense. English-speaking Westerners tend to translate *logos* employed by the writer of John 1:1 as "Word," but it also means wisdom. Athanasius's understanding is helpful for our time. The second person of the Trinity, is Word/Wisdom. God in three persons, Parent or Father, Word/Wisdom, and Holy Spirit create, love, and empower.

Creativity, love, and empowerment transcend gender. Gender belongs to creatures. God, in three persons, is not a creature. God as Father or Parent, Son and Word, and Holy Spirit, Three in One, is our Creator without beginning or end, omnipresent in creation, but transcending male and female existential realities. Neither God who conceives the Son by the power of the Holy Spirit nor the Son are literally male. God is a Spirit and does not have a gender.

The historical Jesus had a gender. Jesus as Word and as the living Christ or anointed one, however, transcends gender-based anthropomorphic understandings of reality. Biblically, Christians are free to speak of the Wisdom of God in either feminine, masculine, or neutral language. Many Christians insist they are "uncomfortable with saying 'she'" for God because it sounds "strange." That makes as much sense as those who argued that there should be no female news anchors (or women preachers) several decades ago, "because their voices sound funny and men sound better." It is illogical and irrational, a very weak excuse for judging those who do use feminine or neutral language for God, for Word/Wisdom, and for the Holy Spirit. While we employ primarily neutral language in this text, because God is a Spirit and neither male nor female in actuality, this does not preclude readers from employing feminine, masculine, or both gendered language as they learn from the content of this theology and move on to write their own work. The Word/Wisdom of God is male and female as the very model of maleness and femaleness in God's omnipresence, yet neither male nor female in God's transcendence of creation. Therefore, Jesus the Christ fully incarnates the Word/Wisdom that biblical writers have written of in feminine and masculine language. No, in response to many who ask, this does not mean that Jesus "was a woman." It simply means that Jesus is fully the Wisdom and Word of God from before the beginning of creation as we know it. This is part of the mystery of what it means for Jesus the Christ to be more than fully human, but truly God who holds all good. In Christ there is neither male nor female (Gal. 3:28), yet God in Christ includes male and female alike.

At the same time, according to John 4:23–24, God is a Spirit and those who worship God must worship God "in spirit and in truth." God is a

Spirit, whom Christians know to be incarnate in Christ, and whose Holy Spirit has the specific function of witnessing to God the Creator. God who is a Spirit, in the Christian worldview, moves in dance with the Holy Spirit and the Word.

The Third Relation of the Divine Dance

God is a Spirit. In authentic worship of God, we worship God in spirit and in truth (Jn. 4:23–24). The entire Trinity is a Spirit, with the exception of the Son who reveals God who is a Spirit through incarnation and living amongst us. The Holy Spirit, or the Spirit of God, is a distinctive *hypostasis* or *relation,* of the one Trinitarian God who is a Spirit. It is the very breath of God, literally *the life inspiring relation* of God. In other words, God, the Spirit who is the source of all life, is Parent, Son and Word, and Holy Spirit. We will discuss the Holy Spirit at length in chapter 7.

Scholars debate strongly today whether or not to refer to the Holy Spirit as the Wisdom of God. Biblically, scripture does refer to the Holy Spirit as instructing the people of God in Christ, guiding them in Wisdom. The Holy Spirit is understood as "the Spirit of Truth."

The Holy Spirit is the Spirit of God that hovers over the waters in the beginning, setting creaturely life in motion (Gen. 1:2). It is important to note that "the Spirit" (Hebrew, *ruach*) at creation is generally understood to be the Holy Spirit in Christian interpretations of Genesis 1. Thus in classical Christian understanding, the entire Trinity is present at creation. The Spirit breathes life into the first human beings and according to Genesis 7:22 and Ecclesiastes 3:19 is the *ruach* or breath of both human creatures and the beasts of the fields.[20] Apparently, it is not simply in the animating breath which is ruach, that we are created in the divine image, a breath that makes us alive, lively, and dynamic. Most likely it is in our ability to live in loving community with creation and serve as God's stewards of the earth, loving it with God's compassion and reason, that we carry God's likeness. All of creation is moved by the breath of God, the *ruach* or Spirit of God. Even rocks are made up of molecules and smaller, subquantum, dynamically moving particles of energy that are invisible to the human eye. Without the Holy Spirit, there is no movement and, therefore, no life in creation. The Holy Spirit infuses creatures of clay with life. The distinction between human beings and other creatures in their original creation is not a matter of spirit. Human beings are distinctive, because according to Genesis 1:26, they are made in the likeness or image of God. They are created to reflect God's own nature, which is loving, creative, just, righteous, relational, and good. We will consider humankind's fall from and distortion of this image in chapters 4 and 5.

First, it is necessary to consider further the divine nature in relation to creation. God, who is a spirit, is first and foremost divine creativity, the initiator of the dance called life.

The Dancing Trinity and Creation

"Creativity" refers to the entire process of creating. The divine process of creating is not just any form of creativity. It is the source and power of creativity. All other forms of creativity are derivative. Divine creativity is everlasting. Without it, finite forms of creativity in nature, including the human process of creating in which peoples of diverse cultures reshape creation for aesthetic and utilitarian purposes, is not possible. Human creativity, like the creativity of birds who build nests, is secondary to divine creativity. Divine creativity is the source of that which we call nature: human beings, trees from which one gathers twigs for weaving, plants from which dyes are made, silicon used for computer chips, water and lemons to which sugar from sugar cane is added. Divine creativity makes the re-creation which creatures engage in possible.

God is three dancing *hypostases* in one divine nature. The first person of the Trinity is more than Creator. All three persons of the Trinity create. "God" creates, the "Word" creates, and "the Spirit of God" creates. As the Greek Cappadocian early Christian writers Gregory of Nanzianzus (330–390) and Gregory of Nyssa (331/40 to about 395) claimed in their interpretation of scripture, all three persons of the Trinity have a common work. Yet, they are distinct. There are three persons or hypostases. Hypostasis is not a person in the static sense, but in the classical Eastern Christian understanding is "a mode of being," dynamic and moving with the power of life.[21] God is a relationship of three modes of being, in dynamic movement and activity, with a common work of love, creativity, justice, righteousness, goodness, and power. As Gregory of Nanzianzus puts it, "Father is a name neither of a substance, O most clever ones, nor of an action, but...the Father is the name of the relation in which the Father is to the Son or the Son to the Father."[22] Similarly, Gregory of Nyssa writes that "the divine nature itself is not noted by any of the names, but that something of its characteristics is made known through the statements."[23] The first person of the Trinity is the one from whom the Son and Word, as well as the Holy Spirit, proceeds.

The name "Father" is not God's name, but the name of a relationship. As Gregory of Nyssa emphasizes, "every name, whether it has been invented from human usage or handed down from Scripture, is an interpretation of the things thought about divine nature and does not encompass the significance of the nature itself."[24] As he further explains, each of the names for God reveals a "peculiar reflection suitable to the thought" or what is "said about the divine nature," without "signifying what that nature is according to its substance."[25] The first person of the Trinity is like a parent, begetting Jesus the Christ who is the Word and only Son of God. The first person of the Trinity also creates heaven and earth, shaping formless matter into the universe we have come to know and have yet to discover in community with God the Word and God the Holy Spirit. God the Word and God the Holy Spirit share the common power and work of creativity as a holy Trinity, three persons of one substance or nature. God is a creating and loving community, in whose likeness human creatures are made (Gen. 1:26). God is one Spirit in three natures. The parenting relation of God is the activity of the first person of the Trinity. The Word and Wisdom of God is the relational activity of the second person of the Trinity. The empowering, teaching, healing, comforting, encouraging, and unifying relation is the activity of the third person of the Trinity.

God in Creation

We may find experiential understandings of God as a Spirit who is present in creation in popular culture as well as in Christian theology and the writings of quantum metaphysics. Alice Walker, a well-known writer-activist, writes that a "womanist 'Loves the Spirit.'"[26] For Walker, to love the Spirit is to love creation. In her Pulitzer Prize-winning novel, *The Color Purple,* the dynamic, integrative relationship of creation and spirit is explicit. The sexually and physically abused Celie learns from blues singer Shug that God is not an old white man in the sky: "it pisses God off if you walk by the color purple in a field somewhere and don't notice it."

> "Here's the thing," say Shug. "The thing I believe. God is inside you and inside everybody else. You come into the world with God. But only them that search for it inside find it. And sometimes it just manifest itself even if you not looking, or don't know what you're looking for. Trouble do it for most folk, I think. Sorrow, lord."[27]

Walker's work implies a relational integrative metaphysics. Specifically, if God is "inside you and everybody else," then we have indications of a panentheistic worldview in which God is in all things. On the next page, however, the text suggests that Shug's God may be pantheistic, that is God is everything. Consider Shug's response to the question "But what do it look like?"

> "Don't look like nothing," she say. "It ain't a picture show. It ain't something you can look at apart from anything else, including yourself. I believe God is everything," say Shug. "Everything that is or ever was or ever will be. And when you can feel that, and be happy to feel that, you've found it."[28]

Feminist and womanist theologians sometimes gloss over this, writing as if Walker, who admits Shug's spirituality is her own, were clearly *panentheistic.* The narrative in *The Color Purple* is ambiguous. Walker may very well be a *pantheist.* Therefore, it is necessary to be selective and critical in employing her work, certainly for Christian metaphysics but also in relation to other religions, including indigenous religions which Western anthropologists have sometimes interpreted as pantheistic, when they were actually panentheistic. Nonetheless, Shug's God reminds readers that anthropomorphic descriptions of God are limited symbols and metaphors, some of them more true than others. Shug's God is very different from the God of Christendom that Celie has learned about in church, where all the pictures in the Bible are of holy looking white men with long beards and no shoes.

Throughout the corpus of Walker's work, she makes no separation between God and creation. Most view Alice Walker as a "pagan." This is the term she uses to describe her spirituality. Anthony Pinn describes Walker as a "humanist." For some, this is disconcerting, because Walker's spirituality is creation-centered, not human-centered. Yet, to be fair to Pinn's analysis, many of Walker's values fit within Pinn's five-part definition of humanism.[29] Moreover, Walker is a recipient of an American Humanist Association (AHA) award. The American Humanist Association defines "humanism" as "a progressive lifestance that, without supernaturalism, affirms our ability and responsibility to lead meaningful, ethical lives capable of adding to the greater good of humanity."[30] The AHA further explains that, "Free of supernaturalism, [humanism] recognizes human beings as a part of nature and holds that values–be they religious, ethical, social, or political–have their source in human experience and culture."[31] Moreover, the AHA is attentive to ecological and environmental concerns. It is concerned about all of creation, not just humans.

Walker's open-ended essays, poetry, and fiction leave readers of her work free to come to their own conclusions regarding how to name her. The spirituality of Walker's characters Shug and Celie wavers between pantheism and panentheism. Kate Talking Tree's spiritual journey in Walker's *Now Is the Time to Open Your Heart* is very earthy. She gains greater awareness of her relationship to the earth itself.[32] Walker describes her personal trinity as Universe, Nature, and Earth.[33] Her poem "Her Blue Body Everything We Know" articulates well Walker's understanding that she finds her spirituality in this earth.[34] In *Living by the Word,* Walker discusses her spiritual relationship with trees and describes herself as an "earthling."[35] As much as humanist Pinn and womanist scholars of religion would like her to be, Walker is not systematic or always consistent in her discussions of spirituality. Where Pinn sees a humanist, others see a pantheist, and still others try to force Walker's work into a panentheistic category. What is most helpful about Walker's writings is that she has increased understanding that if God exists, then God is omnipresent in creation. The weakness of her work from a Christian Trinitarian perspective is that she is very much a pantheist who believes that if God exists, then God is everything–God is nature. God is not nature or creation. God is omnipresent in nature. God is omnipresent in creation.

To the extent that Walker's Shug means that all of creation manifests divine presence, Shug's understanding of God offers an insight that is helpful for an integrative relational theology. Process metaphysics presses one to clarify whether one is panentheistic or pantheistic. In God, there is no separation between heaven and earth. Both are in God. What does it mean to suggest that God and creation are, though distinct, of the same stuff?[36] Shug's earlier panentheistic statement regarding God's omnipresence everywhere and in everyone is helpful, because it suggests that God includes and permeates the many without being finite. God then, can be understood as infinite, in all things without being subject to the finitude and mortality of creation. If this God sometimes "just manifest itself even if you not looking, or don't know what you looking for," then God is omnipresent. Shug says that her first step away from the image of God as an old white man was "trees. Then air. Then birds. Then other people." Then, one day, she explains, "I knew that if I cut a tree, my arm would bleed."[37] God is everywhere.

The God of Walker's Shug is relational. When we recognize relationship with God, we realize that when we hurt creation we hurt God and ourselves. Moreover, process metaphysics presses womanist spirituality and theology to elucidate the term "creation." "Creation," for example, in *The Color Purple* is more than "nature"; it also means creativity. It is noun and verb. Celie finds economic freedom by "entering the Creation" and with a needle in her hand for sewing instead of a razor for cutting "Mister's" throat. Using the term creation as both noun and verb is parallel to Whitehead's understanding of creation as dynamic and as participating in divine creativity. To be creation is to participate in divine creating. First and foremost, God is Creator, then Word, and finally God as Creator and Word relates to God's own self and the world through the power of God's own Spirit. The Word and the Spirit also create. God as Creator, then, might be understood as "Author" or "Maker." There is an implicit Trinity at work "in the beginning," creating the universe we humans have come to experience since the time of our own entrance into creation out of the dust and water in Genesis 2, inspired by the breath of God.

The birth of the cosmos, nature, creatures–all that we call the world–begins with divine creativity interacting with a formless, empty, earth that God has created and continues to create. All that we have come to know as our cosmos begins with the Spirit of God hovering over the dark, deep waters.[38] Genesis 1:1–2 offers an account of the cosmic and ecological nativity of the planet we rely on for sustenance. God creates through Word/Wisdom and Spirit. This is represented in the biblical account of God who commands "Let there be." God, who is a spirit, creates spirit-infused matter. We are because of God, the dynamic creative power that is the source of life. God and creation are interrelational. We are created to reach our full potential in God.

The Breath and Word/Wisdom of God in Creation

Anna Julia Cooper (1858–1964) described God as "an irresistible power not ourselves" and as "a singing something" in human beings, male and female, of every race and nationality. This "singing something" is what makes us *anthropos*. It is what makes us human beings. For Cooper, this "singing something" moves within every human being and rises up against injustice to demand freedom and equality. She employs "singing something" as a synonym for "divine spark" and *imago dei.*[39] A relational integrative theology adds that this "singing something" is the divine, dynamic, omnipresent Word/Wisdom of God that moves throughout creation, recreating everlastingly in communal relationship with God the Author/ Parent and the Holy Spirit. It is God in creation. The earth, its creatures, and the heavens "reveal the glory of God" (Ps. 19:1).[40] Human beings are more complex creatures, yes, but not alone in revealing divine handiwork. Cooper's "singing something" is a relationship of call and response, of breath to breath (Wesley), Spirit to spirit. It is a relationship of divine love to creation and love in creation returning to God. God and creation are mutually responsive. We are created for the purpose of God's enjoyment. We are created to enjoy God. The purpose of creation is to glorify God, not to glorify itself. A moral life glorifies God through praise and worship of God. For Whitehead, the human search for God is "an adventure of the spirit," and the power of God is the worship he inspires."[41] The purpose of creation is to *praise God.*[42] In Luke 19:40 even the rocks cry out! All life, animate and inanimate, is created to glorify and to respond to God. Divine love requires creation's loving response. Our spiritual striving for union with God and right relationship with one another, including the rest of creation, includes worship and praise of the one who inspires us with vision of our full humanity. This fullness of humanity is revealed in Jesus the Christ.

Creatio Ex Nihilo or *Creatio Ex Profundus?*

Scholars of biblical and theological writings ask whether we were created from disorganized matter and energy or out of nothing. Classical theologians employ John 1 to interpret Genesis 1 as suggesting that God created something out of nothing. This is the *creatio ex nihilo* theory. According to John 1:1–3 (KJV), "In the beginning was the Word and the Word was with God, and the Word was God. The same was in the beginning with God." From this basis Christians often think our cosmos and this planet were created from nothing. As I have noted elsewhere, "Early Christian writers employed such philosophical and poetic interpretation to develop *creatio ex nihilo* theory. The author of John claims that God made all things and that nothing was made without God. Even John 1:1–3 does not say that there was nothing before the creation of this particular cosmos. It says that without God, nothing was made."[43]

Genesis 1:1 is not as clear as we would like about whether God created heaven and earth out of nothing or not. In Genesis 1:1–2, the Spirit of God hovers over the waters. The earth was "without form." It was "void or empty." Thus waters existed for the Spirit of God to hover over. It does not say "nothing." Genesis is not at all clear that "void," "deep," and "without form" mean nothing or that they are evil. We are simply informed that these things were present:

> The creation story in Genesis is a birth story…the deep, the darkness, the waters dance in co-creative activity with the Spirit of God. Out of mutual, loving creative activity, all that we call life came into [the process of creative becoming][44]

In looking at the first few words, "In the beginning," it is reasonable to ask, "Whose beginning?" This is not about God's beginning, because God is already present in the story. Moreover, later texts and doctrine claim that God has no beginning or end. On the one hand, Christian tradition emphasizes the chaos or "deep" from which our becoming was shaped. On the other hand, tradition claims that we were created from nothing. The void, the formlessness, and the deep of Genesis are a remnant from the Babylonian *Enuma Elish.* They are a remnant of the maternal in divine creativity. Quoting from *Sisters of Dust, Sisters of Spirit:* "Tiamat's destruction by a male deity represents a misogynist, destructive perspective on women's sexual and creative power."[45] While the Hebrew scripture makes no explicit reference to a matriarchal goddess, Bible scholar Susan Niditch notes that if the Genesis account "lacks a matriarchal goddess, it also does not present the creation of the world as dependent on her death."[46] This early analysis of Genesis is an interpretation that positively values what some might call the feminine aspects of divine creativity.

If there are many heavens, as Pauline literature suggests (2 Cor. 12:2), and if heaven is God's dwelling place, then surely God's dwelling place existed before the heaven and earth we have come to know. Indeed, in much of biblical literature, the word for heaven and sky is the same. So, perhaps it is simply the sky and planet that are part of the cosmos that sustains earthly life that the writer of Genesis 1:1 had in mind.

Creativity, freedom, and depth are revealed in the first verses of Genesis 1 as the Spirit of God hovers over the waters. God creates out of the void or the deep through the Spirit and through a speech or thought act–"let there be." The *word* for early Hebrews and contemporary practicing Jews is very powerful. The Word of God has life and creates. Christians, through our eisegesis of Hebrew scriptures and exegesis of Christian scriptures (especially Jn. 1:1), interpret this speech act to mean that Christ as the Word was with God at creation. Because the Spirit of God is also present, many Christians see the entire Trinity present in Genesis 1. Jewish scholars and Hebrew Bible scholars do not.

One might think of the proposition that the Trinity is present in Genesis as a type of Christian midrash, historically a Jewish practice of reading between the lines to consider the unwritten parts of biblical stories. For Jews, the Torah is the primary scripture to be engaged in midrash. For Christians, the Hebrew Bible and the New Testament are engaged. Scholars rightly call what we Christians do with the Hebrew Bible *eisegesis*–reading into the text, rather than *exegesis* or reading out of the text. *Eisegesis* is a problem when we are not honest about doing it. It makes sense to simply be honest and honor it as a type of midrash. Such midrashic tradition itself carries authority as the work of Christians who have prayed for understanding of the missing parts of the story and experienced divine revelation in *ecclesia* (church community.)

Genesis 1 begins with remnants of feminine descriptions of the divine. A similar understanding of divine everlastingness informs Catherine Keller's emphasis on verse 2 of Genesis 1, with its reflection on the Spirit of God hovering over the deep. This verse, Keller emphasizes, suggests *creatio ex profundus,* rather than *creatio ex nihilo.*[47] *Creatio ex profundus* is undoubtedly an aspect of divine creativity, otherwise it is necessary to ignore Gen. 1:2. Yet, is it possible that if God is indeed greater than all we can imagine, then God creates in ways we can and cannot imagine or empirically observe? Leonardo Boff's analysis is helpful, because rather than enter into the dominant rules of the debates over this issue in which one is either biblically, traditionally, *or* scientifically based in one's analysis, he draws from the quantum physics of Werner Heisenberg and Albert Einstein to develop an understanding of creation that makes it possible for traditionalists to view their understanding of *creatio ex nihilo* as far more than unscientific nonsense. Boff scientifically explores the relationship between particles (matter) and waves (energy) without contradicting, disputing, or belittling classical Christian claims.[48]

Boff reminds the reader that in Einstein's theory of relativity, "energy can become matter, and matter can become energy."[49] His theology does not debate the *creatio ex nihilo* theory, but rather is open to mystery. However, if energy can become matter and matter can become energy, in some sense something can come from nothing–something that is similar to its origins but which enters a distinctive and unique process of becoming. If God is the source of energy itself, the Spirit of life and the very power of creating, then nothing that is made is made without God who is revealed in the Word, the very wisdom, structure, and knowledge of the power to create. In the beginning God created (Gen. 1:1), and without the Word of God, nothing was made (Jn. 1:3). Otherwise, there would have to be some process or entity that is more ultimate than God. God, however, is the universe's ultimate point of reference, "that than which nothing greater can be conceived," to borrow from Anselm of Canterbury (1033–1109).[50] Therefore, it is illogical to posit something more.

The neoclassical metaphysician Charles Hartshorne understands God as creating neither out of nothing nor of unformed matter. In Hartshorne's analysis, God has already been and must always be, not slightly but "supremely creative of the cells in the divine body, including you and me as such cells. Specifically, Whitehead calls his view a 'cell theory of reality,' but he never took the Platonic step of conceiving the cosmos as supreme body." God, for Hartshorne is "supremely creative" of all recent stages of the world process and of its predecessors.[51] In other words, the cosmos is God's body.

While there is truth to this statement, the problem is that, for many Christians, it sounds as if for Hartshorne creation proceeds from creation, rather than from God. This makes Jesus the Christ as the Son of God less novel than the Son of classical Christian thought who is unique by virtue of sharing God's nature. What, then, becomes of the distinction between Jesus the Christ and humankind–or the rest of the cosmos, for that matter. One could argue that there is not such a great distinction, except in the completeness of the divine nature that Jesus the Christ shares with God. In process metaphysics, Jesus the Christ may be understood as one *avatar* or *incarnation* among many. This is not consistent with the understanding of Jesus the Christ in the gospels of Matthew, Mark, Luke, and John. Process metaphysics presents the Christian believer with more problematic questions than helpful insights or answers. Surely if God is everlastingly creative, from eternity before all beginnings into infinity, then God created much more before creating the earth and its galaxy.

Because of his methodological grounding in postmodern science, Hartshorne finds it unsatisfactory to say with the writer of the book of Job that he does not know how God creates. Hartshorne admits, however, that his understanding of God as the "Soul of the cosmic body" is an analogy. It is an analogy, one might add, with limitations like all analogies drawn from human experience and finitude. Jesus the Christ is different from all other "cells of God's cosmic body," which in Christian understanding exists as "the body of Christ." The body of Christ is the church, the community of those who receive salvation through the grace of God, by faith in Jesus the Christ. As "cells" or "members" of God's body in Christ, they share the nature of God through processes of justification in Christ and sanctification through the power of the Holy Spirit. They are not "begotten" of God's very nature, but made.

In the end, in spite of his scientific knowledge of organisms and physics, Hartshorne's theory of divine creativity is no more clear about the issue of nothingness or unformed matter than what we find in scripture. We continue to see through a glass darkly. Boff's analysis is most helpful. It does not try to provide an answer to these questions, but is open-ended. Somehow, God employs God's own energy to create new realities so that energy produces spirit-inspired matter.

A Christian Relational Proposal

A Christian integrative relational womanist appreciates far older biblical and African Bantu Muntu philosophical understandings of the interconnectedness of spirit and matter and Spirit to conclude that of course God creates out of "nothing" and out of "the deep," because God transcends our cosmos and yet is omnipresent. Whatever has been created anywhere in all possible universes is created by God. God alone is not created but Creator who from eternity creates. One finds that in emphasizing that *creatio ex nihilo* does not make literal sense, Hartshorne, for example, loses the poetic sense of the meaning of "nothing."[52] Hartshorne is concerned about an *eisegetical* and overly literalistic interpretation of Genesis 1 and John by the early church writers. His argument is not with scripture itself. To the contrary, he is aware of figurative and literal meanings in scripture. Nor is his issue with the Gnostic influenced words in the gospel of John, which assert that "without God, nothing was made." This is a biblical way of saying that matter is never produced without energy. Likewise creation has not been created without the presence and transcendence of Spirit. Regardless of the early church writers' exegetical strengths and weaknesses, however, there is poetic value and truth in the tradition that says God created something out of nothing. In recognizing that poetry is not meant to be taken literally, one must not lose the truth of the poetry in the process. The poor and the frugal around the globe know what it means to live with a scarcity of resources, a kind of nothingness, and make something out of it.

For those raised by parents or grandparents who talked about "making something out of nothing," "making a way out of no way," and "making do with what you've got," taking the word "nothing" figuratively comes naturally. One can conclude that what looks like nothing to us is something to God. This is the truth behind the story of Hagar in the desert, so often cited by Delores Williams and other womanist theologians.[53] Hagar, thirsty in the desert with no water, sits down to die, despairing that she and her son will not live. A messenger of God appears and reveals a spring of water in the desert–something where it seems nothing exists. One cannot easily dismiss what they have come to know from generations of experience. As is true of the Trinity in relation to Genesis, the problem in the *creatio ex nihilo* debate is that theologians from both conservative and liberal camps fail to acknowledge that we are engaged in midrash–creative, interpretive, sometimes scientifically informed accounts of the story that are not available in the biblical texts themselves.[54] Women globally understand this experience of "making a way out of no way" and "making something out of nothing." Every child or grandchild of a Depression-era parent knows the wisdom of "Making do with what you've got," even if present generations have difficulty implementing this wisdom. God who "makes something out of nothing" and a "way out of no way" is like the poor mothers of the globe, who with other women in their families or communities pull a scarcity of resources together to produce a context of sustenance for their young. God is like those who survive cities torn apart by hurricanes with nothing but the clothes on their back and a scarcity of resources, if any, to begin life anew. The very power of renewing life, individually and collectively, is a divine gift received from a God of courage and grace.

Human Beings, Other Creatures, and the Problem of Evil

Earth creatures are created in "our image," says God in Genesis 1:26–27. God blessed them to be fruitful and to multiply, as well as to enjoy the rest of creation which God calls "good" in verse 23. While questions of *how* God created our cosmos become important for later Jews and for Christians even later, a more important question for the audiences for whom the authors of Genesis wrote was the question of theodicy–"Why does God allow evil?" Specifically, if God is good, then why does God's creation include pain and suffering? Thus the conflict between two accounts: one with God creating Adam, earth creature, in "our image" and another with the woman being taken from Adam's rib. Theories developed showing whom to blame for evil, and questions even arose as to which gender to blame.

In Genesis 1, God views creation lovingly as reflecting God's own goodness. If creation was originally good, then why do we experience evil and suffering? Why is sin such a problem in the world? Why do we humans participate in evil, violating the earth and one another? We human beings are somehow different from other creatures in our consciousness and in our relationship to God, yet we are dust. In Genesis 1:20–24 God commands the elements–the waters and earth–to bring forth creatures of every kind in watery and earthy ecosystems. According to Ecclesiastes 3:19–21, animals and humans alike are made from the dust of the earth and will return to it. What befalls the beasts befalls humankind. As one dies, so dies the other. They have all one breath, the text states. After all, the wisdom writer cautions, all is vanity.

We don't like to remember Ecclesiastes with its dreary proclamations that "all is vanity" (Eccl. 1:1–11). Jewish and Christian traditions alike give it less weight than the Torah and the books of the prophets. Christians rarely preach from it and are eager to move quickly to the resurrection hope of the New Testament. Yet Ecclesiastes has much to teach us, because it returns us to the truths of Genesis, that God breathed life into human beings. It is important to remember to love and care for one another and for the rest of creation, loving God with all that is in us, because it is in our capacity to love and act thoughtfully, with head and heart, toward the entire creation as divinely appointed stewards that we are created in God's likeness. This makes Paul's promise for salvation of human beings and the redemption of creation in Christ all the more powerful (Rom. 8:18–25). It clarifies the transformative meaning and power of the Christ, who for Christians is the promised Messiah.[55]

Creation and Providence

Providence is the work of the entire Trinity and the distinctive action of God the Parent who is Provider/Nurturer. God provides. What God provides is good. This providence is double-edged. God's initial aim is for the well-being of creation, but disobeying the commandments (spiritual laws) to participate in divine love carries consequences. God's providence is not to be taken for granted. We have not been good stewards of the earth. We have not distributed the wealth of resources God has provided well, wisely, or lovingly. God's consequent pole brings judgment. We may continue in God's everlastingness, carried forward in the memory of God; or we may perish, dying a final death.

Creation is called to participate in God's aim for the well-being of creation in spite of the problem of evil. God will continue perfectly well without us if we refuse to participate. Yet, this relational God invites our participation in God's love and aim for well-being. This earth and heaven may pass away, with the creation of a new heaven and a new earth. Many people seem literally "hell-bent" on fulfilling the apocalyptic prophecy of Revelation. But creation is still called to do what it was originally called to do–to participate in the excellence of divine love. We participate in this divine love not because we can erase the consequences of sinful choices, but because we say yes to divine love for its own sake. God does not "need" creation to further this well-being, but God's providence includes order, beauty, a purpose for each creature, and a plan. God may not need us, in the way that we need God, but God does *call* and *choose* us for specific work.

Christ, Creation, and Common Ground

For those who claim to be followers of Jesus, if Jesus exemplifies our full humanity in flesh and spirit, then Jesus is dust and spirit. Jesus as God incarnate has a relationship with creation. To imitate the life of Jesus, then, requires loving and just relationship with the earth and one another. It means that we need to remember that the very dust of the earth is of intrinsic value to God who creates something out of seeming nothingness. It means that we need to remember that "nothing" is "something" in this vast universe of ours and that life begins with the infinitesimal. The earth, redeemed by Christ in the power of the Holy Spirit, is literally part of our common ground. Jesus the Christ, the Word and Son of God, Immanuel or God with us, shares this common ground with us, taking our earthy nature as part of God's own body in loving relationship with creation. In Jesus the Christ, the Word/Wisdom of God who has been with God from eternity, we find salvation, redemption, and abundant life. In Jesus the Christ we find healed relationships among God, the earth, and one another. Our very selves are made complete through adoption to God's own nature in the *relation* of Jesus the Christ.

In returning to the earth, at the end of our moral lives, our bodies do not return to "nothingness" but rather to the original elements that make up cycles of life, death, and rebirth. We are also more than earth. We are spirit, created in the likeness of God, animated by the breath of God with hope for resurrection, and what Paul calls spiritual, glorified bodies (1 Cor. 15:40–44). We have hope for everlasting life in God in Christ. This is the subject of a final chapter. Until then, the next three chapters consider God who hears the cries of earth and the cries of human hearts when blood spills on the ground. If God is dust and spirit, incarnate in creation, then God experiences creation. God experiences the cries of creation. If God is relational, then God responds to the cries of creation. We might, then, consider God's response to Cain, Abel, and blood that cries out from the earth in the book of Genesis.[56]

CHAPTER 4

Even the Rocks Cry Out

Why Evil and Suffering?

According to Genesis 1 and 2, God created the earth, the waters, and the entire cosmos. Biblically and scientifically, it is agreed that humankind was created after the earth, waters, atmosphere, creeping things, and beasts of the fields as the most complex of creatures. God looked at it all and saw that it was good. In classical Christian thought, creation exists within the promise of God's providence. The word providence is related to the words "provision" and "provide." The understanding of providence is based on the presupposition that God is good and that God provides for the ongoing good or well-being of creation. Theologians, clergy, and laity alike ask, "What happened to the good creation?" If what God provides is good and ensures the well-being of all creation, then why is there evil in the world? If the earth and all that is in it, including humankind, were originally created good, then why is there so much sin, the violation or transgression of others that leaves us in a world of broken relationships?

These are perennial questions. They take many forms, but all are grounded in presuppositions regarding divine power, freedom, and the existential conditions of creation. The presupposition is that God has the power to create a world without evil, to make evil go away, and to "make" people not to sin. Why do the righteous and the unrighteous alike experience evil and suffering if God is good? Or more pointedly, some put it, why does God "allow" humans to sin and why does God "allow" evil in the world? This last question, in particular, is similar to the question that Job asked in his story after he lost his loved ones and all he owned.

In the story, God allows Satan, who has been roaming throughout the earth, to test Job. Job remains faithful to God but not without question. Why, Job asks God, has this evil come upon him and his family? "Why me? Why us?" Job asks the question of every parent who has lost a child, of every person undergoing grave illness, of every woman who has been raped, of every child who has been abused, of every soul that experiences hatred from another, and of every innocent who has suffered a tragic accident or crime. Job, like the rest of us throughout time, never receives an answer. He receives instead confirmation that before Job there was God. The strength and power of life is found in God, divine creativity itself, even in the midst of suffering.

Job, who represents every human being who has suffered or who ever will suffer great loss, learns that God created all that existed in the past, the present, and that will come to be (Job 1–3, 27–30, 38–42). Where was Job, God asked, when God created all that has been, is, and will come to be? Job receives no answer as to why there is evil, destruction, suffering, pain, and death in the world. He learns instead that God creates, has created, and will continue to create. The story of Job affirms the power of divine creativity in the midst of evil and suffering. The good news of the story is simply that divine creativity is greater than any other power in its capacity to create. It is also greater in its capacity to instruct human beings in wisdom (Job 40:1–2). One clue to the problem of evil in relation to divine providence and creativity is available in Genesis 1 where we find God as Creator who looks lovingly at creation, declaring it all good. In Genesis 3, however, everything goes awry. Certain spiritual and natural laws are part of God's creation. When violated, these laws result in negative consequences, namely experiences of suffering, pain, and death.

Clues to Unanswered Questions

According to Genesis 3, the desire among human beings to be like gods, possessing the knowledge of good and evil, leads to discord in God's creation. Both men and women, represented by Adam and Eve, were culpable of the arrogance that they could be as knowledgeable and as powerful as gods. Human beings were created to partially determine their becoming as evident in Genesis 3's account that they had the freedom to obey divine law or not. For millennia, human beings have chosen not to participate in divine law. They have chosen knowledge of good and evil in their ambition to attain godlike status. Knowledge is power. The desire to be like gods, then, is a desire for power to do what gods can do.

Human beings, however, are creatures created to be good stewards of the rest of creation. They were not meant to possess godlike power, a greater power than that of human creatures. To possess godlike power is to assume a greater share of power to determine the nature of things. What would human beings, however, do with such power? A greater share of power to determine the nature of the world's becoming means that human beings, for lack of wisdom, can manipulate the becoming of the created order. Divine creativity itself already is at work in the very nature of things, calling it into relationships of well-being. For human beings to possess divine power and knowledge of good and evil means human beings have the ability to manipulate the delicate balance of the cosmos. This, in fact, has resulted in mere interference in the divine and natural balance of things.

Genesis 1–3 is the account of the earliest human beings, who were banned from a paradise of perfect natural and spiritual relationship. It is not history, although every historical account is an interpretation with mythic elements. The stories in Genesis 1–3 are true myths that point to actual human, historical experience. Myth, despite popular misconceptions, is not the opposite of truth. A myth may be true or false. The great myths of classical and biblical literature point to some truth of human experience in relation to divine creativity, love, and judgment. True myths are accounts of macrocosmic events told in microcosmic story form. Are the creation stories and the account of "the fall" to sin true myths? Yes, these myths are true. They point to the truth of the power of divine creativity and to the truth of the problem of human sin as it affects each passing and becoming generation.

No one can deny that human beings are manipulative, wanting more than their share of power, with a terrible propensity for employing their freedom of decision in ways that upset the delicate balance of the created order. Were there really a man named Adam and a woman named Eve? *Adam* is more than a name; it is a description that means, "earth creature." *Eve* means "mother of all." No doubt there was a first earth creature and his mate, mother of all. Otherwise, we would have no human race. The names are descriptive of the earliest, earthly, procreative human beings. It is scientifically true that human beings could not exist without the earlier creation of land, water, the atmosphere with its oxygen, plants that help us breathe as well as feed us, and other creatures who make the ecosystems on which we depend for physical life sustainable.

The stories of Genesis 1–3 indicate the natural processes of creation and the problem of destruction. They point to human beings on the one hand as the most complex of creatures and on the other as the ones responsible for violating the existential balance of things in their desire for godly power. Beyond debates about mythical and literal meanings of Genesis 1–3, the historical human track record around the issue of power and its potential for destructive purposes and consequences, regardless of intentions, is tragic. Look at the history of how we humans have employed our growing knowledge of the inner workings of the universe–biological, chemical, and physical with its basis in energy dynamics. It is patently evident that we have employed this knowledge to create and destroy, to produce beauty and ugliness, well-being and suffering, intentionally and, quite frequently, *in spite of our best intentions.*

Consider, for example, Einstein's sense of woe when his discovery regarding the splitting of the atom was employed both for good and for evil. Some humans used his discovery for healing through such measures as the use of radiation in X-ray readings to diagnose physical illness. Others used it to create the nuclear bombs that destroyed generations of families at Hiroshima and Nagasaki, Japan, during World War II. The power of knowledge in and of itself is neutral. It may be employed for good or for evil, for creating or destroying, for renewing life or as a weapon for death. It seems that the divine wisdom that is ever-present in the very structure of the universe possesses a long-standing awareness about human beings. We, the most complex creatures on the planet, are inherently too limited in understanding to consistently employ the power that comes with knowledge of good and evil with an eye to the well-being of *all* creation. We have a tendency to forego divine wisdom, to act as gods, even claiming to act on behalf of God, when we think that this is best for our most immediate individual and corporate self-serving concerns.

A Relational Analysis of Sin, Evil, and Suffering

In relation to God's power and freedom and the freedom of creation, one must necessarily raise one question: "Is God all powerful"? If God is all-powerful, or omnipotent, as classical theologians have maintained, then why doesn't God prevent evil? Neoclassical process metaphysicians such as Charles Hartshorne qualify the word *omnipotence.* God is not all-powerful in the classical sense of the term. If omnipotence means that God is all controlling, then freedom does not exist. God shares power with creation. If God did not share power, there would be no freedom.[1] Freedom is a form of power. In freedom, creatures have the power to choose whether to assent to God's unsurpassable love.[2] We can choose whether or not to live into goodness or evil.

For there to be a capacity for knowledge of good and evil, both good and evil must have existed before human beings ever went in search of this powerful knowledge. Why is there evil in the universe to begin with? If God is the source of all creation, did God create evil? If God created all that is, then isn't God responsible for evil? This, however, is inconsistent with the understanding of God as good if God is all-powerful. If God is both good and all-powerful, then a good God could not "create" evil. Yet, the world has both goodness and evil as evident in the experience of diverse events. God, then, must not be "all-powerful."

We have a tendency to think of God as being "in charge" and in control of all possible activity in the world. When things go wrong, humans often question God about the divine role in the problem of existential evil. A mother who loses her child in a tragic accident may receive the all too common platitude that "It was God's will." This means that the child would still be alive if God had willed it. Many a bereaved person avoids well-meaning Christian "friends" who offer such platitudes.[3] They find their faith rocked and shaken down to the bone. As many a seminarian involved in internship knows, it is difficult to respond to the "Why" questions of anyone who has suffered or is under threat of a grave loss. The logic that supports a God who "wills" pain and suffering quickly falls apart. It is of no comfort and no good use. All too often such platitudes simply lead the bereaved and the wounded to blame God for their suffering. This is understandable, given the faulty reasoning of the platitude.

If God willed that the mother's child who was struck by a car should be hit and die, then God is responsible. God is to blame, and the mother's anger, at death and at God, is justified. If God were cruel, then who would want to worship God, who seemingly abandons the well-being of some rather than work toward the well-being of all? It is no wonder that the bereaved and the wounded sometimes "just don't feel like going to church." They are avoiding their well-meaning "friends." The church needs a theology that speaks a consistent truth about the goodness of God to help both the bereaved and their well-meaning friends. Such a theology is needed to inform the sermons and Christian education offered in churches.[4]

It is not that God has created, willed, or allowed evil. Nor has God created, willed, or allowed evil's favorite companion, sin, into existence. God's aim for creation is for cosmic harmony, balance, and well-being. This is the divine call to each entity coming into being. Creatures enjoy freedom within the limits of physical, spiritual, divine structure. Creaturely freedom is not the same as divine freedom, although we are invited or called to participate in God's creative, cosmic, loving freedom. Creatures are finite, and God is everlasting. Our only hope for everlasting life is found in God's own everlastingness, the possibility of continuing within God's own infinite experience or feeling.

Evil is a result of the freedom inherent in all of creation. God did not create evil, but God created all of creation in freedom. God is impassible, according to early church fathers, specifically Athanasius (296–373). In this understanding, God is not affected by creation, nor does God need creation. This view conflicts with biblical principles and scientific analyses of reality. In process-relational neoclassical theology, God is not omnipotent in this sense. God is sympathetic. God is not impassible in the sense that God is unfeeling. God is impassible in the sense that we cannot destroy God. God is compassionate, merciful, and feels with creation. The Hebrew Bible speaks of God's *chesed* or unfailingly faithful covenant love and compassion (Ex. 15:13; 34:6; Num. 14:18; Joel 2:13; Jon. 4:2; Ps. 86:5, 15; 103:8; Neh. 9:7).

Jesus' compassion responded to human needs (Mt. 9:36; 14:14; 15:32; 20:34; Mk. 1:41; 5:19; 6:34; 8:2; Lk. 7:13; compare Lk. 15:20). Jesus expressed such compassion in human tears (Jn. 11:35).

In much of modern Christianity, God is omnipotent in the sense that God is a determinist. Logically, one must conclude that God is a tyrant who determines every action. In neoclassical theology, God is omnipotent in the sense that God *influences* creation, but God shares decision-making power with creation.[5] God persuades creation to participate in the infinite possibilities of God's creativity and divine love. Biblically, it is clear that God does not determine everything because Adam and Eve make decisions, Jesus makes decisions, the prophets and the participants in various biblical stories make decisions. The Bible constantly speaks of people being asked to change their minds, change their ways, to *respond to God.*

Neoclassical theology corrects misconceptions about God that are neither experientially true nor biblically grounded. If God were "omnipotent" in the sense of absolute determinism, then creation, and especially humans, would have no freedom. Freedom and absolute determinism negate one another. From the perspective of process metaphysics, if God were fully deterministic, then one could not speak of freedom of the will, the ability to choose to participate in God's creativity or not. God is in control, but God is not a control freak! God is not a "tyrant," puppeteer, or robotic engineer![6]

God is deterministic in that God determines the consequences of our decisions. God gives clear commandments to participate in divine love, without making our decision for us. We can choose to live into goodness or evil. God determines our living and our perishing, based on our concrete choices. God's initial aim is for the well-being of creation. God's consequent pole judges our choices. God freely creates a freely loving creation. God does not make every decision for us, but rather all creation responsively participates in moments of decision in which each individual has agency and power. God partially determines creation, but not absolutely. In creation we find partial determination and partial freedom.[7]

Here again, we run into classical questions and perennial problems. If human beings have the freedom to choose good or evil, to participate in God's aim for the well-being of creation or not, then it sounds as if we are making the same type of claim as the early Christian writer Pelagius (360–420), who was deemed heretical and whose teachings Augustine (354–430) considered anathema.

For Augustine, whatever freedom we human beings may claim is a free gift of God received only through the grace of God. Any freedom of the will that human beings possessed before "the fall" was lost through Adam's sin. Since Adam's "original sin," all human beings are born into "original sin." Since that time, Augustine argues, human beings are utterly corrupt, and only God, through the power of grace, can free us from the bondage of sin. It is not that creation is bad after the fall, because it was created good. It is not bad, but corrupt, so deeply flawed that it no longer knows its original goodness and is incapable of choosing the good without all-powerful divine intervention. Human beings have no capacity to free themselves from sin. Freedom of the will is present only among the saved that have been converted, turned back to God by God. Freedom of the will is a gift of grace, given by God in the process of salvation. Prior to salvation, freedom of the will is not present in human beings. Those whom God predestines for saving grace are delivered from the bondage of sin. To believe, like Pelagius, that human beings inherently possess freedom of the will and the moral power to choose God after the fall is, in Augustine's judgment, a heretical doctrine that the church must anathematize. For Pelagius, Adam's sin did not extend to all generations, which Augustine found ludicrous.

The view presented here is neither fully Pelagian nor Augustinian. It has more in common with John Wesley's (1703–1791) understanding than with any other traditional Christian thinker, and much in common with process-relational perspectives. Pelagius was incorrect not to take the problem of original sin more seriously in his understanding of free will. It would be more correct to say that original sin has not thoroughly compromised human capacity to freely choose the divine good. While we are born into a world of original sin, we are not *completely* determined by sin-laden past events. To imagine that we are as utterly determined by original sin as Augustine implies makes sense only if God has withdrawn the divine presence from the world. Such a God would be so utterly transcendent as to be uninvolved, distant, indeed absent from the world. This goes against the logic of the doctrine of God as one who creates and loves creation. A distant or absent God is not possible within a Christian worldview in which God, according to New Testament literature is Emmanuel (Matt. 1:23; compare Isa. 7:14; 8:8), God with us. If God is with us, then God is present and relational. If God is present and relational, then God responds to creation which means creation must ever be created to respond to God.

Not only did God not create a dead, unresponsive world to begin with, but also nowhere does Genesis 1–3 suggest that the relationship between God and world has ended. The relationship between God and world has changed through sin. It is a broken relationship. A broken relationship, however, is a relationship all the same. Relationship implies capacity for response from all involved. Indeed, the Psalms describe the entire earth as singing to God (96:1,11; 97:1; 98:4; 100:1). There can be no rejoicing and singing out, no praise of God without relationship.

Augustine is correct to say that we have the capacity to love God only through the power of divine grace, the ground of creativity and without whose presence we would not exist. Augustine's logic is faulty, however, on the matter of God's omnipotence or all-powerfulness. Contrary to common misconception, divine omnipotence is not a doctrine found in the Bible or in the empirically observed world. For Augustine, an all-powerful God predestines our salvation. Who will be saved is predetermined.

For John Calvin (1509–1564), who developed the doctrine of double predestination only implied by Augustine, God predetermines salvation and damnation alike. Augustine did not develop a doctrine of double predestination in which some are predestined for perpetual bondage and hell. He did imply the possibility well enough, however, for Calvin, a thousand years later, to develop his own doctrine of double-predestination, in which there is a clear and absolute understanding that God predestines some for salvation and others for damnation.[8] Hope that one is among those predestined for salvation rests, in such framework, in the presence of desire to love and serve God. The very desire to love and serve God indicates that one is predestined for salvation.

Many Christians, Catholic and Protestant, are inclined to hold the contributions of these historical church theologians on this point as sacred and true. Many believe that this doctrine is in the Bible, failing to ask whether or not scripture itself presents such an understanding of human freedom in relation to God's power of salvation. In fact, scripture is ambiguous. In the Old Testament, we find that certain prophets, such as Jeremiah (1:5; 20:17–18; compare Gen. 25:23; Ps. 22:9–10; 58:3; 71:6; 139:13; Isa. 44:2, 24; 49:5), were formed and known by God while in the womb. This is not, however, a doctrine of predestination. If God is forever present in creation, then, of course, God knew the prophet in the womb. This does not necessarily mean, however, that God predetermined Jeremiah's every thought and movement or foreknew every decision the prophet would make.

The weakness in Augustine's thinking is that an all-powerful, all determining God does not make sense in relation to the doctrine of freedom. Calvin's logic falls apart for similar reasons with the added problem that if God predestined Adam to sin and some to condemnation, then the notion of freedom is brutally nullified. In a Calvinist doctrine of predestination, not only are we all born into original sin with some predestined for salvation, but for some salvation will never be a possibility from the moment of conception and birth.

As Hartshorne observes, it is not possible to have both an all-powerful God and freedom in creation. Either God is not all-powerful, or there is no freedom. This, however, would make the altar call itself absurd. It makes sense for Augustine to suggest that our very ability to love God is a gift of grace. It does not make sense that God has already determined that an individual will say "Yes" to God. This would mean that God is compelling and all controlling. If God compels and controls our every decision, then freedom does not exist anywhere in the cosmos. It does make sense, however, to understand such a God as persuasive and constantly calling or luring us into participation in divine love. God determines our living and our perishing, based on concrete choices that are in part self-determined and in part determined by the past. We are not as bound by the sin of past events as Augustine leads one to believe.

In a process neoclassical relational worldview, so the argument goes, it does not make sense to say that God fully and completely determines creation's becoming. God is partly determinative of creation's becoming in relation to the infinite possibilities that are part of God's primordial vision and the free selection of diverse individuals. Moreover, the past becomings of the events, individuals, or entities in the world partly determine their present and future becoming. God is not completely determinative of our actions. As Theodore Walker Jr. observes in his analysis of Charles Hartshorne's *Omnipotence and Other Theological Mistakes* and Alfred North Whitehead's *Adventure of Ideas,* who we become is partly determined by God, partly determined by the past, and partly determined by our own selection of possibilities.[9]

God desires all of creation to participate in God's aim for the harmony or well-being of all creation in freedom. Every entity has the freedom and the power that are inherent in freedom to take God's aim into its own becoming, its own processive self. This happens when one experiences God's aim, which is the divine lure, as one's subjective aim. We are always experiencing the divine initial aim whether preconsciously or consciously. When our experience of this aim becomes conscious and we take it into our conscious being and becoming as our own, it becomes our subjective aim. God's aim and subjective aim enjoy the experience of integration. The subjective aim is the individual's experience or prehension of the divine lure. A helpful synonym for divine lure is "call."[10]

God, who is cosmic unsurpassable love, as Hartshorne reminds us, creates the world in freedom with the aim that the world will freely love God.[11] To suggest that God fully *determines* our actions, including our desire to love, does not make sense because such love would not be free. Calvin is particularly problematic with his doctrine of double predestination. In contrast, Hartshorne proposes a doctrine of dual transcendence with mutual response between God and the world.[12] God's loving desire for the world is that we participate in divine love, without God's making our decision for us. The potential to choose the opposite of God's aim for the well-being of creation is a risk entailed in the freedom that is inherent in all of life.[13] Did God create evil? Is God responsible for evil? If God creates creation in freedom and freedom is evil, then God is responsible for evil. One must ask whether freedom is good or evil.

Freedom as such is neutral, neither good nor evil. It is how created entities employ inherent freedom that leads to experiences of good and evil. Freedom itself is a kind of power, the power of making moment-by-moment decisions, preconsciously or consciously. Human beings and other creatures have always had the power of freedom. In that freedom, we have appropriated the power of knowledge of good and evil, the power of knowledge that we may employ our freedom for the well-being or destruction of others. Moreover, much of what we call evil in nature is not evil at all, but part of the very cycle of life. Without strong winds and hurricanes, for example, waters would become stagnant, and new life could not emerge. Hurricanes are not evil; they simply are part of the divine cycle of recreation. It is up to us to provide safe communal resources for building and moving safely out of the hurricane's path.

Are other events in nature, like cancer, evil? If cancer is nature gone awry, then it makes sense to say that evil is present in this aspect of the free path nature has taken. It is necessary, however, to make distinctions between nature living the life of God's aim, which leads to the well-being of all, and occasions when nature is clearly overstepping its bounds. We must also be careful to acknowledge when it is our own manipulation of nature to serve our own narrow ends that leads to needless suffering rather than well-being. God's initial aim, found in God's primordial nature–God's mental or spiritual pole is for the well-being of creation.

When we violate the well-being of creation, negative consequences ensue, which the world and we experience. We may experience these negative consequences consciously and immediately, like Cain, Abel, James Byrd, and John William King below, or we may experience them preconsciously as we hear about events of violation from a distance. As Suchocki observes, no creature escapes judgment. Negative consequences affect the many when even one fails to participate in God's cosmic love. Judgment exists in our experience of God's "consequent nature," as God responds to the world in God's "feeling of the world's feeling."[14] In other words, because God is compassionate, God feels with the world. God feels the joy and suffering that are part of creaturely existence and in the power of the Holy Spirit in Christ guides the world in realizing the fullness of what it means for Christ to overcome evil through divine salvation, redemption, and sanctification. God freely creates a freely loving creation and "judges" its free "becoming." Whether we fail to realize our humanity or not, others experience the effects of our "becoming."[15] We are called to lives of positive transformation. Within the divine grace of freedom and shared power to make some choices about our becoming, however, it is also possible to choose negative transformation. In negative transformation, we fail to realize our humanity. God and creation experience this negative impact. The latter frequently occurs in spite of best intentions. Human beings know only in part and often harm one another unwittingly. If one has a true desire to respond to and participate in the call of God, however, one learns from these mistakes. One gains wisdom not to repeat past errors. When learning from past errors and correcting them, more positive becoming begins to emerge within the realm of infinite possibilities.

Finally, we must question whether or not destruction is always evil and whether or not God is both creative and destructive. When a bird molts and new feathers emerge, the molting may appear destructive when it is in fact part of a greater creative aim. A child losing a tooth for the first time needs affirmation that this is not some terrible evil but a positive aspect of the growth process. Beauticians and doctors have assured many a woman or man about the normal versus illness-related loss of hair. Moreover, human beings in many cultures cut off parts of our bodies–fingernails and toenails–for more facile use of our hands and feet. Pruned rosebushes grow more lushly with greater abundance of life than those that are not pruned. Fruit trees yield a fuller harvest with careful pruning. The human self, over a lifetime, undergoes a kind of pruning of infantile habits as it matures for the sake of healthy relationship and survival. Further, creatures feed on other created entities to prevent an overgrowth and loss of ecological balance that would lead to the death of entire ecosystems without the process of life eating life to make room for more life. Not all loss and destruction is evil. God, as the very source of life, includes both destructive and creative movements in God's own dynamic life-renewing nature. Indeed the creation of a new heaven and a new earth, which is always in process, points to the dying of the old and the creation of the new.

Yet Isaiah and the Book of Revelation promise a time when there is no more death but only life (Rev. 20:14; 21:4), a time when the wolf shall lie with the lamb (Isa. 11:6). Genesis 2 and 3 point to a paradise state which had no death and where all creatures lived in harmony with one another. Therefore, is death not evil? Is the presence of death in the universe part of God's own destructive nature, or is it a consequence of the sin of God's creatures that God, being the very power of life that overcomes death, simply works to the good of all? Can we imagine a universe without death? Whether we can envision such a universe or not, is such a world part of the aim of God and a promise to hope for?

Process metaphysicians observe the universe as it is to make empirical observations about its internal processes, its inner workings if you will, to draw conclusions about God's own nature. What if, however, the universe is at best a helpful analogy for understanding the nature of God? The process worldview makes most sense based on what we know about the inner workings of the universe as it is. But we must ask whether God is those inner physical, subquantum, energetic workings or something more–"that than which none greater can be conceived."[16] Is God even beyond that which makes empirical sense? That there could be a world without the processes of life and death we have come to experience as natural is difficult to imagine and may not make empirical sense, but we humans admittedly have limits to what we can imagine.

One option is to consider what we mean by "death." Perhaps within the divine aim is an end to death but not to cycles of perpetual perishing and becoming in which entities regenerate through a dynamic process of recreation or renewal as subjects experience the increase of God's own glory or satisfaction. Regardless, there is some form of perishing in which subjects are always becoming new. Such perishing is not necessarily the same as death, which connotes a final cessation of life. In this sense, God is positively destructive, evident as the power of the dynamic movement that is called growth. Baptism is an outward sign of the dying of the old self and the becoming of a new self in Christ. Through the process of sanctification in the power of the Holy Spirit, the new self that is justified and redeemed by God in Christ experiences ongoing renewal. Even those who do not enter the Christian process experience either negative or positive transformation, moving closer either to spiritual death or to spiritual renewal with an increase in abundant life and experiences of divine goodness.

That which needs to cease living in the old self dies. So do false understandings of community within communities, so that a new self and community emerge to participate in divine goodness, love, creativity, and everlastingness. As some churchwomen like to say, "You can get better or get bitter." Bitterness, with its roots of fear and hatred, dies when healing emerges and when love increases in the individual and community. The promise of a new heaven and a new earth is the promise of everlasting newness with no final end or cessation of life. Regardless, within cosmic love exists the power of both creativity and destruction. This is inherent to God's own inherent freedom, which we reflect positively and negatively within our own conscious and unconscious moment-by-moment decisions to participate in God's creativity or not.

Knowledge without spiritual wisdom about how to employ knowledge is deadly, as manifest in human use of power to kill and destroy. When human power of the knowledge of good and evil lacks spiritual wisdom, things go awry in the universe. To possess knowledge is to possess some information about the inner workings of the universe. This knowledge alone is neutral, filled with potential for creativity and destruction according to how one employs the knowledge. In unwise hands, such knowledge leads to gross manipulation of natural and spiritual law. The primary sin of women and men has been the presumption of sufficient wisdom to handle like God the knowledge we have sought to possess. Note that in Genesis 3, human beings seek knowledge of good and evil without divine guidance. Yet, God is the very source and power of life, intimate in and with creation. To will to possess the power to be like gods absent divine guidance immediately creates an imbalance between the human and the divine, one which foreshadows the cosmic imbalance that results from actual surreptitious human possession of the knowledge of good and evil, creating and destroying. There is disharmony in the decision to possess knowledge in this way. Without divine guidance, which is wisdom, human beings fail to participate in God's aim for the well-being of all creation.[17]

Even the Earth Cries Out

In Genesis 4, we read the account of two brothers, one a keeper of flocks and the other a tender of fruits of the soil, named Abel and Cain, respectively. According to the story, God looked with favor on Abel and his offerings of the fatted firstborn of his flock, but not so with Cain's fruits of the soil. It is not clear what this means. How would Cain and Abel know who was more favored by God? Perhaps Abel was more successful in trade than Cain, and this was taken as God's favoring Abel over Cain? Perhaps the sheep were viewed as more valuable in Abel's small community, because they provided wool for warm clothing and blankets, a change from the animal skins we read of in Genesis 3. Apparently Abel was viewed as more favored by God simply because his gift of a lamb was seen as more costly and more generous. Abel is viewed as giving careful consideration in his choice of offering while Cain is viewed as thoughtless, cheap, and halfhearted. The story may reflect a shift from a crop-oriented culture to a meat-oriented culture. This is the first that we hear of blood sacrifices. The perception that God favored one brother over the other was a source of jealousy, resentment, and anger.

Did God really favor one brother over the other? God loves Cain enough to warn him of danger, which suggests that God is caring, compassionate, and present in the lives of both Cain and Abel. According to the story, God warns Cain "if you do not do well, sin is lurking at the door; its desire is for you, but you must master it" (Gen.4:7). In other words, something was brewing in Cain's heart. God, in God's empathetic presence, feels Cain's heart as it is tempted to transgress the divine aim for relationships of well-being. Cain was most likely simmering with anger and resentment, letting his anger grow instead of getting control of it. His anger was growing into rage, gaining control of him instead of the other way around.

Cain asked his brother to go out with him to the field, where he attacked Abel and killed him. In short, violent rage overcame him. This is the first account of murder in the First Testament. It occurs after the first human beings' banishment from the harmonious garden of Eden in response to their eating from the tree of the knowledge of good and evil. Cain, who grew crops, recollects the biblical divine admonition God gives to Adam:

> Cursed is the ground because of you;
>   in toil you shall eat of it all the days of your life;
> thorns and thistles it shall bring forth for you;
>   and you shall eat the plants of the field.
> By the sweat of your face
>   you shall eat bread
> until you return to the ground,
>   for out of it you were taken;

dust you are
and to dust you shall return." (Gen. 3:17–19)

Cain was a tiller of the ground, yet the fruits of the earth that he offered to God were not viewed as earning him favor. God, after all, had cursed the ground. What does this mean? Does God literally curse God's own creation, the earth, because of the sin of human beings? From an intergrative-relational perspective, one would interpret this scripture to mean that through some negative action of human beings came consequences that impacted not only humans but also the environment that sustained them. The environment was thrown off balance through a human disregard for the interrelated structures of the cosmos. Perhaps they anticipated a better way of living in relation to the cosmos in their desire to be like gods and to have knowledge of good and evil. To eat from the tree of the knowledge of good and evil is nothing more and nothing less than the inflated belief that we humans know more than God, more than the empowering Spirit of life itself. We human beings like to manipulate the cosmos, to have control of it, to bend it to our will and our desires. This has happened in multiple societies around the world and throughout the ages. Eating from the tree of the knowledge of good and evil is a cyclical ritual in human history. We experienced it in the twentieth century with the splitting of the atom, replaying thirst for the knowledge of good and evil, destroying enemies on the one hand and "nuking" food in microwave ovens plugged into electrical sockets powered by nuclear power plants (which on occasion leak or blow up) on the other.

Thirst for the knowledge of good and evil spins humankind into tensive intertwining dances of destruction and hope. This is the kind of curse that human beings today, and in the time of Adam and Cain, experienced–a curse not to be blamed on God but on ourselves. We humans simply experience the consequences of our actions when we think we know all there is to know about life, our ecosystems, and one another. The "curse" is simply the response of God's consequent nature after we have chosen to violate God's aim for well-being and harmony in the universe. The "curse" is a consequence, the logical outcome of a violation of natural and spiritual laws, which are within each other. God is not separate from the cosmos, but intimately present within it. This is suggested in scripture. In Genesis 2, God is present in the garden. In Genesis 3, God is responsive to Cain and Abel in their offerings, in Cain's rage, and in the cry of Abel's spilt blood from the earth.

Cain spills his brother's blood into the same ground that he tilled with painful toil and sweat. God responds, "'What have you done? Listen; your brother's blood is crying out to me from the ground! And now you are cursed from the ground, which has opened its mouth to receive your brother's blood from your hand'" (Gen. 4:10–11). The earth itself responds to violence, opening its "mouth" to receive Abel's blood. God responds to the cry of the blood-soaked earth. This is a responsive world, a responsive cosmos, where even in violence and broken relationship the relationship persists nonetheless. Blood and earth cry out to God, responding to acts of violation against body and land. God responds, in turn, calling out to Cain, working in Cain's consciousness to bring him to an awareness of the lasting consequences of his actions. Now, not only is the ground that Cain tilled out of balance, in the throes of some ecological imbalance, but Cain himself is forever changed, no longer at peace with himself, his brother, God, or the land.

"When you till the ground," Cain learns from God who lures or calls to his slowly growing consciousness, "it will no longer yield to you its strength; you will be a fugitive and a wanderer on the earth" (Gen. 4:12). Once Cain fully apprehended or experienced God's aim for the well-being of all creation, he was no longer at peace with the land he once tilled. He was restless, wrestling with internal turmoil, an experiential awareness of his unbalanced self. Perhaps Cain could never look at the land in the same way or till it with the same vigor. From where does evil come? It does not come from any one place but in every disregard of God's aim for creation.

Hope for Cain remained. He experienced God's call to him, evidenced in his awareness that tilling the land would never be the same for him. This is a sign of remorse. God even protects him. God does not desire vengeance against Cain but seals him with a mark that cautions against anyone killing him. The mark is not a curse but a sign of God's protection. In short, Cain experiences forgiveness and loss in the consequent nature of God, in God's healing response to broken relationship. Moreover, the fact that Cain experiences remorse and that he has conscious awareness of God's continued presence in his life suggests that he is still open to experiencing God. What about those without remorse, who are so hardened that they are not open to the call of God in their life? Such as these have no conscious awareness or experience of the lure or call of God; yet the call of God is present in their preconscious experience, deep beneath the barriers they have erected to feel little or nothing. Those who have seen the movie *Dead Man Walking* may remember the nun played by Susan Sarandon and the convicted murderer played by Sean Penn. The nun never gives up on the guilty convict, who is scheduled for execution. She never gives up hope for the redemption of this hardened criminal, who, like some actual convicted murderers, does finally express remorse for the pain he has caused the families involved, repents, and asks God's forgiveness. It is a compelling story that leaves the viewer in wonder at the depth of compassion, mercy, and forgiveness God provides to *all* who sin and *all* who are sinned against.

Marjorie Suchocki defines sin as violence. The word "violence" is a derivative of the word "violation." All sin, she writes is violence against creation and against God.[18] For Suchocki, sin is violence against creation first and against God second. The position of this essay is that if God is present in creation and creation exists only in God, then it is not necessary to determine which is sinned against first. If, from the very moment that creation experiences sin, God experiences it in the same moment, then they simultaneously experience the sin. It is important, however, to clearly distinguish between God and creation. Suchocki's statement does help clarify the process-relational panentheistic view that God is in creation rather than being creation itself. Sin always violates both God and creation, because God is in creation and is in empathetic relationship with creation, not because God is creation.

Cain's murder of Abel is one event among multitudes of events of unnecessary violence that God and the world have come to know. Let us turn for a moment to the problem of human crimes of hate and rape that continue to fill the earth with the blood and cries of our brothers and sisters. Must God continue to experience so much crying from the earth? What is God saying to us about acts of violence now? What can we do to hear and understand God's response? The next chapter considers God's nature in relation to a creation that is both sinful and sinned against. It highlights God's providence in relation to contemporary perpetrators and victims of hate crimes.

CHAPTER 5

Your Brother's Blood

The Dance of Sin, Han, and the Blues

By the rivers of Babylon we sat and wept when we remembered Zion. There on the poplars we hung our harps, for there our captors asked us for songs, our tormentors demanded songs of joy; they said, "Sing us one of the songs of Zion!" How can we sing the songs of the Lord while in a foreign land?"

Psalm 137:1–4 (NIV)

Wherever evil, hatred, torment, and suffering appear, a feeling of living in a foreign or strange land, of not belonging to this world, may accompany them. Yet this world, with its experiences of existential goodness and existential evil alike, as strange as it seems, is our home for the span of our earthly lives. Here in this strange land of goodness and evil we sing songs of praise and lament, thanking God for life and crying out to God with the earth when we witness the wrongful spilling of blood.

Vanessa Baker has written a thesis on African American song as a response to the bittersweet experiences of human existence in situations of oppression. "The singing that I write of pertains to the soul's ability," Baker explains, "to use the Spirit through song and dance to survive and overcome adversity."[1] Baker observes that "Sacred dance, as with music and my writing, is a form of psychological therapy. My ability to use it as a healing, thinking, learning mechanism is grounded in my ancestral history."[2] Influenced in part by Gayraud Wilmore's research as well as by her own experience, Baker explains that during the Atlantic slave trade and modern North American slavery, "through song and dance, tribal histories were passed down; emotional feelings were shared; and intellectual and moral lessons were taught." Moreover, "Once in America, participation in ritual songs and dances quickly became a common denominator in the slave quarters. And this common denominator was essential to the eventual creation of coherent, common traditions for these people."[3] Every culture has its songs of lament and its songs of joy, its songs of sorrow[4] and its songs of celebration. Every culture sings these songs in times of ritual mourning and celebration. Sometimes, in some cultures, and regularly, in others, dance accompanies the songs.

For some, North America has been a foreign land of sorrow, where people lament histories of captivity and inequality. Others have viewed it as a land of promise. Today, many view it as both. We lament for the suffering caused by sin. Divine love and creativity lead the world from lament to healing and eventually from the initial stages of healing to rejoicing. If the "singing something" that Anna Cooper says is present in and amongst us exists, then when we harm one another we harm God.

Womanist theologians have explored the relationship between the presence of God in creation and the violation of creation. Delores Williams, a womanist theologian of culture, offers social-historical analysis of the "violation and exploitation of the land and of women's bodies" which has "led to the destruction of natural processes in nature." Williams analyses assaults upon nature, the human spirit, and the divine spirit, as sin.[5] Marjorie Suchocki's process understanding of the fall to violence which is sin against creation and sin against God is similar.[6] In the understandings of both Williams and Suchocki, then, to lynch, drag, or crucify a man, woman, child, or Jesus is always to lynch or crucify God. When Jesus was crucified, the perpetrators were guilty of sin against creation and sin against God. Here in this land called earth, wherever we may live, we learn not only of the goodness of God in the land of the living but of what it means to resist cycles of hatred and suffering in the face of torment. One learns what it means to sing the Lord's song in a strange land.

What makes this land called earth, with its many waters, strange is the problem of sin. God calls a broken world to harmony, balance, well-being, and right relationship. Yet from generation to generation, the death-producing rage of Cain against Abel repeats itself. It mutates, taking on new form and technology. Human beings are vulnerable to being on both the giving and receiving end of sin. We tend to look at perpetrators of violence as "them," those who are not we, miles apart from our own sense of self. Likewise, we tend to divide persons into two camps: sinners and the sinned against, victimizers and victims, oppressors and oppressed. Sinners and the sinned against, however, are caught up in a common heritage of original sin.

Repentance is part of the daily prayer of the saint–of which there are few–as much as it is the need of the most visibly accused and convicted sinners whose violations are made public in courtrooms and media. The death-producing hatred and rage experienced when sin reveals itself in its full, life-sucking, nihilistic force is rooted in what Marjorie Suchocki calls "the fall to violence."[7] The fall to violence is a fall from harmonious relationship with God to broken relationship and participation in evil.

Monica A. Coleman, a womanist Whiteheadian theologian, considers fallenness in relation to evil and salvation. She notes that, for Whitehead, evil occurs in two ways. First, it occurs in human freedom in various contexts and situations. Second, evil is "the loss of actuality.... That is, when an actual entity becomes a new thing, it ceases to be. It is gone. Actual entities are constantly becoming, but they are also 'perpetually perishing.'"[8] Evil, then, is death. Evil, in a relational theology, is the opposite of life. The nihilistic presence of evil is an ongoing problem in existence, but God overcomes it. In the Christian tradition, believers often refer to this as God bringing good out of evil. Biblically, spiritual death and the loss of life in God is considered the greatest experience of evil. This is what makes sin so painful. Sin produces death. It produces not only death of the body, but those who sin negatively produce a death of the spirit within themselves and sometimes in others. In response to the second definition of evil, one turns to the power of God to overcome evil and guide creatures into abundant life. In response to the first definition, one considers the decisions that creatures make and the consequences of those decisions, particularly in temporal reality–existence in the world.

The first Whiteheadian definition of evil remains as important as the second, because it is precisely the decisions human and other creatures make that lead to experiences of perishing and becoming, death and life. For human beings, this means that through our choices we may contribute to the problem of evil or participate in God's activity for the well-being of creation. To contribute to the problem of evil is to sin.

The Consequent Nature of God

In the consequent nature of God, which in a Trinitarian theology is the economic Trinity, God responds to the world as it is in its becoming, its sin and righteousness, goodness and evil. God's primordial nature and vision, which includes the divine initial aim for the well-being of creation, is graciously constant in the divine response to a fallen world. Moreover, the world experiences God's response. God responds to a world of sinful human beings to lure or call it into healing, saving, redeeming, and sanctifying relationship with God. God responds to the world as it is, gradually restoring those who are willing to receive divine grace and enter into right relationship with God and creation. This does not mean that sin has no consequences in the consequent nature of God. While God transforms all believers who freely and decisively participate in divine love and goodness, sin has consequences. Even in a world of forgiveness, we continue to live with the effects of past sin even as God makes us a new creation. One's own past sins are not all-determining if one chooses to participate in divine love, goodness, and creativity. The evil and suffering that the sinned-against experience, likewise, are not all-determining of the present and future. Hope for salvation is omnipresent in the work and movement of divine creation in which there is strength for renewal. Sin, however, has a powerful, corrupting effect. Only internal renewal through the power of God can overcome the corrosive influence of sin.

Human beings are not the only creatures whose actions result in experiences of nihilism. The tsunami in the Indian Ocean at the end of 2004 is one example of the experience of evil in nature. Hurricanes Katrina and Rita also are examples. Earthquakes, fires, tornadoes, hurricanes, disease, are all examples of what human beings and other creatures threatened by such phenomena experience as "evil." Human beings as complex creatures of high intelligence and consciousness, however, are accountable for their contributions to the problem of evil. Through the omnipresent grace of God who calls creation to participate in the divine aim, human creatures may consciously participate in sin or righteousness. That human beings are accountable for sin is clear. If, human beings are created in the likeness of God and if our humanity is found in God, then the acts of horror humans have committed and continue to commit are not really human or humane.

Many question whether or not nature in its violent aspects is evil as a result of fallenness of an entire creation. Or, are hurricanes, floods, and tornadoes good? Clearly, something is awry in the universe when we consider human destruction of ecosystems that makes tornadoes, hurricanes, and other natural disasters more devastating than they might otherwise be. At the same time, Christian tradition, both Eastern and Western, understands nature itself as fallen and awaiting human salvation so that it, too, may be redeemed. We celebrate whatever paradise-like moments we come to experience in our earthly lives as glimpses of the full reign of God. A full exploration of this topic is the subject for another book. For now, given human contribution to global warming, which exacerbates the perennial problem of nature's moments of violence, it is necessary to focus on human sin against one another and against other creation.

Augustine emphasized the corrupting effect of sin. Sin distorts desire so that desire is misdirected to satiate the self's concupiscence, using the created order in a utilitarian fashion to satisfy this misdirected desire. Concupiscence is the anxious grasping after things in creation.[9] One of the biblical terms that address the problem of concupiscence is "covetousness." For Augustine in the fourth and fifth centuries, sin is pride. Similarly centuries later, for Reinhold Niebuhr sin is the result of selfishness, egoism, and pride. Sin is a fundamental selfishness that plagues all humankind.[10] Paul Tillich defined sin as "estrangement," a term that points to broken relationship.[11] For Tillich, humankind is estranged from God and one another. Marjorie Suchocki's understanding of sin as "violation" and "violence" deepens Tillich's understanding of sin as "estrangement." Not only is sin broken relationship, but it also involves an experience of violence and violation in this broken relationship. Broken relationship hurts. It wounds.

Whether we are speaking about sin as the horror of violent crime or as the often socially tolerated forms of violence that take their toll on the emotions, psyche, spirit, and physical well-being of creatures, sin violates God's aim for well-being and mutual relationship. Not all sin is a matter of misdirected desire or of pride.[12] Humans are capable of "violating" one another and the rest of creation out of feelings of fear, desperation, low self-esteem, and other negative feelings as well as from pride or concupiscence. Regardless of the motive, sin is violation of God and other creatures. Suchocki, in her emphasis on violation, points to the relational effects of sin, regardless of the type of negative feeling (prehension) that motivates it.[13]

Andrew Sung Park's understanding of the Western concept of "sin" and the Asian concept of *han* offers further insight into the problem of human fallenness from righteousness.[14] Park's work encourages people of faith to examine the effects of the fall to violence with reference to both sinners and the sinned against. Some participate in this original sin and its companion, *han,* more tragically, violently, and to a greater degree than others. All, however, are affected. The term *han*, Park explains, refers to the feelings of the "sinned against." The "sinned against" represent what he calls "the other side of the cross." In situations of violence, those who have been violated are the sinned against. The sinned against are the wounded. The Western Christian tradition, Park observes, emphasizes the hope Jesus offers sinners, who through grace, faith, and repentance are promised forgiveness. Yet, Jesus himself represents the sinned against. Humankind, in the event of the crucifixion, sinned against Jesus the Christ, Emmanuel, God with us.

Humankind sinned against God through sinning against Jesus the Christ, who, as God incarnate, embodied God. Reflecting traditional understandings of the sacred heart of Christ, which today are given greater emphasis in the Roman Catholic tradition, Park writes of "the wounded heart of God" and the *han* of God in Jesus the Christ on the cross. *Han* then is the experience of violation and the feelings of woundedness that accompany it. *Han* is what Park calls "the abysmal experience of pain" or "the collapsed feeling of pain."[15] It is also "frustrated hope", a "negative letting go" in which the self is destroyed through resignation or apathy, and what Park terms "resentful bitterness."[16] The latter are all varied, possible responses of "the wounded heart" which is the *han*-filled or *hanful* heart.

The wounded heart is experienced in "the collective unconscious" as Park says,[17] or in the preconscious as Whiteheadians put it. The concept of "preconscious" is more accurate because it signifies a lack of conscious awareness while also pointing to the fact that even when a person has no conscious awareness of various experiences, these *experiences* are still felt. We have many feelings that we are not consciously aware of experiencing. We experience them all the same, consciously or not. Park adds that *han* is evident in racial experiences of woundedness.[18] *Han* is also evident in the experiences of those immediately affected by war in which women and men from each warring nation experience tremendous loss, anger, and resentment.

Han may be active or passive in individuals and in collectives. In active *han*, resentment manifests itself as animosity and even active rage toward the other. Active *han* may manifest itself as verbal or physical assault. We see such *han* evident in those who, having been wounded or having lost someone to the violence of a member of a certain group, will lash out at any member of the group responsible for perpetrating the wounds whether said member is guilty or innocent. This is the type of *han* Park has in mind when he speaks of racial experiences of woundedness and that we might extend to include national experiences of woundedness. Biblically, one might say that Cain, as an individual, was filled with active *han* toward his brother.

Passive *han* manifests itself as lamentation and may be expressed in music, poetry, and art. In Asian understanding, in contrast to Western understanding, there is activity within passivity and vice versa. Active *han* is active in the sense that it is more aggressive and violent but contains underlying resentment and woundedness that are also passive. Passive *han* is less aggressive. It is certainly active in its artistic expression but more creative than destructive. It is helpful to consider Taoist influence here and the metaphor of the waxing and waning of the moon. A connection exists between the Korean understanding of *han* and the expressions of existential suffering and hope arising from slavery and segregation found in the spirituals and blues of African American culture. Each understanding of existential suffering and hope, though different in the details of cultural form, relays a similar message that has universal meaning for both sinners and the sinned against. Park puts it this way:

> Passive collective unconscious *han* signifies *the ethos of racial lamentation*. Hundreds and thousands of years of oppression mold a race into a certain mode of moaning spirit–the dark soul where the suffering people share their agony. The crucible that melts the anguish of a certain people into this unconscious solidarity expresses itself in art: music, poetry, and pictures. The blues and

> Negro spirituals of African-Americans epitomize this passive sad collective unconscious *han*.[19]

Each cultural articulation of the problem of suffering in a world characterized by a wavering dance between tragedy and hope speaks to questions regarding struggle with the global problem of evil. Park's emphasis on both sides of the cross–sinners and sinned against–requires theologians to develop a thicker understanding of the passion of the world and the passion of Christ.

For many, the passion of Jesus Christ during his torture and crucifixion has meaning because they take comfort in the incarnation of God, a God who empathizes with their own experiences of being sinned against. Womanist theologian Delores Williams emphasizes that we need to learn from the life and ministry of Jesus rather than glorify his crucifixion. Such glorification often results in behavior detrimental to health and healing among black women and others who are taught to be self-sacrificing by submitting to oppression. Williams's emphasis rings true.[20] Yet, as I noted previously, it is still necessary to address the problem of crucifixion.[21] It is "glorifying" the cross that Williams questions.[22] One can agree with Williams that a problem emerges when believers unwittingly render abuse, torture, and killing as a holy rite to bring those willing to suffer closer to God. One might also argue that the resurrection of Christ makes the cross a two-edged symbol–at once a symbol of the human capacity for violence and a symbol of God's power in Jesus Christ to overcome evil, hatred, and suffering.

Park observes that *han* in Asian culture, particularly in Korean culture, shares some common ground with the African American cultural understanding of the *blues*. From within the tradition of black theology and African American culture, James Cone aptly clarifies for theologians what African Americans and sensitive listeners have always known about the Negro spirituals and the blues in the black musical tradition. These two art forms, born from the experiences of slavery, Jim Crow segregation, economic poverty, and political disenfranchisement, express the tragedy-burdened yet hoping against hope souls of black folk.

Whereas W. E. B. DuBois, at the turn of the twentieth century, was critical of the blues and focused on the spirituals in relation to the "souls of black folk," James Cone observes that the blues are "secular spirituals."[23] In listening to *han* music, one recognizes what many cultures, including the Irish, call a type of "keening"[24] in the notes and voices as well as the moaning, blue tones that characterize the spirituals and the blues. One is reminded in these diverse cultural forms of the universal experience of human pain and suffering.

The experience of the sinned against continues to have meaning for Christian theology and spiritual growth. Humans tend to look at perpetrators of violence as "them," as "monsters" as Ricardo Ainslie puts it,[25] born enemies who are not human. Although it is not uncommon to speak as if it is possible to divide persons into sinners and the sinned against, sinners and the sinned against are caught up in a common heritage of original sin and its companion, *han.* In a world where sin is a daily experience, *han*–the blues, feelings of keening and lament–afflict the sinned against. *Han,* the spirituals, and the blues represent a mixture of wailing, lament, anger, resentment, resistance, hope, love, even tempting seeds of hate. Unresolved, this experience of lament–with its thread of hope and love to which the sinned against cling–may give way to hate. In processes of resolution, however, it may give way to participation in the full power of divine love.[26] It is not enough to think about these issues in the abstract. It is helpful for those engaged in faith seeking understanding to engage in theological reflection on actual historical events and to participate in theological analysis of a more contemporary event of hate and woundedness as a kind of case study. Therefore, before turning to the passionate heart of God found in Jesus the Christ in the next chapter, I turn to historical and contemporary stories of the nihilism of hatred and the grief of wounded hearts.

Ida B. Wells-Barnett, W. E. B. DuBois, and other participants in the antilynching movement protested the tradition of killing African American suspects. Thousands of men, women, and children were lynched for alleged criminal behavior and minor offenses without privilege of due legal process and a fair trial. Very few of the offenses were serious enough to consider a death penalty even if the accused were found guilty beyond a reasonable doubt in a fair trial. Every state had at least one lynching. White Americans lynched other white Americans even in states where there were no documented lynchings of African Americans.[27]

According to research documents created by Jana Evans Braziel at the University of Cincinnati, some of the reasons given for lynching were:

> Acting suspiciously, gambling, quarreling, adultery, grave robbing, race hatred, race troubles, aiding a murderer...rape, attempted rape, arguing with a white man, incest,...arson, inciting to riot, resisting a mob, assassination, inciting trouble, robbery, attempted murder, indolence, running a bordello, banditry, inflammatory language, sedition, being disreputable, informing slander, being obnoxious, injuring livestock, spreading disease, boasting about a riot, insulting a white man, stealing, burglary, insulting a white woman, child abuse, insurrection, swindling, conjuring, kidnapping, terrorism, courting a white woman, killing livestock, testifying against a white man, criminal assault, living with a white woman, throwing stones, cutting a levee, looting, train wrecking, defending a rapist, making threats, trying to colonize blacks, demanding respect, miscegenation, trying to vote, disorderly conduct, mistaken identity, unpopularity.[28]

In the past, people practiced lynching to vent hatred against those they feared for all manner of reasons, ranging from being suspected of assault to exercising the basic human right to demand respect. Today, as in the past, hate crimes are committed against human beings because the perpetrators are simply angry that their victims exist. Their rationales include anger at victims who "demand respect" or who "talk back," as in the case of James Byrd Jr. For 2003, the FBI *Hate Crime Statistics* cited 7,485 reports of single bias hate crimes and 4 reports of multiple bias hate crimes in the United States. Of these, 51.4 percent were committed because of racial bias, 17.9 percent because of religious bias, 16 percent "attributed to sexual orientation bias," and 13.7 percent because of the offenders' ethnicity/national origin bias, with disability bias motivating 0.4 percent of single bias hate crimes for 2003.[29] Of the 12.9 percent of hate crimes committed out of offenders' sexual orientation bias, 11.9 percent of such crimes were committed on college and school campuses.

Today, the nation struggles with "hate crime" in the form of the rape of women every two minutes somewhere in the United States.[30] Contrary to past mythologies, a rapist or molester is generally of the same race as the victim or survivor. Other forms of hate crime are racially motivated violence, family violence, violence against gays and lesbians, terrorism, and, as in every century, a multitude of wars. One of the most infamous hate crimes of the last century was the fatal 1998 hate crime against Matthew Shepard, a twenty-one–year-old student who was homosexual. Shepard was brutally beaten by two straight men, tied to a fence, and left for dead on the outskirts of Laramie, Wyoming. He later died from his injuries.

A Passion Story in a Contemporary American Town

On June 7, 1998, John William King–with the assistance of Lawrence Russell Brewer and Shawn Berry–lynched James Byrd Jr. by dragging him from the back of a truck during the deep quiet and opaque early morning hours. The complex sequence of events has been the subject of several books, a cable television movie, and a Public Broadcasting System film presentation. What actually happened at a spiritual and social-psychological level is a complex, existential reality. Who can make sense of the presence of evil and the deep capacity for sin among human beings? Who can adequately describe the *han* of victims of hate crime?

The story of the dragging of James Byrd Jr. and the men who lynched him is part of the larger story of good and evil found in creaturely existence. The story, as journalist Joyce King has found,[31] is a tragedy for which the answers to the question of how and why anyone could commit such evil are forever unsatisfactory. The answers belong to the void or what Augustine called "the absence of the good."[32] Hope cannot be found in that void, but only in knowledge of the power of goodness, which overcomes evil.

In the wee hours of Sunday morning on June 7, 1998, James Byrd Jr. left a party of forty people or more at a friend's house in Jasper, Texas. Byrd's old friend, George "Billy" Mahathay, later reported that between 1:30 and 1:45 a.m. he saw Byrd walking down Bowie Street, near Mahathay's house. Byrd was well known in town. He had served time for a nonviolent offense–petty stealing–but was harmless, peaceful, musically gifted, and well liked.

Steven Scott, an eighteen-year-old, was heading home after leaving a different party and easily recognized James Byrd Jr., "very drunk, meandering" down the road without having to think twice about who he was seeing.[33] Byrd kept ambling down the streets toward one of the two places he called home, his apartment or his parents' house, which were near each other.[34] John William King, Lawrence Russell Brewer, and Shawn Allen Berry had been partying together and joyriding when they saw a black man walking in the road.

Joyce King writes that moments after tying a chain to a wooden mailbox, uprooting it, and dragging it:

> the pranksters discovered a black man walking in the road, minding his own business. Their next diversion was about to begin. The unwitting victim believed someone would finally help him find the way home. "Hey, you need a ride?" Berry called to Byrd, a man he knew by sight but not by name. No response. Berry tried again: "Do you want to go home or what?" Byrd was not so drunk he didn't recognize at least one friendly face, the one behind the wheel. "No. I'll hang out with you white boys for a while," he responded. Byrd, who served time for theft, and Berry had the same parole officer; their paths may have crossed before. Feeling safe, James Byrd, Jr., climbed on the back of Shawn Berry's truck. He had no reason to fear. After all, everybody in Jasper knew everybody else.[35]

James Byrd Jr. had no reason to imagine that he would become the victim of one of the most horrendous and unforgettable crimes of murder in United States history. The young men who picked him up were out on a Saturday party night like Byrd. They even offered him a beer. As Joyce King writes:

> The hospitality ended before Byrd could even consume the whole can of beer. Berry's simple offer to give a black man a ride home set King off. Livid, he turned to Berry, red-faced and suddenly more sober than drunk, and made an announcement: "That's some ho-ass shit, picking up a f**king n****r." Apparently unfazed by the tone or by the kind of racist language he heard all the time, Berry drove on, laughed it off, wound all the way down Martin

Luther King Boulevard, picked up FM 776, a farm-to-market road, then turned on State Highway 63 and traveled east.[36]

Joyce King observes a quick escalation of events after John William King's initial outburst. The men stopped at a local convenience store off of the highway. Finding it closed, they relieved themselves in the open. Then, King and Brewer invited Byrd to sit up front in the cab of the truck. King and Brewer sat in the back of the truck. Back in the truck, Berry continued as the driver. Suddenly Berry made a wild turn from the main road onto an old logging road, following King's suggestion for a joy ride. King banged on the roof for Berry to stop.[37]

There, in the woods, King and Brewer began to abuse Byrd while Berry, according to testimony, made a feeble attempt to stop them. They "violently pulled at Byrd to tear him from the truck…Byrd, disabled, a chronic arthritis sufferer, about 5 feet 9 and 160 pounds, was trapped and suddenly in the battle of his life."[38] According to testimony, King was so angered by Byrd's efforts to fight back that King "stepped back and shouted, 'F**k it, let's kill this n****r.'"[39] They finally managed to rip Byrd from the truck, pull him down to the ground, beat him, and kick him about his head and body. Brewer sprayed black paint into Byrd's badly beaten eyes and face, blinding him as he flailed in resistance to the torture.

The beating and kicking alone were a horrible crime, but King and Brewer would never have faced the *death penalty* for that. The beating and torture constituted the first tier of an even more brutal, premeditated crime that took thought and willfulness. Could it be that, as in the biblical story of Cain, King and Brewer–along with their passive, aiding and abetting companion Shawn Berry were warned in the spirit to turn away from an evil that would leave them forever marked for making the earth cry out to God? If so, then they did not heed that voice of wisdom. In a rage, King and Brewer grabbed a logging chain from the back of the truck. They chained Byrd, whose pants and underwear were pulled down to his ankles, to the back of the truck. "Before they snatched loose his clothing, exposing Byrd in the most cruel, physical way, King took a moment to explain that the same thing was done in the old days to 'n****rs who messed with white women.'"[40]

More accurately, the same was done to men of color who were mere suspects of "messing with white women." King, Brewer, and Berry jumped into the cab of the truck and drove off, dragging Byrd's chained body until Byrd slipped from the chain. The driver slammed on the brakes and backed up, possibly running over Byrd's body. An eager member of the three jumped out to rechain Byrd to the truck. The three men dragged Byrd's body, while Byrd desperately tried to keep his head up by placing his arms beneath it but to no avail. Eventually his head was decapitated from his body by a concrete culvert on Huff Creek Road. Stripped of skin, the chained remains of his body were finally released and dumped at the local black cemetery.[41]

Berry claimed that King took over the wheel of the truck for the dragging while he sat frozen with fear in the middle of the seat of his own truck.[42] Each of the three men had opportunities to stop participating in these violent events–before the beating began, after the beating, after Byrd's body came loose from the chain. But all three gave way to the power of violent rage.

During the dragging, Byrd's genitals were torn from his body, recollecting the practice of castration in historical lynching. One arm was ripped off of his body. Bits of his flesh were found in the side and chassis of Shawn Berry's truck. His face was unrecognizable.[43] The persecution, mocking, beating, and torture of James Byrd were a full-scale lynching, with the thirty–foot chain that dragged him down Hull Creek Road as the lynching rope.

When Berry offered Byrd a ride, he was, according to his own report and the report of those who knew him, unaware of King's and Brewer's potential for racial *violence.* He had not seen King in years. He had never known King to be a killer and was perplexed by King's new, white supremacist rhetoric. As Joyce King observes, Byrd's acceptance of the offer of a ride indicates that the overall racial climate in Jasper was not dangerous enough for him to feel suspicious or afraid. Brewer, however, was not from Jasper. John William King had met him in prison.

King took over and directed the increasingly violent course of events. Of the three men, King has always pled innocence and has never shown remorse. The "kites" or messages that King and Brewer sent to one another in prison while awaiting trial, however, reveal pride in their crime. White supremacist literature was found throughout King's apartment.[44] His body was covered with white supremacist and satanic tattoos, including depictions of Woody Woodpecker wearing a Klan robe and of a lynched black man. One tattoo on the back of his head featured an upside down pentagram.[45] At the scene of the crime, Brewer left Ku Klux Klan (KKK) paraphernalia behind for investigators to discover.

A sheriff testified that he figured out pretty quickly the accident he was investigating was no hit-and-run–especially after a lighter with three interlocking K's was found along the bloody trail left by a black man who had been dragged to his death. "I'm a brand-new sheriff. I didn't even know the definition of a hate crime, but I knew somebody had been murdered because he had been black," Billy Rowles said.[46]

The crime in his view was clearly a hate crime, an anomaly for the town of Jasper.[47] Historically, the purpose of lynching has been to terrify the surrounding communities of black, Jewish, and general populations of color. The objective of white racial supremacists who lynch is to emasculate men of color or Jewish men. Moreover, the objective is to proclaim the supremacy of whites.

Byrd liked to sing and play piano, which his church-going family loved about him. His love and gift of music made him a favorite at parties with his friends. Byrd's Christian parents were active as a deacon and Sunday school teacher at Greater New Bethel Baptist Church, pastored by Rev. Kenneth Lyons. That Byrd was on disability for his poor health, barely able to fight back,[48] makes it clear that King and Brewer chose a very easy victim.

Brewer, Berry, and King all were intoxicated the night of the dragging. None of these men was a saint. Berry had served time in a juvenile boot camp with King as a teenager. All except Berry were unemployed. Whatever flaws any of these men had, however, all were known as nonviolent. What led these nonviolent offenders to brutally and fatally assault their human kin?

Joyce King indicates that an essential ingredient in their fully brewed hatred was their experience of abuse in prison. She conducted interviews, observations, and in-depth research on the conditions at the George Beto Unit of the Texas Department of Criminal Justice. These convinced her that the primary impetus for the hate crime against Byrd was the stew of violence that John William King and Russell Brewer experienced in prison. Both King and Brewer had been recently released from Beto at the time of the Byrd murder. In prison, inmates form gangs organized along lines of racial identity. Serving time for nonviolent crimes, King and Brewer were housed in a unit with prisoners convicted of violent crimes, and they joined one of the unit's hate groups, the Confederate Knights of America, for protection against other gangs. This led to radical shifts in their personalities. According to King, a group of African American convicts attacked him in Beto.[49] Joyce King notes certain state's witnesses insinuated that "as a consequence of serving time there, King has become a hard-core white supremacist."[50]

For convicts of every race in prison, the culture of violence and the expectation to participate in it or die is another type of experience of being nailed to a cross, not as innocents but like the guilty men whom Rome crucified on either side of Jesus. Joyce King describes the southern sector of the Beto Unit as "a tranquil place, its painted tower of green and brown, strikingly similar to a guard watchtower, features a superimposed male figure with outstretched hands, pierced by nails. The palms of his hands are marked by crimson stains. It is the Christ, inviting, suffering, loving, and forgiving: artwork done by Beto inmates."[51] In a violent prison system, such an image is filled with paradox.

One cannot assume that seeing an image of the suffering, loving, and forgiving Christ evokes feelings of comfort from prisoners who daily face the threat of assault and the demand to prove themselves by fighting back or assaulting first. Such an image could evoke anger, rage at God for "allowing" the hellish experiences of inmates' lives. One can imagine that for the most positive of prisoners, the effect of such an image of Christ is like "waiting for Godot."[52] One can easily speculate that such an image simply further fueled the rage of John William King and/or those like him. In Beto, King rejected his biological mother's Christianity, choosing instead tattoos of satanic images to protect himself from various gangs. Convicts know the pain of torture and the potential for crucifixion. For King, and others like him, the forgiving, loving, inviting Christ failed to make sense in a context where survival is a matter of belonging to warring gangs.

King and Brewer received death sentences. Are such men, in all their guilt, like the prisoners Rome crucified alongside Christ? Do such men have time to repent and receive redemption in the courts of divine judgment? Such men are slow to show remorse. The hope that they will confess, repent, and find redemption is slim. Yet if God forgave Cain in his remorse, then redemption of those like King is a possibility within all the possibilities of God's consequent aim for creation. Persons like King need only yield to the persuasive power of divine love and justice, even in the last days and moments of their lives, to leave a little more peace, comfort, and closure in the world for those who mourn the James Byrds, Abels, and crucified women of this Earth.

King, Brewer, Berry, and Byrd each are reminiscent of impoverished characters in Victor Hugo's famous novel *Les Misérables*. Clearly King, Brewer, and Berry failed to rise to the nobility of character, high virtue, and compassion of Hugo's hero, Jean Valjean, who helps his fellow *misérables* rise from fragmented rubble of poverty, crime, deception, and misbegotten justice of eighteenth-century France with its economic and political absurdities.[53]

Byrd, well-liked for his musical ability, friendly manner, and kindness, came closest to such virtue, but did not live to realize his dreams of reaching his fullest potential. Whatever his imperfections, Byrd recalls for thinking, feeling people of faith the open heart of Jean Valjean. Byrd, like Valjean, had a heart for the Christian values Valjean came to embody. But Byrd never reached the *imitatio Christi* proportion of virtue found in Hugo's epic hero, a quality found only in saints. One can see Byrd as a member of that chorus of *les misérables* who struggle to embody kindness over cruelty, peace over violence, and beauty over ugliness of heart and mind. Byrd chose the beauty of music to heal his blues. He chose creativity, joy, trust, and kindness in the midst of his struggles against poverty.

Who are "*les misérables*?" They are the bluesy, *han*-filled, keening, barely and sometimes desperately hopeful people of the world. They are the poor of the world, the disinherited and dispossessed. They are those who learn the ugliness and beauty, the hardness and broken promises of the world in the midst of pain, suffering, strange justice, and violence in contexts of economic inequality and absurdity. Men and women in these conditions make choices in a world where beauty and ugliness are evident in all their rawness, where the choices are nakedly visible. King, Brewer, and Berry chose the ugliness of violence to vent their unresolved rage. Given that officials refer to King as "the smartest" of his murdering trio, one wonders if King imagines that he is as clever as, say, Rodion Romanovitch Raskolnikov, the young man in Fyodor Dostoevsky's *Crime and Punishment,* who commits a murder because he arrogantly believes he can hide his crime. Raskolnikov, however, was not very clever. Like King and every other criminal, he revealed his unconscious wish to be discovered by legal authorities.

Dostoevsky's famous psychological study remains a favorite among criminologists, criminal psychologists, forensic scientists, judges, and lawyers. Perhaps Dostoevsky's Raskolnikov struggled, like King, with a bipolar or manic depressive disorder given descriptions of his mood swings, morbidity, and grandiose sense of self.[54] That is a matter of conjecture. We do know that King endured conflicted feelings of pride and guilt. He took care to hide his crime, yet wanted to be known for his brilliance in covering it up. On the other hand, the crime King instigated was famously sloppy. King and his comurderers made no attempt to carefully conceal evidence in a world where forensic science and DNA evidence are far more advanced than during Dostoevsky's days.

King's favorite criminal character is Hannibal Lecter from *Silence of the Lambs* by Thomas Harris. Lecter, played by Anthony Hopkins in the film version of the novel, enjoys not only killing his victims but also eating them.[55] While King admires Lecter's intelligence, King does not exhibit a brilliant criminal mind himself. One of the few characteristics King shares with Lecter, aside from a descent into evil, is the desire to be caught, resulting from a strange sense of grandiosity and repressed feelings of guilt. King has not admitted to the latter, which is very common. Repressed feelings of guilt are unconscious. King, at the time of this writing, neither feels nor admits to them. The desire to be caught is evident in the sloppiness of King's crime and in the prison kites (messages) he sent to his friend Russell Brewer after their arrest and imprisonment as suspects in the Byrd dragging case. The fictional Lecter, unlike the very real King and the fictional Raskolnikov, enjoys wealth. Raskolnikov, like King, has something more in common with *les misérables*–poverty and the persistent threat of eviction.

Some have commented that "Byrd was a criminal," a reference to previous arrests for stealing and drunkenness, as if that means his murder does not mean so much. That is one trait that Byrd deeply shares with Jean Valjean. How much are we affluent Christians like the judgmental wealthy good citizens of Hugo's morality tale? While those of us who are "good" affluent Christians may have never spent time in jail breaking society's laws, we cannot claim to be morally superior to Byrd in the eyes of God, who experiences with the wounded the slights, darts, and oppressions we release into the world through legal but morally selfish words and actions.

Byrd's sin of stealing landed him in jail, while the same sin of covetousness that afflicts us, the affluent, in our gross consumer appetites is equally sinful in the eyes of God. While Byrd stole with his eyes open, we steal with our eyes closed to the conditions in which the poor, who make our affluence possible, live. We covet what our neighbors have and want more of the same. In spite of that, Byrd's murder matters to God as much as would our own.

As for Byrd's slayers, their values and actions were not always so monstrous, so deeply steeped in evil. King and Brewer both had friends from all racial groups when growing up. To enter Beto 1 Unit was to enter, as Joyce King learned from her research, "the gladiator unit." Something happened to King while in the Beto 1 Unit to turn him violent. As a small young man he was vulnerable to rape. However, if he was raped, he has refused to tell.[56] Telling would make him more vulnerable in the prison system.

Byrd's dragging was a form of lynching and of crucifixion. To enter the Beto 1 Unit also entailed forms of torture and cross bearing. The racially structured violence of prison begot more violence along racial lines. Young men in prison learn to confront persecution, torture, and extreme violence from racially identified others by engaging in persecution, torture, and extreme violence against them. Violence begets violence. This does not mean that those who perpetrate violence against another have an excuse. Nor does it mean that they should not face disciplinary consequences for perpetrating violence and perpetuating the cycle. It does mean that what society perceives primarily as a moral choice is that and more. It is part of a larger psychosocial and *spiritual* problem. It is a glimpse of the depths of the potential for hatred, violence, and death present in the existence of original sin. Sometimes, victims of violence and abuse become victimizers and abusers. Regardless of the trauma they have experienced, they bear responsibility for their behavior. It is also important, however, to diagnose and treat the conditions that increase the probability of such behavior. It is necessary to recognize not only the psychological, biological, and moral predispositions that make such behavior possible, but also the environmental conditions that could trigger such behavior.

According to Augustine, from the time of Adam we are all born into conditions of original sin. Cain realized the potential for such violence when he failed to repent from his first feelings of jealousy and hatred to redirect the whole of his desire toward God. Unchecked, his jealousy moved to hatred, from hatred to an attitude of violence, and from that attitude to murder. He killed his brother. According to the story, Cain was aware of the presence of God when God spoke to Cain, warning him of his violent potential. Apparently then, it was possible for Cain to hear or experience the presence of cautionary wisdom. The experience of the reality of sin and its violent potential is palpable to an extreme in certain prison and other environments. It is not difficult to see why for some, perhaps many, it overwhelms one's perception of the reality of God's presence even in the depths of earthly hell.

Was it possible for King and Brewer to experience such cautionary wisdom in the Beto 1 Unit? It is easy and extremely tempting for this African American theologian to judge King and Brewer and to desire an eternal hell for them. God in Christ alone, however, is the final, merciful judge who descends even to the depths of hell to offer salvation to the lost. Regardless, the ground that soaked up James Byrd Jr.'s blood surely cries out to God in the postmodern world just as it cried out when receiving the blood of Abel. Violence against one another is violence against God and creation.

In the depths of hell on earth, persons of diverse backgrounds become overwhelmed by the pervasiveness of evil, deeply cynical about the power of God, and conclude that violence is their only means of justice and survival in a dog-eat-dog world. The brutal slaying of James Byrd Jr. in 1998 was so sloppy, with so much evidence left behind, that the perpetrators appear to have been suicidal, preconsciously at least, as well as homicidal. Their actions were self-destructive *and* destructive of another. Their actions were those of nihilistic men, quite similar to those of youth gangs in North American cities and suburbs in which young men and women kill with the expectation that they will be killed at a young age in the name of protecting their turf and gang "family."

Byrd's killers, like other desperate young men around the world, gave up on the possibility for meaningful lives. Such men frighten us not only because they can kill our bodies, but also because they are a visible reminder of the worst possibilities for fallen humankind's potential within the condition of original sin that plagues us. Is it for this reason that society seeks their bodily eradication through execution? Does society imagine that the horrible depths of the potential for violence will go away if we dispose of those who embody its visible manifestations? Do we doubt the providence of God when we rationalize that the potential for such violence is overcome only by execution, killing those among us who have killed others among us? In the process do we become more like those from whom God protected Cain? Or are we correct to recall Deuteronomic laws in which killing of those who break certain laws is permitted, over and against that of one of the great Mosaic laws of Exodus 20, "Thou Shalt not Kill"? Meeting violence with violence perpetuates the cycle of violence.

Meeting violence with serious disciplinary consequences, up to the consequence of life in prison, has the potential to transform a life for the well-being of all rather than destroy another life. Where does the death penalty make sense? Is it within the logic driven by God's compassion for the weakness of humankind given the existence of original sin in which a hard-hearted humankind is incapable of resolving its problems nonviolently? Is it within the logic of the mercy, providence, and grace of the God of the cross who forgave those who killed Jesus, Emmanuel, God with us? During the trials, James Byrd Jr.'s son wanted the death penalty for King and Brewer. Over time, he came to believe that the death penalty would neither help nor change anything. In March 2004, he held a vigil with Martin Luther King III and other advocates of nonviolence asking for a repeal of John William King's death penalty.

"When I heard King had exhausted his appeals, I began thinking, 'How can this help me or solve my pain?' and I realized it couldn't," Byrd said. Jasper County District Attorney Guy James Gray said King has unsuccessfully used every state appeals option available.[57]

Within the providence and grace of God are mercy and compassion for each path. There is no evidence in scripture that God *condemns* believers who exercise the death penalty in response to the conviction of the violent. Biblically, there is evidence that both the path that Deuteronomic law offers *and* the law of Moses found in Exodus are permissible, and Jesus the Christ distills the laws into the Two Great Commandments (to love God and neighbor). Not everything that is permissible, however, leads to the *best* possibilities for healing and transformation. The logic of the crucified God in Jesus the Christ, who forgives those who kill and offers hope for redemption, points to the better path. It is in this second, more difficult and challenging, path that one becomes more than forgiven, but more fully in the image of God. The promise of God in Christ is not only that mercy, compassion, and forgiveness are available to a sinsick world, which is an ever-present lesson in both the First and New Testaments. The promise of God in Christ is the restoration of full humanity in God's own likeness, deliverance from all distortions and corruptions of that likeness. Karl Barth emphasizes that Jesus the Christ reveals the humanity of God. In God we find our humanity. In God we become more completely human as we recover likeness to God.[58]

When the larger society imprisons those convicted of crimes, it bears responsibility for the conditions in which convicts find themselves. The effects of these conditions clearly came to haunt the wider community as a whole in the case of Byrd, King, and Brewer. King and Brewer sought protection in prison. Protection at Beto is drawn along racial lines. King and Brewer were not welcomed into the Aryan Brotherhood and started their own division of the Confederate Knights, another white supremacist group. Having suffered their own experiences of torture, they sought to torture another, perhaps someone who reminded them, however fleeting, of those who they felt threatened them the most. Their decision was not rational or wise. They made an irrational decision, in part, because a violent environment corrupted their capacity to reason. Society cannot lock the doors and throw away the key with an attitude of "good riddance" when it sends people to prison. When we do this, we pay a grave price in the long run. Nor ought we to place those convicted of nonviolent crimes with violent offenders. Such a practice amounts to promoting nonviolent offenders to a school of higher education in criminal behavior.

In her analysis of her research findings, Joyce King comes to the following conclusions regarding what she calls "the production of hatred":

> What I have learned is stark and sobering; we have much work to do in what is now the *second*-largest prison system in the country, after California. At the time of the crime, numerically, the Texas system was still the most populous. No matter what transpired behind prison walls before the crime, nothing can excuse the murder of James Byrd, Jr., or the tragic method utilized by the convicted killers. Nothing. But we must look at anything connected to the production of such hatred, whether it is the experience of men in prison or institutional racism from other sources.[59]

In other words, Joyce King, an African American familiar with the longer history of lynching and a native Texan, finds it important to examine *all* of the conditions that led to the hate crime against James Byrd Jr. Jasper, Texas, may have its racial tensions and divisions, but the normative lesson of engaging in hate crimes is peculiar to the culture of certain penal institutions. Jasper does need healing from its passive *han,* its "ethos of racial lamentation."[60] Hate crime, however, is not the norm for Jasper. It *is* the norm of prison systems. Hate crime is a form of active *han* in which woundedness emerges as active animosity and open bitterness to the point of physical violence. This is the type of *han* that King and Brewer experienced in Beto 1 and that they came to embody in their own lives.

The greatest concern Joyce King lifts up is the racial climate in the prison system. She observes, "An ex-warden tended to agree, calling prison nothing more than 'racial hotbeds' for breeding hatred."[61] Where does one learn such hatred and how to imagine such violence? What Joyce King has found is that, in their own way, John William King, Russell Brewer, Shawn Berry, and James Byrd Jr. each represent at-risk persons in society. In the anger that their crime elicits, it is not easy for all to consider the at-risk realities of King, Brewer, and Berry. Yet in raising questions on how to prevent such events, these realities require attention.

The Cross of the Perpetrators

Race hatred is a mutated form of Cain's bitter resentment and hatred toward his brother. To kill another human being is always to kill a sister, a brother, and one's own blood kin. Violence in response to violence not only perpetuates the cycle of violence, but also perpetuates and intensifies the cycle of *han* or *the blues,* which is the cycle of woundedness. King, Brewer, Berry, and Byrd had all felt *han* in response to various experiences of evil and suffering. Byrd responded to his *han* by turning to alcohol and music.

He wanted to be a singer. Like many artists, Byrd mixed the passive destructive behavior of alcoholism with the creativity of music. He was a blues man of the quiet passive sort. King and Brewer's response to woundedness meets the definition of active aggressive *han.* They turned their *han* outward toward any random person who represented those they felt to be at the source of their woundedness. Their *han* did not turn into the creativity of the blues, but into a raging, drunken, blood bath. This is an extreme form of active *han.* Their *han* destroyed self and others.

The families of all four men, the murderers and the murdered, have felt *han,* the abysmal pain that parents experience when they lose their children. King's father laments that he has lost the son, Billy, that he raised. His son became someone who is painfully different from the person he thought he knew, resulting in feelings of shame as well as loss. The loss to the Byrd family, through the brutal murder of their son James Jr., is the nightmare every parent hopes will never happen. Theirs is the deepest *han* of all in this particular story.

King and Brewer have increased their own *han,* because they are back in the violent environment of prison and two are on death row. They spread *han,* woundedness, to their own families and to the family of James Byrd. As we shall see in subsequent chapters, however, through faith in God in Jesus the Christ, the Byrd family have not been overcome by *han,* because there is hope and promise for healing in the God to whom they have turned. King and Brewer did not know how or where to find a positive resolution for their *han.* Byrd's family, in contrast, has not remained in bitterness, but moved on to be healed *and* to heal others. *Han,* the experience of pain and suffering in the lives of the sinned against, does not have the last word. The past does not fully determine the present. Through the divine omnipresent grace that moves in and beyond time, God shares power with creation. Persons may choose to overcome negative past influences.

The Omnipresence of God in a World of Sin, *Han*, and Blues

God, who is all-inclusive in God's love for the world, experiences the suffering of all and graciously offers transformative visions of faith and courage to the world. Joyce King suggests the effects of this transformative grace in her public lectures, stating that she was transformed by the Byrd family and by the town of Jasper. She went to Jasper expecting the type of racist environment she experienced as a child when she and her mother were stopped on a dark, rural Texas highway by a Texas sheriff and detained with threat of jail or a fine for no reason other than the color of their skin. Instead, she found a town she came to love. Following the lead of the Byrd family, her current work is committed to healing hate. For the Byrd family, this is an ongoing process. Byrd's family founded the James Byrd Jr. Foundation for Racial Healing, which provides training in racial healing, and, in 2002, began an oral history project on racism, gathering 120 oral accounts. Part of the Byrd family's healing is to engage in a measure of tough love, such as actively supporting Texas Governor Rick Perry in passing a hate crime act in 2001:

> James Byrd Sr. and his wife, Stella, say they have to clean their son's grave of racist vandalism every month. They say hooded members of the Ku Klux Klan have posed for photos at the cemetery in Jasper, the East Texas town where James Byrd Jr. was dragged to death behind a pickup by three white men because he was black. The Klansmen "left a placard there saying, 'We've been here,'" Stella Byrd said Friday, minutes before Gov. Rick Perry signed into law legislation strengthening penalties for crimes motivated by hate.[62]

The legal definition of "hate crime" is that it is a crime that the perpetrator(s) enact against a person or persons because of bias against their ethnicity, religion, disability, gender, nationality, or the color of their skin. Federal and state acts prohibiting hate crime make it clear to potential perpetrators that such behavior will not be tolerated.

We need to think of what one might mean by "hate crime" theologically, when appealing to a higher power than any the world offers and than any state or nation can produce. In the end, there is one race–the human race. In this respect, any violent crime against another human being is a hate crime borne out of racialized loathing. Rapists engage in a form of misogynist hate crime against the sisters of the human race. Child abuse is a hate crime against the offspring of the human race and emerging generations. Such violence is always violence of kin against kin and kin against God in the eyes of God. The human race is God's kin. Humankind is created in the likeness of God. Sin corrupts and distorts that likeness. Still, because the image of God is present in every human being, no matter how corrupted and distorted, when we violate a fellow human being we violate God. The violation of James Byrd Jr. is a violation of God, humanity, and of the groaning, blood-soaked earth. The earth cries out to God, looking for healing and wholeness.

The consequence of sin and evil is that James Byrd Jr., like all the beaten, maimed, and murdered of the world, will no longer eat with friends and family, sing songs for them, or smile. It is a tragic consequence of evil that loved ones lost the temporal, physical presence of the men, women, and children who were lynched from 1882 to 1964. A consequence of evil is that vast numbers of those who committed lynchings before 1964 were never held accountable for their actions. This left many loving survivors filled with the blues, *han,* and the weary struggle to overcome resentment, anger, bitterness, and the strong temptation to hate in kind.

The consequent nature of God, however, is greater than the consequences of sin and evil. In the midst of the consequences of sin and evil, the consequent nature of God overcomes pain and suffering to create new healing realities. Those who survive evil to become healing agents in God's creative activity are witnesses to reality as described by Whitehead, in which we must contend with evil while holding fast to God's saving vision of truth, beauty, and goodness.[63] As Monica Coleman puts it: "The implication is that we will always have to deal with evil in the temporal world. The eradication of evil, the perfection of the actual world can only happen in the consequent nature of God. God does, however, provide ideal visions to the world through the initial aim."[64] The consequent nature of God, replete with its initial aim of well-being for creation, is revealed in the healing of the Byrd family members. God's providence is not evident in the slaying of another but in the evidence of the presence of divine love, healing, and creativity among the living. In other words, God does not will that human beings hate, maim, and kill one another. It was not God's initial aim for James Byrd Jr. to die by dragging. His lynching was the choice of three men who gave in to nihilistic desires and thoughts. It was the will of John William King.

Forgiveness, Repentance, and Prayers for Salvation in the Grace of God

A broken world raises a cry for salvation. "Salvation" is derived from the Latin word *salus*, which means healing and wholeness. The world is in need of healing and wholeness. God persuasively calls the world to realize healing and wholeness, because God's initial aim is for the well-being and wholeness of an entire creation. God also calls the world to participate in God's work of salvation. Victims and survivors of hatred are often asked to forgive perpetrators as if forgiveness were a simple act. Confusion reigns about "forgiveness" and what it means to forgive. Forgiveness is a lifelong spiritual discipline. The sanctifying power of God makes it possible. Christians understand this power to be the work of the Holy Spirit who is the power of comfort, teaching, and healing in the nature of God. In and on this earth, human beings feel the wounds and joys of the past, continuously recovering when choosing to move in the consequent nature of God's aim for well-being in creation. Forgiveness of sin on the part of believers when sinned against does not require the forgiver to trust those who have wounded us. Rather it is a matter of freeing one's own heart from the corrosive embittering effects of hatred. It takes time for the negative effects of the past to perish to the point that their influence on the world is negligible. In Ireland, people waver between recovery and entropy from hundreds of years of violent conflict. In the Middle East, thousands of years of hateful conflict are negotiated only to enter into a vicious cycle of falling apart. In South Africa, "Truth and Reconciliation" is a *process*. For the Byrd family and the town of Jasper, as well as for a nation where hate crime, abuse, murder, and rape are ongoing problems, healing is a *process*.

We are a world in recovery from hatred. We are a world crying out for healing. We are a world perplexed by the question of whether or not forgiveness is possible for human beings, and what it requires of us. There is so much confusion about what forgiveness is, that it is necessary to clarify what it is not. Forgiveness does not require human beings to *trust those who have deeply hated them and sinned against them.* It is impossible for the Byrd family, the nation, and the world to *trust* those who have violently hated and continue to hate. In the selectivity involved in finding one's humanity in God, forgiveness does not require close intimate relationship with those one forgives. We cannot deny that we are all interrelated, but God created human creatures to be selective. We are empowered by God to select the degree to which we allow others to become part of our lives, part of our own sphere of becoming. Through divine creativity, we are empowered to create our most intimate environments. There are degrees of relationship, intimacy, and distance. Forgiveness *does not* require close personal or social association with those who wound. It never entails accepting sin.

What is forgiveness? From the example of James Byrd Sr., his wife, Stella, and from the example of James Byrd Jr.'s son Randy, one gets a glimpse of what forgiveness *is.* James and Stella Byrd demonstrate that forgiveness is a desire for healing and justice in a broken world. Forgiveness does not accept evil but demands transformation. Byrd's son Randy demonstrates that the power to forgive is something we can pray to receive for as long as it takes the heart to heal enough to receive that first touch of forgiving power. God is omnipresent in the life of the heart that questions whether forgiveness is even possible. God is present in the midst of doubt and resentment about forgiveness, feeling the *han* of the sinned against who, like Jesus on the cross and the psalmist, cry out the prayer of doubt: and seeming abandonment: "My God, my God, why have you forsaken me?" (Mt. 27:46; Ps. 22:1). Forgiveness is grounded in love that demands justice. Forgiveness is a God-given grace that frees the sinned against to pray for the salvation of sinners to free the world from further hatred, violence, and desecration. Forgiveness is, most succinctly, the act of praying for another's salvation rather than for their everlasting damnation. It is the act of desiring divine overcoming of evil while also desiring the salvation of those who have been seduced by it. Forgiveness is grounded in a tough divine love that prays for the power of righteousness to persuasively, powerfully move sinners into righteousness against all visible odds so that evil is overcome.

In contrast, hatred desires the permanent annihilation of the other. Hatred has a negative capacity to infect the souls of well-meaning people of faith and the faithless alike when they are on the receiving end of sin. Hatred tempts the hated to hate. Forgiveness frees the sinned against, liberating them from continuing the cycle of hatred they have experienced. The pain of woundedness in forgiveness does not simply evaporate. That would be a denial of creaturely and divine humanity. To the contrary, the pain remains but is transformed into the healing force of compassion for a deeply wounded world and to joy wherever a witness to healing appears.

Forgiveness is a personal matter in the lives of the sinned against. Not even the church can push anyone to forgive. God does not coerce us to forgive. God is persuasive and is simply with us in blues-filled, *han*-filled existence, empathizing with our pain and suffering. God is present, simply being with us in love and compassion, sharing our anger, guiding us to use the power of anger creatively and constructively for justice. God is present, leading us into resolution, persuasively moving us out of feelings of hatred toward those who have wounded us. Under God's leadership, a moment in time comes when we are so filled with God's patience, love, and peace that we are ready to forgive, because we genuinely know and feel through the experience of God that we can let go, let God, and forgive. For some people the process is very long, for others it is shorter. Some choose to be witnesses to God's loving, divine wrath against injustice. Biblically, God does hate evil, injustice, and crimes against humanity, expressing wrath against them and calling the world back into righteous relationship. Some people are called to be prophetic, embodying divine indignation as activists for justice, hating evil actions, not the persons who commit the evil. We have no right to demand anyone to forgive, because this request is God's right alone in loving spiritual relationship with each individual as God in empathy heals each of us. God alone truly knows where any of us are in the healing process. The timing belongs to God. The timing is not in the control of those who wish an individual or community would hurry up, get healed, and forgive so that everyone else can feel comfortable. God is gentle, understanding, and empathetically encouraging of the healing process. Instead of getting impatient with the healing process and demanding that victims and survivors forgive, we need to focus on participating in divine activism for justice in a world of sin.

Forgiveness, the divinely empowered work of people of faith, directs the heart outward to a world of wounded souls rather than to the entropy of cycles of hate that imprison hearts in unrelenting bitterness. While repentance and forgiveness are possible, certain consequences of the evil actions of King, Brewer, and Berry necessarily remain in place. Because they committed their crime in a state with the death penalty and were dealt death sentences, they will die by lethal injection–unless the death penalty in Texas is repealed. Repentance– which in this case would include compassion for their victim and his family plus encouraging youth not to hate, torture, maim, or kill others–will not change the fact that they killed a man. It will not and ought not change the fact that in any state of the United States they would have to serve at least a life sentence for the safety of the larger society.

Repentance and forgiveness are a matter of internal change, regardless of external circumstances. It is a matter of living the remainder of one's life in tumultuous, separatist, nihilistic rage or in relationship with divine love and its companion–internal peace. Divine love alone can prevent and save individuals, families, and communities from perpetuating cycles of hatred. Whereas forgiveness is always personal and social as a matter of choice, repentance always must be social. If it is true that we reap what we sow, then divine love is tough. One may experience the power of divine love as a warm flame of comfort, when one is the sinned against, or as a forge in which one experiences the pain he or she has caused others when one is the sinner. In divine love, we experience ourselves as others experience us. Divine love alone can shape sinners into compassionate human beings. Repenters must reach the goals of restitution and reparations. Repentance means entry into a new life, a life of healing and a life working to make amends.[65] Repentance must be social, because it involves making amends by sharing the wisdom learned from the errors of sin with others who are at risk of making the same mistakes.

God's consequent nature is evident in the predominantly white jury that found King, Brewer, and Berry guilty of the dragging murder of James Byrd Jr. That trials of the men who beat and dragged James Byrd Jr. to his death did not simply mimic early cases of lynching also speaks to the healing power of God in a nation and region. The fact that just enough people are open to healing from hatred and to abundant life is evidence of God's initial aim and of the lure of God, in the grace of divine providence for creation's well-being at work. Although some view King as a monster,[66] he is more accurately a fallen human being who rejects divine grace in a fallen world. To be born a human creature is part of an ongoing process, requiring continual birth in the Spirit. One can know what it means to be fully human only by knowing God, who is the fullness of humanity. In failing to know and understand the humanity of God, human beings–who are really human becomings–fail to act humanly and humanely. They gradually lose their humanity and die an internal death. While King may be a human being, he did act monstrously. Or, in the language of Paul Tillich, he allowed himself to be motivated by "the demonic," a condition in which a finite individual or social structure claims divinity. The demonic suppresses obedience to structures of truth and distorts humanity.[67] King chose inhumane devolution, rather than an ascent into the humanity of God. Only in God do we find our humanity. To be human is to accept and to reflect God's likeness. Put in Wesleyan terms, rather than in Tillich's recast Lutheran language, to reject God's prevenient, justifying, and sanctifying grace is to descend into inhumanity. Humanity is a goal that humans are called to realize through the power of divine grace. King, in his descent into demonic rage, rejected the divine call to realize full humanity in God revealed in Christ in the power of the Holy Spirit.[68]

If our humanity is found in God, what does Jesus the Christ reveal to us about what it means to become fully human and humane? What healing does God in Jesus the Christ offer a world afflicted with multiple manifestations of hatred? Racism is one of many excuses to find someone to blame for one's own fears and weaknesses. For King, as for others, his hatred of another was a manifestation of feelings of alienation, internal turmoil in response to his birth parents' failure to accept him, rage at his lack of clarity regarding his own identity, and most important pure *self-hatred*.[69] If it is true that human beings are created in the image or likeness of God, then hatred of another human being is also hatred against self and God. Hatred is the root of violence. Hatred leads to unjust suffering. Its consequences are spiritual and physical death. Hatred is sin against God and creation. All murder constitutes a hate crime against God and humanity. Hate is an existential reality to overcome. Therefore, the next chapter examines God as incarnate Spirit, Jesus the Christ, Emmanuel or God with Us, who promises hope for overcoming hate in response to the laments of the keening, *han*-filled, blues-filled world.

CHAPTER 6

The Pulse of God

The Passionate Spirit of God

Trees

Girls
Dressed in brown,
dance, bend
dance, wind
dance, curve,
dance, wave,
dance, dance, dance,
green leaves twining
'round slender,
arms
falling, weeping,
rising, twining,
reaching,
hands and
feet
stained
red,
blood on
leaves and
blood on

roots,
dancing
the dance
of poplar trees
that weep,
of trees
that protest,
desecration
of earth,
flesh,
sap,
blood,
dancing
memory
of
breath
a brush
of wounded
green
re-member-ing
children,
12, 13, 15, 16,
9, 10, 11
with whom
we have sung praises,
for whom the word
has sounded,
with whom we have
broken
bread,
shared
wine,
whose breath
has fluttered
against our breasts
our children,
upon whose
brown heads
we have
breathed,
"I love you,"
our children
who we
SEE

ropes on necks,
waiting, hushed,
we wait, hushed,
seeking redemption
not in suffering,
not in death,
but in an entire earth
that shouts God's,
"Noooooooooooo........"
in this moment
where we tarry
for
God's will
to be done
on earth
as it is in heaven,
where we tarry
for
resurrection.

Incarnation and the Dynamic Nature of Christ

In the Western tradition, systematic theology often begins with the person of Jesus the Christ and then moves to the work of Jesus the Christ. An integrative, relational theology may or may not write of Christ in this manner. Traditionally, African American Christian theologians do not separate Jesus' person from Jesus' work. Instead they find ways of speaking and writing about Christ in a truly integrative manner. This makes sense for the theological task of understanding what it means to dance with God who is in communion with God's own nature as one holy Trinity. Therefore, our discussion of Christ will not actively separate Christ's personhood from Christ's works. Christ offers all hearers, believers, and receivers of the Word/Wisdom of God communion with God. It is most important to honor this communion.

Jesus the Christ: Incarnate Word and Wisdom of God

Jesus the Christ is the incarnate Word/Wisdom of God, who was with God at creation. The incarnate Word/Wisdom of God, who is the second person of the Trinity, loves human beings and the rest of creation, promising salvation to human beings and redemption of creation (Rom. 8:18–22). Jesus, the incarnate Word/Wisdom of God, promised salvation to women and men, children and adults, proclaiming that the realm of God is "at hand." Jesus as incarnate Word/Wisdom of God, as the embodiment of

Hokmah/Sophia, which in the gospel of John is Logos, shared the Word/ Wisdom of God with Jews and Gentiles alike.[1]

Jesus' life and ministry bring the good news of the living Hokmah/ Sophia to the poor, to captives, to the sick, to the lame, to the outcast, and to all those ready to receive forgiveness for their sins. Jesus, the living Word of God, the living Hokmah/ Sophia of God breathed abundant life into those willing to hear his embodiment of Hokmah/Sophia through his teachings. His call was simple, "Follow me," just as Wisdom (Hokmah) shouts, "Follow me," in Proverbs 1–8. Jesus the Christ (anointed one/ messiah) is living. Jesus is "God with us" who shares and feels our joys and pain, who cries for Lazarus, who eats and drinks with the masses, who associates with sinners and prostitutes, and who rejoices at at least one wedding, turning water into wine. Jesus is God to whom you can talk and with whom you can walk.

Classical Debates

Theologians traditionally have asked how to make sense of the divinity and humanity of Jesus, asking whether or not Jesus is and was fully human *and* fully divine. In the fourth century, Arius argued that Jesus was not God, but a creature and intermediary between God and other creatures, divinized but not fully God. In orations against Arius, Athanasius argued that Jesus was fully God and fully human. This led up to the Council at Nicea in 325 C.E., which concluded that the Logos is fully divine and fully human, begotten not made. Pope Leo led the Council at Chalcedon in 451 C.E. in an attempt to reconcile the Antiochene position and the Alexandrian position regarding Christ's divinity and humanity.

The position of the Alexandrian school, espoused by Cyril was that Christ is one hypostatic union, fully human and fully divine. The Antiochenes understood Christ as two separate natures, one human without a human soul and one divine, with Christ's humanity separate from Christ's divinity.

The Council at Chalcedon reinforced the decision at Nicea and defined the Logos as one hypostasis in two natures. The definition of Christ at Chalcedon also clarified that Mary, mother of Jesus, is the Mother of God–*theotokos* (bearer of God), rather than *theodochos* (receiver of God)–deeming the Nestorian view of *theodochos* as heterodox. If Mary is not the mother of Christ yet Christ was conceived by the Holy Spirit, then Christ is fully divine but not fully human. Mary for Nestorius was simply *theodochos,* the recipient of the divine Logos, the second person of the Trinity. Jesus is simply the vessel for the Logos in this scheme. There is a separation between Christ's divinity and humanity. There is no integration of Christ's humanity and divinity. The Nestorians maintained a two natures doctrine in which God could not have a human mother; therefore, they strongly separated Christ's divinity from Christ's humanity. The Nestorians were strongly committed to the Antiochene "two natures doctrine" and split from the Chalcedonian Christians. Those most committed to the Alexandrian school also split off to emphasize the one nature of Christ and became the Monophysites of the Middle East and North Africa.[2]

A neo-Chalcedonian position notices that the meaning of one hypostasis in Christ is not clear in the Chalcedonian definition of the second person of the Trinity. While the Chalcedonian position maintains Christ's two natures, their union remains vague. Robert W. Jenson notes that in Eastern Orthodoxy and "in some Reformation theology," an effort has been made to indicate that the one hypostasis is "a plausible active protagonist of the gospels' total narrative." This position, which becomes a Neo-Chalcedonian position, gives greater emphasis to the union of Christ's humanity and divinity, further correcting Chalcedon's lack of clarity regarding the relationship between Christ's two natures.[3]

The Neo-Chalcedonian understanding makes better sense of biblical understandings of Christ available in the gospel of John: "I am in my Father and my Father is in me" (Jn. 10:25–30, 34–38),[4] than the rather sketchy definition offered at Chalcedon in the fifth century. There is no separation between the Christ and the first person of the Trinity, whom Jesus lovingly called "Abba"–"Daddy," or "Father." Another problem in the Chalcedonian position is that, like Athanasius at the Council of Nicea, it maintains the concept of the impassibility of God, a Platonic idea that is not biblical. In this Platonic, but unbiblical understanding, Jesus' human nature, not his divine nature, experiences joy and suffering. Traditionally, impassibility has been understood to mean that we do not affect God. How can God be "compassionate," fully empathizing with creatures if God is impassible in this sense? The argument for impassibility makes little sense unless we carefully define it to clarify that what we mean is that we can do nothing to *destroy* God. In this sense, God is omnipotent, because as the very power of life God is the very power of resurrection, present in the healing miracles and the forgiveness of sins found in Jesus.

Therefore, God is different from all creatures in that ultimately we cannot destroy God in any sense, incarnate or not. Yet, in some sense we affect God if God has passion *with* the world, not just for the world. The God of Israel has passion with the world in the First Testament, as does God in gospel depictions of Jesus and his teachings in the New Testament. Therefore, an absolutist doctrine of impassibility that loses sight of divine compassion is not biblical and makes short shrift of the meaning of Immanuel. It makes better biblical sense, then, to understand Jesus' humanity and divinity according to the Neo-Chalcedonian doctrine. The gift of Chalcedon is its clarity regarding Mary as Jesus' mother and its understanding that Jesus had a human body and soul. This is retained and fleshed out in Neo-Chalcedonian Christian doctrine.

Experience of Christ

Jesus, who is dust and Spirit, matter and divine energy, body/soul and Spirit, feels or prehends our joy and sorrow, our well-being and our suffering. God incarnate has concrete, experiential knowing. Only God who is Spirit knows the world completely, as the world knows itself. Only God knows each event, individual, entity, or person fully. That Jesus had this type of knowledge speaks to Jesus' incarnation of Spirit. There is hope in the knowledge that God is compassionate, not sympathetic, but empathetic. God is passionate *with* us. God feels with us, lamenting in death and rejoicing in new life. Jesus' divine power of life continues to affect us in its loving response. For these reasons, it makes sense to follow Jesus while also challenging Western Christianity's adulterous relationship with oppressive, Western global economic power and expansion.

Every time a child is born or a woman or man dies of cancer, or is whipped, assaulted, murdered, lynched, dismembered, or raped, Jesus the Christ is present in these human experiences of joy and suffering, empathizing with us. Jesus is remembered as one who has survived to feel with us and to bring the good news of God in the land of the living. Jesus and God are judge. Jesus the Christ is experienced through the Spirit. Jesus the Christ is in God, and God is in Jesus the Christ. Jesus the Christ is Prince of Peace, Bright Morning Star, Healer, a Heart-Fixer and Mind-Regulator, Savior, Redeemer, and Deliverer. Jesus the Christ is fully human and fully divine, perfectly and without division. An integrative understanding of spirit and creation precedes the encounter with Western Christianity. It is an interpretive lens and type of logic that corresponds well with the internal logic of scripture, making scripture seem more familiar than foreign. Historically, people of African descent have not separated the material and spiritual realms, but have viewed them integratively and relationally.

Jesus is found by Sojourner Truth and others in the hush arbors and in secret meetings. Sojourner first learned about God from her African mother, Mau Mau Bett, who told her to look to the sky with its stars when she prayed. Truth began with an understanding that God is in the heavens. Truth, whose full name means Walker of Truth,[5] prayed for someone to stand in between her and God as she petitioned for her children's freedom and her own freedom in the hush arbor. In a vision she saw a figure standing next to God and received comfort that this was one who mediated between her and God, advocating her plight. Shortly thereafter, through the teachings of Quakers, who helped her, she came to understand this figure as Jesus. She became a powerful preacher, abolitionist, and speaker on women's rights. Her favorite sermon was "When I Found Jesus." Moreover, she was very clear that Jesus came from "God and a woman" and that "man had nothing to do with it."[6] The point here is that God in Christ in the power of the Holy Spirit is not only revealed in scripture, which frequently refers to theophanous experiences of others, but God reveals God's own nature in present experience to comfort and guide those who seek God.

In traditions that emphasize personal *and* social liberation, Jesus is loved for freeing mind, body, soul, and spirit. God's presence and movement in the lives of freedom fighters become sacred stories alongside scripture and interpreted through the wisdom of scripture. The biblical canon is supplemented by the wisdom and power of Christian stories that guide, sustain, and liberate.

There are diverse starting points in experiential understanding of God in Christ, and they are interconnected. Some first come to know Jesus the Christ through scripture and tradition. Others first come to know God in Jesus the Christ through the experience of seeking God and experiencing a spiritual sense of one who advocates or mediates the seekers' relationship with the one whom they are seeking. Still others first come to know Jesus Christ through various combinations of these types of experiences. There are yet others who come to an understanding of God in Christ primarily through reason as a form of logic, another aspect of human experience, concluding that there must be a God whose presence is both metaphysical and incarnational for the very principles of interconnectedness, the relationship between energy and matter, the intricacies of ecosystems, and the very ideas of love and justice to exist.

Truth's starting point on the surface seems more dramatic than that of many others, but her intentional request for someone to stand between her and God indicates her openness to an integration of reason and experience. She was already thinking deeply and implicitly, raising questions about how to approach God. Moreover, she actively sought teaching, learning scripture and tradition. Eventually, because she kept asking reasonable questions and through a type of catechesis,[7] she made sense of her earlier experience, concluding with conviction that she had "found Jesus" and that Jesus liberates people from bondage and gender-based oppression. At this point she becomes an integral part of the Christian tradition in North America.

Jesus the Christ draws the world into deeper relationship with God, specifically with the human sense of the "High God," "Great Spirit," "God beyond our words," or God of all gods found in many ancient understandings throughout the world. As God with us, Immanuel, Jesus the Christ convinces the questioning, seeking human heart of the omnipresent love, compassion, and healing heart of God. Moreover, while Sojourner Truth did not necessarily hold an orthodox view of God in which Jesus *is* God, she was clear that God is revealed in Jesus and that God revealed in Jesus lives with us and identifies with us in our existential experiences of goodness and evil. In short, God is "a spirit" for Sojourner Truth.[8] Jesus, who embodies the Spirit of God, makes intimate communication with God possible.

Sojourner Truth was not concerned about debates regarding Jesus' humanity and divinity in the way that many theologians steeped in traditional arguments regarding orthodoxy and heresy are engaged. She simply knew God through relationship with Jesus and knew what God through Jesus can do, based on her own experience and the experiences of others in scripture. As she moved into her life as an itinerant preacher, Truth was very particular in her Bible study. Unable to read English, Truth's Bible study was a discipline of hearing, interpreting, and memorizing scripture. She did not like for adults to read scripture to her. She would have a child read the Bible to her. She found adult readers imposed too many of their own suppositions on her. In part influenced by Quaker practice, she relied on the Spirit to help her interpret. She came to a deeper understanding of Jesus through hearing the New Testament. She came to a deeper understanding of the God who Jesus mediates to the world through hearing the First Testament as well. Then, through interpretation and understanding guided by the Spirit, she preached the freedom available in life with Jesus.

While debates regarding Arian, Antiochene, and Nestorian understandings vs. Nicene and Chalcedonian understandings, or Chalcedonian vs. Neo-Chalcedonian doctrines of God and Christ are helpful for clarifying what we mean when we speak of Jesus' humanity and divinity, in the end it is intimate relationship with the God of whom we speak that is at the heart of the four gospels. Jesus says, "follow me" and reminds us to love God with all within us, and our neighbors as ourselves. In following Jesus, we come to know the true God. In following Jesus we come to know the Christ, the promised Messiah. In following Jesus, we come to experientially understand the wisdom he embodied and taught. In following Jesus, we come to know the living Word with joy and rejoicing. Scripture and firsthand revelational experience of divine presence are Sojourner Truth's primary authoritative sources for proclaiming the teachings of Jesus, more than the creeds of tradition. For Wesleyan African American and Euro-American evangelicals in the nineteenth century, creedal understandings are, seemingly, more influential with emphases on the Trinity and processes of prevenient, convincing, justifying, and sanctifying grace. Is one type of understanding better than the other? The most important point for Truth and evangelists in the Wesleyan tradition is that Jesus saves. Jesus does what God can do.

Therefore, it is important to find Jesus and be in relationship with Jesus, who lived, died, and rose again to be everlastingly present with us. Abundant life is found in Jesus the Christ. He advocates for us. He empathetically shares our suffering and transforms it into joy beyond words. He forgives our sins. He heals our wounds. He justifies us to share in the realm of God. He frees us from every type of bondage through grace and faith from generation to generation. Jesus' life and ministry manifest God's gift of abundant life for all who open their hearts to receive it. In the midst, Jesus experienced suffering and persecutions, temptation and sorrow. He suffered not only on the cross but as a member of the Jewish tradition in the Roman Empire and simply as a citizen in the world, daily dealing with the problem of sin and evil that is part of human existence. Sometimes Jesus became tired and needed time alone to pray, meditate, and rest with God his Abba, just as God rested after creating our cosmos and just as God asks us to take rest from our labors. But the needs were endless; when a woman in the pressing crowd touched the hem of his garment, Jesus knew she had touched him, because he felt power go out of him and into her to heal her (Lk. 8:43–47).

The crowds who sought him affected him, but the power of God within him, and that he was in, and who he was, ongoingly resurrected him to do what only God can do in communion with God as three hypostases in one nature: (1) prevent evil, (2) save through justification and forgiveness, and (3) renew life in the midst of death, which is to heal. The power of overcoming physical and spiritual death is evident throughout Jesus' ministry, not just at the moments of his crucifixion and resurrection from the dead. Yet, the crucifixion is an important event for Christians who live in a world in which it does not always appear that Christ has overcome the evil of crucifixion. As we shall see, Jesus the Christ is not simply "dust and Spirit." Jesus the Christ is "dust and Spirit" resurrected. He holds the free gift of the power of new life for all.

Theodicy and Christendom

The Problem of "Redemptive Suffering"

Is suffering redemptive? Such questions recall the title of Anthony Pinn's humanist theological study, *Why Lord? Suffering and Evil in Black Theology.*[9] For deep questioners like Pinn, the understanding that God in Christ suffers with us is not enough. One cannot avoid questions of theodicy in relation to the persistent problem of violence, which Christians say Christ has overcome on the cross. Where is the material evidence for this overcoming? Pinn raises profound questions regarding the Christian faith in relation to the realities of evil, sin, and the blues, experiences of *han* and lament that afflict the world. Growing up, Pinn heard the members of his African Methodist Episcopal church, particularly "the church mothers," testify of "God's mysterious ability to 'make a way out of no way.'"[10] He remembers the Sunday morning prayers of "'Lord, you never said it would be easy…and so, if I'm going to wear a crown, I must bear my cross.'"[11] Pinn wrestles with a cognitive and experiential dissonance between the church's "struggle to make sense of a meaningless world," raising questions "concerning the tension between lived reality and Christian truths." He asks, "Does the

Christian message say anything liberating to suffering humanity? Does theological conversation serve to make a positive difference in the way the oppressed respond to their existential plight? Do Christian explanations of human suffering make a 'material' and concrete difference?"

Pinn addresses these questions "within the framework of theodicy, or, more, generally, the problem of evil."[12] In his early work he identifies with the "strong form of humanism," which denies the existence of God and is, therefore, "free from the dangerous doctrinal and theological obligations inherent in theistic responses to suffering." For Pinn, this form of humanism, in contrast to weak humanism, which is agnostic, "values experiences above any allegiance to theological categories and platitudes."[13] For Pinn:

> Life for African Americans has been historically defined by oppression and suffering. Reflecting upon this reality, Black folklore and modern Black literature often bring into question the theistic beliefs held dear by Black Christian religion. A system of religious thought truly committed to dealing with oppression must hold in tension the existence of God and operate according to a new hermeneutic–nitty-gritty hermeneutics–in order to avoid the theological dilemma through which suffering is inevitably, and dangerously, labeled redemptive. Only such a system is of value in the struggle for liberation.[14]

It makes sense to ask Pinn's questions in reference to christology, without expecting that one necessarily will share his conclusions. If evil, lynching, and crimes of hate were overcome on the cross, why, then, is there still so much evil in the world? If Christ overcame evil on the cross, then why should church mothers ever pray that they must still bear crosses? Is this the true Christian faith? It seems more plausible that if Christians find salvation in God through Jesus the Christ, then Christians must name the crosses of the world, confront them, and overcome them in the power of the Spirit. If Jesus the Christ did not simply bear a cross, or suffer on a cross, but overcame the evil of that cross, then participating in the divine aim includes a call to overcoming the evil of crucifixion in all of its forms.

Pinn's argument is, "Suffering is evil and it must end; contact with it and endurance of it do not promote anything beneficial. To think otherwise is to deny the value of human life by embracing a demonic force that effectively mutates and destroys the quality of life. *Suffering has no redemptive qualities.*"[15] Pinn's thesis is, "Approaches to Black suffering that leave intact God's goodness and existence are doomed to collapse into redemptive suffering apologetics." For Pinn, "Only a questioning of God's existence provides a working resolution (that is, a full rejection of redemptive suffering)." Pinn questions all writings that result in "the theodical dilemma," the tendency of many Christians to label suffering as redemptive.[16]

Crucifixion and Lamentation in African American Writings

Pinn is not the only one who raises questions regarding whether or not concrete, material, liberative meaning exists in Christian faith. As Pinn observes, many have cried out, "Why Lord?" As Celie puts it in Alice Walker's novel *The Color Purple,* God seems "deaf and dumb," never answering the prayers of those who struggle to survive. Celie, who was incestuously abused by her stepfather and physically abused by her husband Mister,[17] laments, "All my life I never care what people thought 'bout nothing I did, I say. But deep in my heart I care about God. What he going to think. And come to find out, he don't think. Just sit up there glorying in being deef, I reckon. But it ain't easy, trying to do without God. Even if you know he ain't there, trying to do without him is a strain."[18]

Pinn views Walker, as well as her characters Celie and Shug, as humanists. The character Celie, like Shug, Sophia, Harpo, and Mister are, Walker explains, based largely on composites of actual people from her own family history.[19] In interviews, she describes Shug's spirituality as representative of her own.[20] In this conversation, Celie has just about given up on God, concluding that even if God does not exist, "trying to do without him is a strain."[21]

In her definition of "womanist," Walker explains that a womanist "loves the Spirit."[22] Walker is ambivalent, however, desiring to believe there is a God, but unsure God exists, unless God is nature and nature is God. Walker consistently defines her spirituality as pagan, deeply connected to both human and nonhuman nature. For example, in *The Same River Twice,* she writes: "It is my habit as a born-again pagan to lie on the earth in worship. In this, I imagine I am like my pagan African and Native American ancestors, who were sustained by their conscious inseparability from Nature prior to being forced by missionaries to focus all their attention on a God "up there" in "heaven."[23] Like Pinn, she reminds readers that an honest examination of responses to human and earthly suffering acknowledges that not everyone who has witnessed evil and suffering chooses Christianity or finds meaning in the cross.

That suffering is redemptive is an oft-heard theme in Christian writings and preaching. Is that theme, however, an authentic teaching in the good news attributed to Jesus the Christ? Or, does the good news–the gospel–of Jesus the Christ point us in a very different direction? How might one find meaningful answers to questions regarding evil and suffering in a world where crucifixion takes place again and again–from the rape of women by soldiers in war around the globe, to the torture of prisoners, to contemporary hate crimes? Historically, those who have been the subjects of extreme suffering have questioned Christendom's claim that suffering is redemptive. They have questioned forms of Western Christianity that perpetuate crucifixion.

Howard Thurman wrote of his journey to India to meet Mahatma Gandhi in the 1940s when the United States was segregated and many black men were being lynched. A Hindu lawyer asked Thurman how he could be a Christian when this religion had oppressed so many people of color around the world. The man said that for Thurman to be a Christian made him a traitor to all the darker peoples of the earth. India had been colonized by the British, who were Christian. Thurman responded, "I am a follower of Jesus."[24] He focused on the fact that Jesus was a poor Jew. Thurman was speaking and writing during a period when millions of Jews suffered and died under the violence of Nazis. Moreover, he was concerned with the psychological torture of slavery and the global disinheritance of people of color in the Two Thirds world. Biblical scholars today have corrected Thurman's understanding that Jesus represents poor, disinherited Jews *in contrast* to Paul, who Thurman casts as a representative of the Roman Empire. Jesus *and* Paul, Abraham Smith reminds readers of New Testament literature, were oppressed Jews within the Roman Empire.[25] Thurman's analysis of Rome's imperialist impact on the content of Christian faith is well worth heeding, however, even given the correction that Paul, in fact, was critical of pro-Roman aristocracy in Thessalonica. Therefore, while Thurman's analysis of Paul has its flaws, his critique of the Roman Empire, as Smith seems to agree, remains relevant as we consider the temptations among empires today and in every age to compromise Jesus' good news *to the poor.*

Those who are African Americans and connect with this violence perpetrated by many so-called Christians, and yet remain "Christian," find themselves in paradox. They connect through and identify with the social-historical experiences of the millions of Africans thrown overboard during the trans-Atlantic slave trade, and with the brutal whippings, tortures, lynchings, and slayings of black bodies. Thurman's decision to name himself "a follower of Jesus" encourages all Christians to think about what it means to be a disciple of Jesus. What does it mean to love Jesus and his intimate relationship to God who is Spirit when Christianity as a Western institution has been so destructive toward people of color and women? Even Walker is clear that it is Christianity with its history of conquest and oppression that she finds troubling more than Jesus. She comments parenthetically:

> (Everybody loved Jesus Christ. We recognized him as one of us, but a rebel and revolutionary, consistently speaking up for the poor, the sick, and the discriminated-against, and going up against the bossmen…We knew that people who were really like Jesus were often lynched).[26]

Easter mornings in black churches have long been events of passion not only because of the crucifixion of Jesus, but because of the memories of black people who were whipped at whipping posts and hung from trees.

The understanding is that the world is a place of such hate and evil that it even hung God's own Son from a tree. If it happened to the Son of God, then it could happen to anyone in a world full of evil, especially those who are subject to oppressive powers.

Walker inaccurately refers to the "bossmen" who killed Jesus as "the orthodox Jewish leaders and rich men of his day." He may have been killed by wealthy, ruling powers (Rome), but not by orthodox Jewish leaders. Walker is not a biblical scholar. Contemporary biblical scholars see Herod and Caiaphas not so much as "orthodox Jewish leaders" as much as pawns of a Roman empire entrusted to keep peaceful relationships within an empire subject to Caesar as god. Rome, not Jews, crucified rabbis like Jesus. What is true about Walker's inherited understanding of Jesus is that he is very much like the lynched of the world. Jesus, like other rabbis during the same period, was known to publicly resist the claims of an empire to be the divine kingdom and of an emperor to be god. There was nothing unusual about this belief in Judaism, orthodox or otherwise. Rome was threatened by any leader who relativized its power. African Americans connected lynching with crucifixion, because both the lynched and the crucified defy the claims of empires no matter how small or large the empire may be–a sharecropping town in the deep Southern United States or an imperialistic nation.

Christians must ask who they believe Jesus the Christ is. Is this Christ the Jewish rabbi Jesus who was crucified by the Romans? Is this Christ we are talking about the Jesus who was Mary's son, that Peter knew, and that Sojourner Truth found to help her preach powerfully to others in her freedom journey with entire communities? Or is it the Christ of conquering, enslaving, Western economic imperialism? If the one we are talking about is the latter, then the speaker is an idolater who does not really know Jesus, the one Peter called Christ and Messiah. If the one we are talking about is the former, then this is the one whose words turn the world to the reign of God. This is the one who brings deliverance, healing, freedom, and good news to the poor, widows, orphans, the blind, the captive, and most simply, to the least of these. This Jesus the Christ is not of Rome or of any worldly empire. This Christ is of *basilea tou theou,* the kingdom, reign, or realm of God.

Walker appreciates the power of love revealed in Jesus, a power that she finds attractive in her native black culture, which is deeply attracted to Jesus. She writes:

> It is fatal to love a God who does not love you...Indeed, it was because the teachings of Jesus were already familiar to many of our ancestors, especially in the New World–they already practiced love and sharing that he preached–that the Christian Church was able to make as many genuine converts to the Christian religion as it did.[27]

Walker proposes paganism as an alternative to Christianity. Her argument for paganism, however, rather than for christocentric faith is not persuasive. If the love taught and embodied by Jesus is the same love many ancestors knew, then *why not* follow Jesus? Moreover, if that love is fully embodied in Jesus the Christ, then why refer to the God of the Bible, of Moses, Joshua, and Jesus as some "foreign" God? Our "pagan ancestors" were attracted to the power of this Son of God and son of Mary, Walker admits, because he was familiar. Jesus, Son of God and of a woman, like the child of so many black mothers, was whipped and hung from a tree. They found power in Jesus, not simply out of shame towards their old gods, but because Jesus spoke to their present situation in ways the old gods did not.

This God of Jesus is the God of love who moves throughout the ages. If this is Jesus' God, in whom Jesus the Christ lives and who lives in Jesus the Christ, then there is no need to replace Jesus with worship of Earth/Nature. The overarching biblical story cannot be reduced to the texts of violence that trouble Walker, but rather it is the story in which divine love and relationship to creation have the literal ultimate Word. Walker attests to the power of the Word of Love Jesus taught and embodied.[28] That Word is omnipresent in the Earth that Walker worships and in the "Nature" that Walker believes is its Spirit, but it cannot be reduced to Earth and Nature.

Earlier African American writers also have challenged hypocrisy in Christendom. Countee Cullen's poem, "Christ Recrucified," published in 1922, speaks to a weariness of the unrelenting presence of hatred and suffering. He describes the South as "crucifying Christ again." Moreover, "Christ's awful wrong is that he's dark of hue, / The sin for which no blamelessness atones." The poem also describes the practice of burning lynched African American bodies and crowds who fight over the burned bones to keep as souvenirs.[29]

Cullen, like Pinn, appears to be asking, "Why Lord?" If God does indeed exist, "Why such evil in the world?" A lingering tone of unresolved bitterness and resentment regarding the problem of theodicy is evident in the poem. Cullen is sarcastic–"The South," with its deep, Bible-Belt profession of Christian faith, "is crucifying Christ again." Cullen is calling the "good" Christian people who encouraged and participated in lynchings hypocrites. Again, while the emphasis of the anti-lynching movement of the late nineteenth and early twentieth centuries was on "Southern horrors," such horrors were also taking place in other regions of the nation. A postcard of the lynching of Laura Nelson at Okemah, Oklahoma, on May 25, 1911, is extant in the Robert W. Woodruff Library at Emory University in Atlanta, Georgia.[30] For a time, similar postcards were available for viewing at the *Without Sanctuary* Web site, created by James Allen, author of an exhibit and book by the same title.[31]

W. E. B. DuBois, like Cullen, compared lynching, a form of hate crime, with crucifixion. In 1920, DuBois wrote and published a short story entitled "Jesus Christ in Texas" about justice, redemption, and lynching.[32] The story is a parable about the ways in which the problem of the sin-filled violence of crucifixion repeats itself. Moreover, it is a story about how the compassion and forgiveness of Christ extends to the poor, the outcast, and the prisoners (Lk. 4:18–20; Mt. 25:31–46). In the story, segregationist characters do not recognize a stranger who turns out to be a mulatto as they search for a runaway black man convicted of stealing. The female protagonist is startled after the stranger asks if she loves all of her neighbors, turns on a lamp, and for the first time sees the curly hair and dark face that identify the stranger as a mulatto–a colored man. By his voice and in the dim light, she had believed him to be white. Startled, she runs down the path outside her door. In her panic, she runs into the runaway black convict the segregationists have been hunting and falls. The woman's husband accuses the black man of attacking her, and the man is lynched by moonlight.[33] Looking out her window, the woman gasps, because:

> A fierce joy sobbed up through the terror in her soul...behind the roped and swaying form below hung quivering and burning a great crimson cross. Her dry lips moved: "Despised and rejected of men."...There, heaven-tall, earth-wide, hung the stranger on the crimson cross, riven and bloodstained, with thorn-crowned head and pierced hands...His calm dark eyes, all sorrowful, were fastened on the writhing twisting body of the thief, and a voice came out of the winds of the night saying: "This day thou shalt be with me in Paradise!"[34]

Only when the mulatto appears in the sky with outstretched arms saying to the lynched man, "This day you shall be with me in heaven," does the poor, confused woman recognize that the stranger who has asked her if she loves *all* of her neighbors is Jesus Christ, who looks either very Semitic, or "colored," or both. DuBois's vision of Christ calls readers to overcome hatred and to participate fully in loving the neighbor and the stranger. The consequence of sin is broken relationship with God, self, and others, which results in less abundant life. The consequence of participating in divine love is abundant life.

DuBois's short story functions as a parable that asks one to think about Jesus Christ in present situations of violence and injustice. It offers a microcosmic view of Jesus Christ in the world. It also questions the practice of execution in relation to God's love for life. Specifically, DuBois's parable evokes readers to love *all* strangers and neighbors completely and in truth (Mt. 19:16–22; 22:34–39; 25:31–46; Lk. 10:25–37). "Crucifixion," in DuBois's parable, becomes a metaphor for lynching and other forms of unnecessary violence forged in the nihilistic furnaces of hatred. One can extend DuBois's metaphor, which is deeply steeped in the African American experience of lynching, to include all aspects of the cycle of violence, whether against human beings or the rest of creation. The parable functions as an incisive critique of false faith.

For Christians, DuBois's parable recalls John 3:16–21:

> For God so loved the world that he gave his only Son, so that everyone who believes in him may not perish but have eternal life.
>
> Indeed, God did not send the Son into the world to condemn the world, but in order that the world might be saved through him. Those who believe in him are not condemned; but those who do not believe are condemned already, because they have not believed in the name of the only Son of God. And that this is the judgment, that the light has come into world, and people loved darkness rather than light because their deeds were evil. For all who do evil hate the light and do not come to the light, so that their deeds may not be exposed. But those who do what is true come to the light, so that it may be clearly seen that their deeds have been done in God.

Like John 3:1–21 and the parable of the good Samaritan in Luke 10:25–37, DuBois challenges readers to rethink whether or not they are truly disciples of Christ. Readers must reexamine what it means to walk in the light instead of in darkness, in the Spirit rather than in evil, and in love instead of hate. Whoever does not love does not know God revealed in Christ, who is love. Christians who are familiar with New Testament literature would immediately recall 1 John 4:7–9, 20–21:

> Beloved, let us love one another, because love is from God; everyone who loves is born of God and knows God. Whoever does not love does not know God, for God is love. God's love was revealed among us in this way: God sent his only Son into the world so that we might live through him…Those who say, "I love God," and hate their brothers or sisters, are liars; for those who do not love a brother or sister whom they have seen, cannot love God whom they have not seen. The commandment we have from him is this: those who love God must love their brothers and sisters also.

As African American deutero-canonical literature, "Jesus Christ in Texas" challenges readers to read their Bibles again. It functions as a novel type of altar call, calling readers to be born again in the love of Christ they have poorly professed and failed to follow. Christians are left to ponder the irony that an agnostic has written such a profound Christian parable.

While some may think of the poetry and other writings of anti-lynching intellectuals as "literature" and not "history," one might also think of creative expressions of lament as "deutero-canonical texts" of African American faith. DuBois intentionally created a parable to question the false Christian faith of those who either actively or complicitly affirmed lynching and "Jim Crow" segregation. His parable focuses on Texas for its illustration, because Texas, at 352 documented lynchings from the late nineteenth through twentieth centuries, had one of the largest numbers of lynchings of African Americans after Mississippi (539) and Georgia (492). DuBois, along with Ida B. Wells-Barnett, was a leader in the anti-lynching campaign of his era.[35]

Lynchings were community events with crowds in attendance that sometimes numbered in the thousands. Participants treated lynchings as a form of entertainment. People brought food. Men brought their wives and small children of all ages. It was a spectator event, where many watched the torture and killing. Whereas in popular film, lynch mobs are portrayed as rather small and isolated groups, lynchings were not always such private affairs. As for the history of the term "lynch," Baker and numerous other sources note that the term comes from a Virginia planter and Revolutionary War officer named Col. Charles Lynch, who served as Justice of the Peace in Bedford County during the mid to late eighteenth century. Baker notes, "Through extralegal means, Lynch meted out punishment to Loyalists who favored the British rule over the colonies." Over time, most Americans have come to associate the term with racial violence in the post-Civil War South.[36]

It was not uncommon to publish notices of planned lynchings in community newspapers, inviting white citizens to attend the event.[37] Morbid participants, as part of the entertainment, took photographs of men, women, and children hanging from trees, duplicating them to circulate as postcards.[38] Lynch mobs did not simply hang their victims from trees; they also beat them and tortured them in other ways. Sometimes they burned the body after taking it down from the tree. In the first century of the Christian era, crucifixions were, likewise, public events, occasions that were entertaining for Roman citizens and soldiers. Lynchings as public spectacles were every bit as similar to the crucifixion of Jesus as poets and songwriters indicate. Cullen's title for his poem, "Christ Recrucified," is fitting. It is meant to challenge so-called Christians who participated in such horrific events.

Langston Hughes's poem, "Christ in Alabama," first published in 1931 expresses keen bitterness at the horrors that Cullen wrote of in more flowering language a decade earlier. For Hughes, "Christ is a N**** / Beaten black–O, bare your back. Mary is His Mother / *Mammy of the South, Silence your Mouth.*"[39] In Hughes's poem, God is the lynched man's father who judges from above like a white slave master or segregationist boss. In other words, Hughes criticizes those who lynch for killing their own descendants, given that many African Americans are offspring of a system of forced concubinage.[40] The references to God as "White Master" and to the Christ figure as "bastard" are a reference to the fact that so many people of color are the rejected progeny of Caucasian slave masters, borne of raped slave women or, during segregation, raped domestic workers.

The poem's rancor is self-evident. The wording and tone are meant to shock and awaken the reader into awareness of the deep ugliness of it all. This is a difficult poem to quote, hear, or read, even in part. Yet, no discussion of lynching and hate crime is honest without careful attention to the depths of bitterness such horrors can produce in a people. Just a look at a few of the documented pictures and postcards of lynchings are enough to tempt bitterness and doubtfulness of the existence of God in Christ within viewers years, decades, and even a century after given events. What does it mean to speak of Christian faith as the solution to unjust suffering, when Christians have too often been the source of that problem? Pinn's question, in concert with the laments of Cullen and Hughes, along with the rejection of Christendom by Thurman and Walker and the altar call of DuBois, remains: "Why does God allow evil?" God's suffering, weeping, walking, eating, hearing, speaking, loving, healing, and rejoicing in Jesus' ministry to the oppressed peoples and cosmos speak to God's omnipresence in the universe.

In a more hopeful note that affirms Christian faith, James Cameron writes of barely escaping a lynching in Marion, Indiana, on August 7, 1930. The mob was eagerly waiting to witness the killing of this last of three men accused of rape and murder as the rope was being placed around Cameron's neck. Then, all of a sudden, Cameron says, after he prayed for God to forgive him of his sins, he heard an angelic voice above the crowd saying, "Take this boy back; he had nothing to do with any killing or any rape."[41] Still, Cameron witnessed his two friends, Tom Shipp, 18, and Abraham Smith, being beaten unconscious and then hung from a tree that was meant for him as well. The men were hung before a crowd of 15,000.

Initially, Cameron became bitter and began to internalize the hatred he had experienced. Through the prayerful faith witness of his mother and a white sheriff who helped him beat the injustice of an unfair system, he overcame the temptations of bitterness and hatred. He founded the Black Holocaust Museum, Inc., established in 1988 in Milwaukee, Wisconsin. The Black Holocaust Museum is a nonprofit museum devoted to preserving the history of lynching in the United States and the struggle of black people for equality.[42] Like African American poets, prose writers, and scholars, some who were humanists or agnostics, he put his righteous indignation to work in creative projects and committed his life to racial healing. Cameron's life demonstrates that suffering is not redemptive, because it easily leads to bitterness and internalizing one's experience of hatred in the world. To the contrary, *overcoming evil* is redemptive.

Atonement

The cross, an *enduring symbol* of Jesus' and humankind's suffering, is also an *enduring problem*.[43] The cross is the most controversial aspect of *christology*–the study or knowledge of Christ. So often, discussions of christology in relation to the problem of the cross are written prior to consideration of more recent historical and present, ongoing events of "crucifixion." For many suffering people in the world the material evidence is not immediately apparent that the hatred, evil, and suffering that Christ is said to have overcome has been overcome. From the crucifixions in Rome during the first century, to the lynching of Emmett Till in Money, Mississippi, to the fatal beating, car-dragging, and decapitation of James Byrd Jr. in 1998 in the small town of Jasper, Texas, to twenty-first–century attacks in the United States and bombings in the Middle East, Christians have pondered the meaning of violence in relation to the sacredness of life.

On the one hand, the Christian tradition teaches that God has overcome death and evil through the crucifixion of Jesus on the cross and the event of resurrection. On the other hand, the tradition is left with the difficult task of maintaining the credibility of its claims by responding to questions regarding continued death and destruction. At first glance, the New Testament accounts of the Son of God dying on the cross do not seem very promising. Moreover, as the church enters its third millennium, a long history of world violence since the crucifixion of Jesus gives the appearance that he is only one of millions of victims.

For some, the thought that God forsook God's own Son, the incarnation of God's own self, makes God seem cruel and abusive. "Why has not God stopped these cruel acts of violence?" such voices ask. Victory over evil, death, and suffering is a process, an ongoing event, not a static moment in history. In every present moment, God is overcoming evil. This divine process now does not appear to be soon enough, quick enough, or static enough. It is like changing the chemical balance in a polluted body of water only to be told that it will be many generations before fish can live in it, anyone may drink from it, or children may swim in it. The necessary transformative events have occurred, but the effects appear to be absent.

According to atonement theories developed in scripture and in later church writings, God sounds rather tyrannical. Early indications of a "ransom" theory in New Testament literature can be read as suggesting God is rather cruel, using God's own Son as a ransom to Satan to pay for the sins of the world. Later Christian thinkers draw on such texts to develop a full ransom theory that is more confusing and nonsensical to many than the New Testament verses the theologians derive these theories from. God and the Son of God do have the last "Word" in this theory, because God in the Word who is the Son of God, Jesus the Christ, tricks the powers of evil in the resurrection. It does not make sense, however, given biblical emphasis on divine justice and glory, that God would owe Satan anything and therefore pay ransom to Satan. For those who choose this theory, however, one might note that in African, Caribbean, and African American Yoruba religions, the *orisha* Legba is a trickster. The notion of the divine as trickster is not uncommon in many indigenous religions.

In the 1100s, Anselm of Canterbury developed the satisfaction theory, along with its derivatives. This theory is equally problematic, in its suggestion that God required a blood sacrifice to satisfy the sins of fallen humanity. As the Mennonite theologian J. Denny Weaver points out in *The Nonviolent Atonement,* Gustav Aulen's "Christus Victor" model is more tenable, more biblical, and more ancient. He also observes that womanist theologians make similar claims in their christologies. For Weaver, the "Christus Victor" narrative found in scripture, in the early church centuries before Anselm, and in the writings of womanist theologians, offers a nonviolent understanding of the atonement that is in keeping with biblical principles.[44] In this understanding, God does not need to pay a ransom to Satan, because the overarching biblical principle that God is more powerful than Satan holds. God does not demand satisfaction through the blood sacrifice of the Son, who must pay for the sins of the world. The latter, many today readily admit, makes God sound abusive, which is inconsistent with the metaphorical understanding of God as a loving parent, in whom those who sin certainly experience consequences for wrong actions, but who is not abusive.

It is important not to misunderstand what Weaver means by "nonviolent atonement." This expression does not mean that Jesus did not suffer on the cross or that crucifixion is not violent. To the contrary, it means that Jesus the Christ, in communion with the Trinity, is nonviolent. Moreover, it means that the *only reason* why God knows Jesus must die and rise again, is because the world is so filled with evil, sin, and violence that this is the logical outcome for God incarnate, Immanuel, with sinful human beings in a world of evil. Jesus does not die on the cross because God crucifies God's own son. Jesus dies on the cross because few in the world either recognize God or love God, neighbors, and strangers. Jesus' atonement is an event that emphasizes the power of life and goodness over the false "power" of evil and death.

The Christus Victor narrative *does not deny* that Jesus gives his own life in the name of God who loves Israel, humankind, and all of creation. The question for Weaver is whether or not God *causes* the Son's crucifixion, suffering, and death. God does not *cause* Jesus' death, because God is good. Evil, which is God's adversary,[45] causes Jesus' death. God sent God's own Son into the world that we might have abundant and everlasting life. God sent Jesus "into the world to die" only in the sense that any parents send their children out into an unfair world already filled with violence. *God is not like an abusive parent who demands a son's blood, but rather is like a loving parent who knew that the incarnate second person of the Trinity faced sacrificing his life in a world that was already crucifying Jews for speaking the truth about the one God.* Previously, I have, with Sharon Welch, referred to this as an "ethic of risk." A deep exploration of "ethic of risk," however, reveals a more profound understanding of "sacrifice" in which Jesus still gives his life in the name of speaking the truth, a risk for rabbis in his time.[46] The entire Trinity is in agreement in this sending forth of the incarnate Word/Wisdom of God, knowing that it holds the power of resurrection.

The point of contemporary theologians who, like the early church, turn to the Christus Victor doctrine of atonement is that God overcomes evil on the cross. The gift of Jesus' life is precisely that life. Jesus' gift, in relation to the entire Trinity, is the power of life in an unfair, often brutal world. The significance of Jesus' blood is that throughout his life, crucifixion, death, and resurrection Jesus the Christ shares the power of life, which blood represents, with the world. Womanist theologians like Joanne Terrell do not reject the biblical understanding of "Jesus' sacrifice," but carefully define the uniqueness of Jesus' sacrifice. Terrell emphasizes that Jesus is cosufferer who overcomes systemic structures of evil in the world. In particular, womanist theologians emphasize that Jesus' sacrifice does not endorse or affirm the violent practices of empires toward indigenous peoples, the poor, or any subjects of worldly empires, beginning with Rome's abuses of the meaning of sacrifice.[47] To employ Jesus' sacrifice in ways that endorse worldly greed, power, and conquest mocks Jesus' overcoming worldly evil and violence on the cross. Put another way, Jesus' sacrifice is once and for all. Accompanied by the risen Christ, in the power of the Holy Spirit, men, women, and children are to overcome suffering and evil. They are not to return to situations of abuse and bondage, but rather they are called to walk fully within the power of the entire Trinity, revealed in Christ, to live into freedom from abuse, suffering, and bondage. Therefore, God the Parent and Jesus the Christ understand that this is inevitable given events that were taking place during Jesus' life on earth and the consequences of those events. The Divine Nature knows of all possibilities for the lives of each of the many that make up the universe that we live in. Jesus was clear that his own crucifixion was inevitable, given the events of his world. Jesus pays a debt for us only in the sense that Jesus functions as our justifying advocate in relation to God, saying, "Father, forgive them. They know not what they do."

Mary's Song of Wisdom

In the interstices of Anselmian and Christus Victor debates, we find the wisdom of Mary's *Magnificat,* her song of praise to God her Savior who has blessed her and whose Son she will bear. She is filled with praise for the abundant life of God's promise to her, in her, and for the world. From the words of her song of praise, one gleans that she has a divinely given mother's vision of her son's life. In the life and ministry of Jesus that Mary prophesies in her song we gain insight into the nature of Jesus, the type of person he was before the crucifixion, and, therefore, what type of person would be able to forgive even his enemies. Jesus was a teacher of Torah and a follower of spiritual discipline. He did not suddenly become the Christ on the cross. According to the gospels of Matthew and Luke, Mary, his devout Jewish mother, understood him to be the Son of God from his conception. Jesus was Christ from his conception, in birth, in childhood, and in adolescence, not merely in his adult ministry (Mt. 1:18–2:18; Lk. 1:26–36, 39–57). Mary raised Jesus with the understanding that he was her son and the Son of the Spirit of God. She rejoiced in God her Savior who chose her to bear this special child. In believing this child was of God, she both rejoiced and experienced a foreboding that a sword would pierce her heart. She would bear and raise this child in a world that was unkind and could be cruel to the Jews. Jesus grew up in a world of crucifixion. He also grew up in a world where Jewish women, men, and children rejoiced. He also rejoiced, turning water into wine at the wedding at Cana, sharing wine and food with all manner of followers, not only his closest disciples, but with crowds of thousands of people.

Jesus' mother, Mary, knowing the type of child she would bear and raise, knew what Jesus would have to face in the world. According to Luke 1:46–55, Mary said or sang words like these to announce her good news of Jesus' expected birth to her cousin Elizabeth, mother of John the Baptist:

> "My soul magnifies the Lord,
>   and my spirit rejoices in God my Savior,
> for he has looked with favor on the lowliness of his servant.
>   Surely, from now on all generations will call me blessed;
> for the Mighty One has done great things for me,
>   and holy is his name...
> He has brought down the powerful from their thrones,
>   and lifted up the lowly;
> he has filled the hungry with good things,
>   and sent the rich away empty.
> He has helped his servant Israel,
>   in remembrance of his mercy,
> according to the promise he made to our ancestors,
>   to Abraham and to his descendants forever."

In her *Magnificat*, Mary praises God her Savior and is thankful for the son she has conceived by the Holy Spirit, confident that in this event God is victorious over evil rulers and delivers the oppressed. She proclaims what God will do in Jesus. Mary was a faithful Jewish woman, faithful to Torah and to the God of Israel. The words attributed to her by the writer of this text paint a portrait of a woman who would raise her son to be unwavering in faithfulness to Torah and to the God of Israel. Torah, the law of the God of Israel, would come before Rome for her and the son that she bore. Jesus lived in a time when he would not be the only Jewish teacher and leader to face persecution and death. The world was troubled, and the likelihood of death for any man who spoke of "a kingdom not of this world" could prick the ears of Roman rulers commissioned to squelch any suggestion of treason.

Mary knew that her son would teach the Torah and the prophets. Jesus is God incarnate who suffers with us, but this does not mean that suffering is redemptive or sacralizing. Suffering does not make us more holy, and suffering is not what makes God, God. *God's empathy in Christ is redemptive. God's overcoming evil in Christ is redemptive. And God's forgiveness in Christ is redemptive.* We are called to overcome the production of hatred and violence. We are called to live into the resurrection life promised to us and given to us in the here and now. The cross is symbolic of all weapons of hatred and violence–physical, emotional, mental, and spiritual. The significance of Christ's response to weapons of evil is not a passive bearing of it all, but it is God's profound "No" to evil. In following Jesus, we participate in the divine "No" to evil and suffering. For these reasons, it makes sense to follow Jesus while also challenging an adulterous relationship with worldly power, greed, and violence.

Matthew 20:28 and Mark 10:45 portray Jesus as giving his life as a ransom for many; 1 Timothy 2:6 continues this theme. The doctrine of Christ's victory over evil does not dismiss these biblical understandings, but takes them very seriously. If humankind is in bondage to sin and evil, clearly Christ cannot pay a ransom to Satan. Therefore, in a variation of the Christus Victor understanding, the world of evil does not recognize Christ hidden in human flesh, assumes Christ is easy prey, and swallows the bait; and thus God tricks Satan.[48] The gift of the Anselmian doctrine of atonement is that Jesus does not pay a ransom to Satan. Rather, Jesus the Christ dies to satisfy God's offended honor, as a substitute for sinful humankind. Scripture itself is never clear about who Jesus pays a ransom or debt to. Anselm's suggestion that Jesus pays humankind's debt to God for us takes care of earlier problems in the notion that Christ, in human disguise, pays a ransom to Satan, which is untenable given that God cannot pay a debt to one God rules.[49] The problem with the Anselmian doctrine is that biblically, it seems that God in Christ forgives sin rather than pays the debt of sin. In the gospel of Luke, Jesus the Christ, as the divine second person of the Trinity, *forgives our great debt, just as Jesus teaches his disciples to pray for this same forgiveness.*[50] God owes no debt, ransom, or sacrifice to Satan. Nor does God demand that the second person of the Trinity pay this debt. Jesus asks God to forgive; and God forgives, rather than condemns, the world that crucifies God. Whatever debt human beings might speak of owing to God cannot be paid; therefore, God wipes the slate clean by simply forgiving the debt owed through Jesus Christ's words on the cross. God can afford such forgiveness of debts, because God is the very power of life. Jesus overcomes Satan–the power of systemic structures of evil in the world–through God's resurrecting power.

A synthesis of the Anselmian doctrine and the Christus Victor understanding works well for an integrative, relational theology in which we do not want to lose the sense that Jesus does indeed give his life for a debt we can never pay, but also want to recognize that his divine mission of gracing the world with abundant life is victorious over the false, so-called "power" of death-dealing evil. If we take the Latin word for power and virtue, *virtus,* seriously, then Christ removes the masks that evil parades in. *There is no power in evil, because evil literally has no virtue.* The point is that Jesus' sacrifice is not based in what we today call "a martyrdom complex," in which men, women, and children feel they must function as doormats, accepting abuse because uninformed ministers have taught them they must do this, because this is what Jesus did. The point of this synthesis of the Anselmian and Christus Victor understandings of Christ's atonement is simply this: One can easily imagine Jesus visiting some churches with a big sign, reading, "I already did this for you, once and for all. Do not try this at home! Drop everything and follow me. Come, eat and drink with me. I will give you bread that is not of this world, drink from a well that never runs dry, peace that passes understanding, joy that is not of this world, and rest." If greater emphasis is given to Jesus' suffering than to his humane, rigorously loving ministry, which is unsurpassable, then the understanding of Jesus' humanity and divinity becomes lop-sided. The understanding that God in Jesus the Christ *suffers and overcomes* speaks more precisely to the *full humanity and divinity* of Jesus the Christ. Jesus' suffering, like Jesus' celebration meals and Jesus' sharing of divine wisdom in his ministry on this earth, is evidence of the full humanity found in God with us, Immanuel. The humanity found in Jesus the Christ, the anointed one, *is* divine, because true humanity comes from God. It is not Jesus' suffering that is redemptive, but the life leading up to his crucifixion, his words on the cross, his resurrection, and the abundant, everlasting life he graciously gives to the world that is redemptive. We must remember Mary's song, her Holy Spirit–inspired prophecy of the God-son she bore and his overcoming of the world. Let us, then, be of good courage!

Mary, Mother of God and Dancing with God

Mary's wisdom of redemptive overcoming sings today in the hearts of women and men who are engaged in the task of spiritual striving with Christ to overcome evil. The poetry and prophetic contributions of past and older generations echoes in the creative works of new generations. The poem opening this chapter is a response to a Christian liturgical performance created by Vanessa Baker and Cheryl Swann for St. Luke

"Community" United Methodist Church. While the writings of Dubois, Cullen, and Hughes were filled with pathos, contemporary interpretations offer hope of overcoming. In introducing the task of our theology, which is to understand the God of grace and courage, we noted that the dance and poetry Baker created, along with choreographer Swann, were performed during African American History Month, February 10, 2002, to commemorate the lamentation and the resurrection hope of Mamie Till-Mobley. In 1955, Mamie Till-Mobley's son, Emmett Till, was the victim of a hate crime by white racial supremacists who hated black Americans. At the tender age of 14, Emmett Till was brutally beaten, disfigured, hung from a tree, and thrown into the Mississippi River. Till's blood, like the blood of many before and after him, fell on the leaves, branches, and roots of the trees that God created.[51]

Baker, who wrote the poem "Sacrificial Food" and who developed the concept for its performance, writes, "There is a direct correlation between the acts of lynching and crucifying, for lynching–the unlawful killing (most commonly hanging) of a person by mob action–is a form of a crucifixion (execution by way of cruel, severely painful, and agonizing torture)."[52] Baker found it important to create poetry and dance that commemorate Emmett Till and his mother, because, "Today, Emmett's story is still alive, but not as much in the fore as it and other courageous ones should be. And the impact of Emmett's lynching on youth seems almost non-existent. Their voices only speak during February of each year, unless they find a heart to indwell that will sing for them; one that embraces the past, realizing that it makes way for the future. There aren't enough."[53] Therefore, for Black History Month, she created a performance that would involve youth and adults to share the Till story.

The Till story is an important one. The Baker/Swann choreo-poem (a mixture of music, dance, and poetry) moves from Mamie Till-Mobley's mourning to praise for God's resurrecting power in Jesus the Christ. In this choreo-poem a young, teenaged boy performed the part of Emmett Till. A mature woman danced the part of Emmett Till's mother, whose dance represents both lament and a courageous "No" to evil. Teenaged girls played the parts of poplar trees with blood on the leaves and blood at the root. At the end of the choreo-poem, the young man playing Emmett Till is not alone. Not only do mourners surround him, but the dance of the mourners turns to rejoicing as he is carried out of the sanctuary in cruciform by a taller adolescent male who represents the crucified but resurrected Christ who overcomes evil and suffering. "Sacrificial Food," with its compelling poetry and elegant sacred dance, is not just about lament. It is also about resistance, hope, and renewal of an entire community, the dead and the living. It does not glorify evil and suffering, but rather protests evil and suffering. It does not present suffering as redemptive, but as a problem to actively overcome.

Mamie Till-Mobley is famous for holding an open-casket funeral for her son, insistent that the world confront the evil of his perpetrators in a demand that a passive society wake up and refuse to comply with such hatred and violence. When black women artists and Christian thinkers approach the cross in this way, it is a refusal to bear any more crosses and a demand to resist the production of crucifixion until it is overcome. Baker writes, "Both crucifixion and lynching are heinous executions where the victims' suffering is a crucial part of the act. In both cases, victims were mutilated. Victims were taunted and jeered. They were sometimes stripped bare before the crowd; then tortured alive, thus community attendance was encouraged…[I]t served as a scare tactic to divert others from repeating the crime; and it afforded entertainment for those sick enough to view the acts as *sport*."[54]

In overcoming the sickness of the world with Christ, Mamie Till-Mobley did not let the world forget the sin of violating her son's life even as she participated in divine love. Moreover, the process of healing included seeking justice for the crimes against her only son and child. She included an entire nation in the task of remembering the sin of unnecessary violence in the divine work of overcoming hatred. The cross, like the lynching rope and Emmett Till's battered body, then, becomes not a glorified, pseudo-holy, sado-masochistic fetish, but, to employ a colloquial expression, a righteously indignant, "in-your-face reminder" of humankind's deep potential for destruction of one another, which is sin.[55] Likewise the commemoration of Good Friday becomes a ritual practice of what womanist theologian Evelyn Parker calls "holy indignation"[56] at the wrongness of it all and an indignant call for radical transformation.

The Baker/Swann production of "Sacrificial Food" functions as a Spirit-led counter-performance of resistance, protest, and testimony to God's power, which overcomes evil and suffering. It is a performance of dance, song, and poetry that demands the world rid itself of lynching ropes, crosses, and other tools of unnecessary violence. It calls communities of faith to participate in activities of overcoming evil. The players in the sacred dance and poetry created by Baker and Swann represent an intergenerational black communal experience of resistance. They resist the ongoing problem of the existence of crucifixion, of crimes of hatred against those who offer any appearance of stepping out of one's place in relation to emperors, Caesars–representations of worldly, oppressive powers be they racial supremacists or economic forces that rob the poor. They danced to Billie Holliday's song, "Strange Fruit," whose lyrics and music were written by a Jewish schoolteacher, Abel Meeropol, who published the song under the pseudonym Lewis Allan in 1940. The lyrics of Meeropol's song describe lynched African American bodies as "strange fruit" that swing from ropes on trees. The song also recounts the practice of burning lynched bodies and the smell that filled the air. Finally, it refers to lynched bodily remains as a macabre harvest for scavenging birds to pick at and eat as well as for the elements to decay. Meeropol employed pastoral imagery and the aesthetics of nature as a sharp contrast to the lynched, burned, and decaying African American bodies.[57] In Till's case, he was thrown into the river for the waters and the sun to make his body rot.

The poetry, music, and dance of black culture, which weave through the interstices of evil and suffering in creative movements of lament and hope against hope, are resources for the "nitty-gritty hermeneutics" of which Pinn speaks. The poetry of Countee Cullen, Langston Hughes, Vanessa Baker, and the sacred dance of Baker and Swann, along with the music sung by African American artists like Billie Holliday, sometimes authored by themselves and sometimes by those who intimately know similar suffering, like Meeropol, tell the truth of the human dance with existential evil. In the very creative power that fuels such crafting of experience into rituals of story-telling through movement, sound, color, and words, the artists reveal longing for more abundant life with questions and sometimes answers about the possibilities for such life to be realized. If nothing else, hope for life abundant is evident in the will to sing, to dance, to write, to compose, and to choreograph. Such art, whether in forums of secular or sacred ritual, speaks to the possibility of healing and renewal, however thin or thick faith in such resurrecting power may be.

Redemptive Overcoming

If Christ has overcome the world in the event of resurrection, then how can writers speak of "recrucifying Christ," "a world of crucifixion," and "redemptive overcoming"? Are we really crucifying Christ again? No. God in Christ, however, does have the memory of crucifixion and suffering. Therefore, God in Christ does empathize with our suffering and pain whenever and wherever the world persists in acts of persecution and crucifixion. Christ as cosufferer accompanies us through our pain and suffering to help us overcome it and to help us live into resurrected life in the power of the Holy Spirit. The great gift of the resurrected Christ is the availability of the resurrecting power of the Holy Spirit to all who believe in and confess Christ. So, we are not alone when we suffer, because the entire Trinity is with us, leading us into redemptive overcoming of evil. Christ has already overcome evil and is in the process of creating a new heaven and a new earth. The problem is, while Christ has "overcome the world," all the world does not yet worship God in Christ. Much of the world still resists the reality of the power of life over death and the divine power of goodness over evil. The full reign of God has not been fully realized yet, even though the reign of God is near at hand, and very present in the actuality of God.

According to Paul in 1 Corinthians 15:12–18, Christian faith is vain faith if Christ is not resurrected. As Paul puts it,

> Now if Christ is proclaimed as raised from the dead, how can some of you say there is no resurrection of the dead? If there is no resurrection of the dead, then Christ has not been raised; and if Christ has not been raised, then our proclamation has been in vain and your faith has been in vain. We are even found to be misrepresenting God, because we testified of God that he raised Christ–whom he did not raise if it is true that the dead are not raised. (1 Cor. 15:12–15)

In other words, some Christians at Corinth could not make sense of a bodily resurrection. Therefore, while in liturgy they proclaimed Christ crucified and resurrected, some also questioned whether or not God raised Christ from the dead. Later, as we shall see below, Paul speaks of spiritual bodies as the bodies of the resurrected.[58] For the moment, it is necessary to focus on the issue of how we can say that Christ has overcome evil given that the world is still filled with evil.

In verses 24–27a of the same chapter in Corinthians, Paul writes that "Then comes the end, when he hands over the kingdom to God the Father, after he has destroyed every ruler and every authority and power. For he must reign until he has put all his enemies under his feet. The last enemy to be destroyed is death. For 'God has put all things in subjection under his feet.'" In other words, Paul believed that God resurrected Christ. Moreover, Paul believes that the work God began in Christ does not end with the resurrection. God has put all things under Christ's feet, yet the world continues to reject God in Christ and continues to reject worship of God in Christ. Paul suggests resurrection is part of a process of overcoming evil, in which the world resists accepting that the evil in it has already been overcome. Because many get distracted by Pauline language of "subjection," "rule," and "kingdom," perhaps Johannine language of what it means to be born of the Spirit might be helpful for engaging in Christian midrash here. (See Jn. 3:1–16.) One might say that the world is in a process of rebirth and that Christ's reign is a reign of labor pangs, in which the world resists the truth that evil is overcome and that the world is already in the process of being born again in the Spirit. When all the world accepts Christ's victory over evil and participates fully in the reality of the divine realm, which is yet and not yet, present and yet to come, then all the world will worship God in Christ. Christ has overcome death, hatred, and evil. Yet, the world continues in the delusion that Christ has not overcome these things and that the power of evil is real. The notion that evil has real power, as we concluded above, is a lie and the absence of truth. All the world, however, has not recognized that the so-called "power" of evil–with its greed, hatred, and violence–is a lie. As some preachers in the African American Christian tradition have taught, "We must remember who we are and whose we are." We are created by God, and we belong to God.

Everyone and everything in the world was created by God and belongs to God. Until all the world accepts that, Christ continues to reveal the truth that God has "put all things under his feet." In other words, Christ has the power of judgment until all repent of evil and worship God, our ultimate authority, who is love, goodness, and righteousness. Paul refers to an end to the world's acceptance of the illusory power of evil when the world realizes the truth not only of Christ's reign, but of God's reign when the fullness of God's glory is revealed. One might describe Christ's reign as a reign of spiritual labor, in which the world is being reborn in the power of the Holy Spirit. One might describe the full reign of God in the Trinity as the fulfillment of rebirth and God's creation of a new heaven and a new earth. In Christ, we courageously encourage the world to accept divine authority and to realize the realm of God in worship, praise, and reflection of Christ's righteousness over and against evil. Whether we contemporary people of faith and people who have just begun seeking God struggle with the ancient language of "kingdom," "reign," and "subjection" or not, Paul did the best he could in the language that people of his time could understand to make the following point: God is our final, ultimate authority. God reveals this truth to the world in Jesus the Christ. Christ died, was resurrected, reigns with God, and God has given Christ authority over the world. Much of the world still rejects divine authority. In the end, the world will recognize God's authority, given to Christ. When that happens, the full reign of God will be realized; and the full body of Christ on earth as in heaven, in communion with God, will witness to the glory of God's reign with all of creation, proclaiming God's ultimate authority forever.

CHAPTER 7

More than Suffering

The Healing and Resurrecting Spirit of God

The Spirit, for Alice Walker and other womanists, is omnipresent in creation. The Spirit, in this integrative and relational theology, is the power that brings life out of death. This is possible because Spirit, the power of life, is omnipresent, intimately related to the world and the many bodies in it, in and beyond time. If God is omnipresent in the universe, then there is, as the psalmist writes, no place where we can hide from God or fail to find God. Howard Thurman quoted Psalm 139 as a meditation, recollecting to the heart and mind of the wounded searcher for justice the psalmist's experience that:

> Whither shall I go from thy Spirit?
> Or whither shall I flee from thy presence?
> If I ascend up into heaven, thou art there:
> If I make my bed in hell, behold, thou art there.
> If I take the wings of the morning,
> And dwell in the uttermost parts of the sea;
> Even there shall thy hand lead me,
> And thy right hand shall hold me.
> If I say, Surely the darkness shall cover me;
> Even the night shall be light about me.
> Yea, the darkness hideth not from thee;
> But the night shineth as the day:

The darkness and the light are both alike to thee.
(Ps. 139:7–12, KJV)[1]

Is there a place where God is not present? All who have felt that God is absent in a world afflicted with evil have asked this question, including Jesus on the cross. On the cross, Jesus experienced feelings of forsakenness. In such experience, one feels that divine goodness, justice, and righteousness are absent in the presence of unrestrained evil. The writer of Psalm 22, quoted by Jesus on the cross, cries out, "My God, my God, why have you forsaken me? / Why are you so far from saving me, from the words of my groaning? / O my God, I cry out by day, but you do not answer; / and by night, but find no rest (Ps. 22:1–2). The writer beseeches, "O LORD, do not be far away! / O my help, come quickly to my aid!" (Ps. 22:19). The writer of Psalm 22 gradually comes to the conclusion that those who seek, praise, and confess God as the ultimate power of life and all nations shall find life in God. The writer of Psalm 139, like the writer of Psalm 22, has contemplated whether or not the understanding of God's distance or absence that emerges in human suspicion of divine abandonment is true. Is God truly absent?

According to the psalmist and Thurman, even in the seeming absence of goodness and divinity, God is there. Even in the depths of hell (*Sheol* in more current translations, which in Hebrew understanding is simply the neutral concept of the place of the dead), God is there. From sea to land–in height, breadth, and depth of creaturely and spiritual existence and experience–God is there. The longed for, consummate integration of heaven and earth is present and yet to come in the saving love that permeates the universe. There is hope for all creation. If the power of life is omnipresent and if it can inspire love of the hater regardless of the temptation to hate the hater, then it is all-inclusive love. It is all-inclusive love because it is more powerful than the temptation to hate, loving even the hater, persuasively luring, to use Whitehead's term, or calling, to use the church language of the folk, all into right relationship.

Such love neither fears nor gives in to oppression. To the contrary, such love overcomes fear and resists oppression. John Cobb and David Griffin are not the first to observe that liberation movements require an understanding of God as responsive to the world, as loving and continuously creating.[2] For several centuries, black mothers have taught this wisdom to sons and daughters encountering the violence of hatred for the first time. Divine, loving, creative activity is the power of divine salvation and deliverance from every form of bondage. This unsurpassable, cosmic love unites God and the world in an ongoing, consummating process to fully realize the reign of God. This love is embodied in Jesus, who, according to New Testament literature, is Christ–the anointed one of God who is the very power of just love.

The Spirit of God is present in the First Testament and the New Testament as the creative, prophetic, and renewing power of God. It is by the Spirit of God that the prophets and the Messiah speak (Isa. 61; Lk. 4:16–21). It is in the Spirit that David sings and dances (2 Sam. 6:14; 22:1–51). It is in the Spirit that the apostles and the early followers of Christ are able to overcome evil with Jesus as they await Christ's final appearing and the full reality of the reign of God. It is by the Spirit that the apostles are empowered to develop Christ's church in response to Peter's leadership. Theology is incomplete without seeking understanding of the event of Pentecost, after Christ is risen, and Christ's promise that his followers will receive the Holy Spirit after his ascent. At Pentecost, the Holy Spirit becomes fully present in the lives of the apostles.[3] By the Spirit Paul is overcome by Christ on the road to Damascus, and by the Spirit Christ transforms Paul from a persecutor of Christian Jews to a leader of Christian Jews and Gentiles. Finally, by the Spirit Paul is able to teach the early church that the greatest gifts of all are faith, hope, and love. Our first introduction to the "*Holy* Spirit," however, is found in the story of Mary in Matthew 1:18–25.

The Holy Spirit and Mary, Womanish Bearer of God

In Matthew, an angel appears to a virgin, Mary, and tells her that she will bear a son who is conceived by the Holy Spirit. The first story we read in the canonical New Testament, then, is about the Holy Spirit's life-giving power. The Holy Spirit makes Christ's conception and incarnation possible. How this is possible, the narrative does not say. We only know that Christ is a gift from God to Mary and to the world. We only know that the Holy Spirit makes this possible. Later, in John 3:1–16, we learn that we all must be born of the Spirit to enter the reign of God and that Mary's son, Jesus the Christ, makes this possible.

Protestants have given little attention to Mary as *theotokos* or mother of God. Yet, the question of Mary's relationship to Christ was very important for the early church writers. Diana Hayes notes that Catholic womanists offer important insights in this area. "Too often seen as a docile, submissive woman, Black Catholic womanists, instead," writes Hayes, "see a young woman sure of her God and of her role in God's salvific plan."[4] Hayes identifies Mary, mother of Jesus, as a "young, unwed, pregnant woman" who "proclaims her allegiance with God and with her brothers and sisters with whom she lived, as a Jew under Roman oppression."[5] She is not a symbol of passivity, but "courageous and outrageous authority" who gives a "prophetic 'yes' to God, standing alone yet empowered."[6]

Hayes describes Mary as a woman attuned to the existential realities of a young Jewish woman living in an empire that had its own quest for power and maintenance of that power at heart, rather than her or any other community's understanding of its own best interests. She describes the experience of Mary's community as "a poor and marginalized existence similar to the existence of Blacks in the Church for so long a time," explaining that Black Catholic women "relate to her [Mary] by sharing in her experiences as women who are also oppressed but who continue to bear the burden of faith and to pass on that faith to generations to come."[7] For Hayes and other Roman Catholic women, Mary is a "role model, not for passivity, but for strong, righteous "womanish" women who spend their lives giving birth to the future."[8] Hayes's work indicates that this future is not a future of death, but of cultural and community preservation, perseverance, and hope in liberation. God in Christ, for Hayes, is a symbol of liberation. Although Hayes does not say it in exactly these words, one gathers that Mary is a symbol of what it means to intimately bear the power of liberation, which is the hope for the future. Hayes, like other Roman Catholic women, sees power, authority, and liberating hope in Mary that Protestant women often miss.

It is reasonable for Protestant womanists to take interest in the understanding that some Korean women and Catholic womanists have of Mary. Delores Williams is concerned that the virginity attributed to Mary as mother is something that ordinary mothers cannot identify with.[9] There is something even more important, however, to learn from Mary. So many Korean women and black American women have lost children, sons, and husbands to violence like Mary. From Mary's story, Korean women learn to overcome the *han* experienced by such loss. African American women learn to overcome the *blues* experienced in such loss. Protestant womanist theology could deepen in wisdom by taking Mary more seriously.

The Holy Spirit and Dancing with God

In her work as a producer and performance artist, Vanessa Baker feels led by the Holy Spirit to create Christian art. In the artistic representation of Mamie Till-Mobley in the Baker-Swann choreo-poem, as well as in images captured by photo-journalists, one finds parallels between Mamie Till-Mobley before the coffin of Emmett Till and the Pieta, the image of Mary holding her son at the cross. Mamie Till-Mobley had an open-casket funeral. She had her son photographed in his casket to be viewed in magazines. She was like Mary, mother of Jesus, asking the world to look and to repent. She was like many other black women who had seen the horror, and couldn't bear another look. But Mother Till-Mobley found courage to say, "I'M NOT TAKING THIS! LOOK!" "Look, world, don't you see?" "Look at my son's face! Look at his body!" "World, get delivered of your demons and Look!" The viewing and funeral lasted four days. Thousands came to look. The world began to change until it forgot. Then the families of Medgar Evers, Martin Luther King Jr., and James Byrd Jr. followed, issuing calls to stop the hate that produces unnecessary violence. The struggle continues.

So, over the years the story of Emmett Till and his mother has been retold in scholarly publications, through Internet publications, community events, and educational programs to keep the story within the collective consciousness. The story is significant not only because of its tragic dimensions and moral challenge to cease hate crimes, but because of the faith of Till's mother.[10] She found courage to shout, "NOOO!" to hatred of another's life and unnecessary violence through her faith in a resurrecting God. She refused to merely bear the cross Money, Mississippi, gave her when they lynched her son, and instead sought justice to overcome it, bravely appearing at the trial of her son's accused killers at the risk of her own life. If we can ever speak positively about what it means to "bear one's cross," then she demonstrated it in her Christlike willingness to risk her own life by making every effort to bring her son's lynchers to justice. If there is any positive meaning in what it means to "take up your cross and follow me," it is what we learn through Mamie Till-Mobley.

To overcome the cross with Christ, then, includes being willing to risk your own life in the process in the call for justice. Yet, this is not a path that glorifies suffering and rationalizes that suffering is redemptive. Suffering is deepest and most severe when it is the spiritual suffering called despair that leads to cynicism. That is the worst kind of suffering. It is part of the problem that perpetuates hatred, injustice, and unnecessary violence. To overcome the cross by taking up one's cross is to claim divine and personal power over all crosses. It is the power that turns the cross into two pieces of wood instead of a tool of destruction. It is to choose the path of the old spiritual, "I shall not be moved."[11] It is the path of resistance against evil. It is the path of confronting evil and staring it in the face. This path is not death-loving. This path is life-loving. Where there is courage and truth, there is life. Where there is a call for justice, there is life. Where there is a call for love instead of hatred, there is life. This life resurrects itself again and again. Mamie Till-Mobley lived in the knowledge of resurrection faith.

Resurrection faith is the source of power and courage to say "No" to evil and destruction. Mamie Till-Mobley, who became a church mother in the Church of God in Christ, chose to carry the message of overcoming racial violence and hatred, in effect a message that crosses, hanging people from trees, are to be overcome. She was clear that such acts should not be repeated. In memory of her and of all women from the time of Christ who have mourned loved ones hung from trees, the teenage girls of St. Luke's performed a sacred dance. It gave everyone a new vision of human community, of God, and of trees. Protestant Christians need to remember Mary, because we continue to hear her story through the stories of Merlie Evers, civil rights widow of activist Medgar Evers. We continue to hear her story in the biography of Mamie Till-Mobley and the story of Stella Byrd. We continue to hear her story in the story of every woman who has survived the unjust killing of a loved one.

If Mary were not the mother of God, then Christ's humanity would come into question. Was Christ fully human and fully divine or not? If

Christ was not human and Christ does not continue to live in the hearts of believers like Mamie Till-Mobley today, then Christianity is a dead religion. However, it is not inevitable that we come to that conclusion. Mary *was* the mother of Jesus the Christ. As Hayes reminds us, she bore the humanity of God into the world in the flesh. In a process-relational understanding, energy produces matter, and matter produces energy. Likewise, spirit produces matter, and matter produces spirit. So of course Jesus is matter and spirit, divine and human, creature and creating, beloved and loving. Moreover, Mary is an integration of matter and spirit, who experiences the full possibilities of bearing and raising a child who is the full embodiment of God, who is the all-inclusive power of life, abounding in love, and continuously creating and renewing. She is therefore an appropriate bearer of God who is Spirit and who is embodied in Jesus the Christ, because God is omnipresent in creation. Mary at the cross witnesses the life and death of her own flesh and blood, because Jesus is flesh of her flesh and heart of her heart.

The blood shed on the cross takes on new meaning. It is Jesus' blood, it is Mary's blood, and it is the blood of Immanuel, God with us. The heart pumps blood to give life. Life flows from God's heart, to Mary's heart, in Jesus' heart, to all humanity. This God on the cross suffers with us in persecution and oppression. This resurrected God rejoices with us in victory over evil and suffering. Jesus' blood is a symbol of abundant life and unsurpassable love. I spent some time as a young girl in a Roman Catholic school. I was taught by nuns for three years. They always linked Jesus' love with Mary's love as mother of God in Christ. From them I learned about the sacred heart of Jesus. Paintings of the sacred heart of Jesus as well as paintings of Mary have influenced my Christian consciousness, although I am Protestant. To preach Christ and him crucified, it is necessary to focus on the heart of Jesus the Christ and on the heart of Mary. This is a new idea for Protestant womanists, but I believe it is essential. Otherwise, we literally lose the heart of the Christian message, and the relational understanding of womanist theology becomes compromised.

Vanessa Baker's production of sacred dance, music, and poetry moves beyond the moaning of past generations to a prophetic lament and shout. This lament and shout functions as a call to resistance against evil and to action for a world in which crucifixion is no more, a world in which we are no longer forced to bear crosses. Emmett Till is mirrored in Baker's sacred dance by the Christ figure that carries him lifted up in the cruciform of Christ like arms. Even so Mamie Till–Mobley evokes memories of the story of Mary, mother of Jesus, who kneels at the cross and, who, in Christian artwork, holds his body as could only one who loved him from conception. Similarly, women, including Christian women, have fought to change rape laws and domestic violence laws, seeking justice in rigorous love. These are people who do not simply bear the crosses placed in their paths. They pick up these crosses to overcome them and to overcome the production of crosses. They actively seek to bring an end to unnecessary suffering and violence. They refuse to acquiesce to evil.

Some Mother's Child, Some Sister's Friend

Jesus, like Emmett Till, James Byrd Jr., and Laura Nelson, was some mother's child and some sister's[12] friend. Womanist scholars of religion like Cheryl Townsend Gilkes and feminist theologians like Elisabeth Schüssler Fiorenza maintain, "If it wasn't for the women," to use Gilke's words, much of the work that God in Jesus the Christ has called the church to do would not get done.[13] Jesus' mother, Mary, raised a son who kept the prophetic principles of the God she worshiped, knowing the world was unfair to worshipers of the God of Israel. The God that Israel worshiped and worships created all that has been, is, and will be. Followers of Jesus believe that, in Christ, this God is the God of all nations, available to all nations. Mary knew her son believed this. Since she had a role in raising Jesus, a son she believed was God's own Son, Jesus was truly a son of her own heart. Mary went to publicly mourn Jesus' public death by crucifixion. Mamie Till-Mobley imitated Mary's public mourning some 2000 years later when her son, Emmett Till, was lynched. It is in a woman, Mary of Magdala, that we first hear the realized, resurrected presence of Jesus the Christ preached in an unfair world.[14] Mamie Till-Mobley taught and practiced the power of Jesus the Christ's present, resurrected divine love and justice in a climate of hate. Women are important in Jesus' story. Women are important in teaching and practicing Jesus' love and justice in each generation in a world that is infected with hate and unnecessary violence.

The activist Christian faith of Mamie Till-Mobley recalls the faith of Mary, Jesus' mother, the faith of the women at the cross, the faith of the women at the tomb, and the faith of Mary Magdalene to proclaim the gospel. When we consider the relationship of the heart of God who is Spirit in relation to Mary's own heart as she bears and raises Jesus the Christ, then the Christian understanding of God's relationship to the world becomes more clear. It is through the heart of Jesus the Christ, son of Mary and son of God, that we find dynamic, living, abundant hope and love to overcome violence and suffering in the world. We are embraced in the power of this unsurpassable love that permeates the universe, even when we are not conscious of it. In this unsurpassable love, we have hope for healing and abundant life. The stories of overcoming crucifixion and living into resurrection justice shared here bear witness to the power of love, life, and creativity embodied in Jesus the Christ. We, too, if we are followers of Jesus, are part of God's body, the body of Christ in the world today, with edifying stories to live into and to share. God wants the *whole earth* to find a new kind of courage–the courage to stop acting ugly and to start acting beautiful, to stop playing with evil and to start working with God, to start being a healed and whole creation. The healing, resurrecting Spirit of God, which is the power of the Holy Spirit, also known as the Spirit of Truth, was with Jesus in his ministry. It is the power of his healing ministry. Note that in New Testament literature, Jesus is said to raise Lazarus from his grave before Jesus' crucifixion and resurrection. The prophets Elijah and Elisha are also said to have this gift of healing and renewal of life. What makes Jesus' ministry significant is that this gift is available to all of those who love God in Jesus' name, once Jesus Christ is reunited with the first agent of the Trinity in the everlasting realm of God, which is omnipresent on earth and is a spiritual realm.

The Healing, Resurrecting Power of the Spirit on Earth

Resurrection is not just an event of the past, but of the present and the future. Evil, suffering, and death have not, cannot, and will not overcome the world. Sin is a handicap that God in Christ, through the power of the Holy Spirit, overcame and continues to overcome. God, through Christ, in the power of the Holy Spirit, has overcome the evil that is in the world. We know this because love and creativity still exist in the world. We know this because Word/Wisdom is omnipresent in the world. We know this because comfort, healing, and encouragement to heal others are omnipresent in the world. The goodness of God in the land of the living is omnipresent and permeates creation, ever renewing and recreating. There is resurrection promise and resurrection hope in the world. Resurrection begins with the Spirit and ends with the creation of a new thing that is integratively physical and spiritual, a new, spiritual body, visibly incarnating past and present loving ways of being and becoming, visibly embodying future possibilities of becoming, creating faith, hope, and love in others.

The earliest Christian theologian, Paul, responded to questions about resurrection. New and prospective Christians in Paul's day were as perplexed as many today about resurrection. It made no more scientific sense in Paul's time than for many today. Paul, as pastor and theologian, said, "But someone will ask, "How are the dead raised? With what kind of body do they come?" Like many pastors today, he must have heard this question more times than he could count. Like some pastors and evangelical theologians today, he responded impatiently: "Fool! What you sow does not come to life unless it dies. And as for what you sow, you do not sow the body that is to be, but a bare seed, perhaps of wheat or of some other grain." Paul goes on to explain that God gives it a body as God has determined, "and to each kind of seed," God gives "its own body." Moreover, "Not all flesh is alike, but there is one flesh for human beings, another for animals, another for birds, and another for fish. There are both heavenly bodies and earthly bodies, but the glory of the heavenly is one thing, and that of the earthly is another" (1 Cor. 15:35–40). In other words, the resurrected body is a spiritual body. It has its own splendor or beauty. It integrates body and spirit in a new way, a way that many find difficult to imagine. "So it is with the resurrection of the dead," Paul continues (1 Cor. 15:42a). This spiritual body is everlasting and will not perish. The resurrected body is a spiritual, imperishable body that is not subject to decay.[15]

Similarly, Monica Coleman observes that Whitehead in *Process and Reality* defines evil as the fact of perpetual perishing, the element of loss in every process of becoming. We are saved from "the fact of perpetual perishing, the element of loss in every process of becoming, by immortality." Specifically, "salvation is effected by assuring everlasting life for the actual entities that are lost and by God's lure of the temporal world towards specific goals."[16] In other words, God's grace is saving in that there is promise of everlasting life in God, which overcomes temporal perishing and death. Suchocki puts it another way in her discussion of resurrection and redemption, writing, "Applied to God, God receives the world so fully that God resurrects the world, and then integrates the resurrected world into the depths of the divine being according to the divine character." In other words, God judges the resurrected world according to God's own loving, just, creative nature. God does this within God's consequent nature, which, like the economic nature of the Trinity, is the divine response to the world. The world is continuously resurrected. Moreover, God continues to feel the positive and negative effects of the actions of the entities that make up the world, discerning which are consistent with divine love, creativity, and justice. Specifically from Suchocki's Whiteheadian perspective, "Applied to God, God evaluates, contrasts, judges the world according to God's own character till the world is conformed to God."[17] For Suchocki, this means that God, who feels the feelings of the world, feels the agony and joy of the world. Resurrected subjects, knowing themselves as God knows them, feel the effects of their actions, agony or joy, on others.

Suchocki paraphrases 1 Corinthians 13:12, observing that in resurrected, everlasting life with God, "We shall know as we are known." We shall experience ourselves as God experiences us. This indeed, Suchocki concludes, would be judgment. Her theology suggests that God is both heaven and hell."[18] At this point, problems emerge in Suchocki's understanding. The strength of her understanding is that everlasting life is relational and that we know ourselves as God knows us. The weakness of her understanding is the notion that God is both heaven and hell. Psalm 139 simply says that God is even in the depths of hell, with emphasis on the fact there is no place where one can flee or hide from God. Psalm 8:1 describes God's name as "majestic…in all the earth," and says that God has set God's glory "above the heavens." The writer of Psalm 108:4–5 describes God's love as "higher than the heavens," and says "let your glory be over all the earth." First Kings 8:27 describes Solomon's prayer dedicating the temple he built for God as asking, "But will God indeed dwell on the earth? Even heaven and the highest heaven cannot contain you, much less the house that I have built!" Moreover, Isaiah 66:1 describes Isaiah prophetically speaking as God's mouthpiece,

> Thus says the Lord:
> "Heaven is my throne
> and the earth is my footstool;
> what is the house that you would build for me,
> and what is my resting place?"

The point is that, scripturally, God who dwells in heaven and earth also transcends heaven and earth. According to Genesis, God created heaven and earth. This theme is carried forward throughout Hebrew Scriptures, particularly in the Psalms and in the book of Job. Neither heaven nor earth can contain God. Therefore, God is not heaven as Suchocki states. Nor is God hell. God, the Creator of all things–who continuously, everlastingly, dynamically creates–is not heaven, earth, hell, nature, or the universe. The latter are God's creations, not God.

God is in all places, but God is not a place. Suchocki fails to attend to the fact that "heaven" and "hell" are metaphors that describe the joy or agony of God's experiencing the feelings of others in resurrected experience. These are not metaphors for describing God. They are metaphors for describing the experiencing of joy and agony, the effects of every entity of the world on other entities. They are metaphors for divine judgment and selectivity regarding these experiences of freely and consciously participating in divine creativity or rejecting it to participate in the evil of harming others. Suchocki's understanding of the redemption of evil is also unclear and problematic. She claims, "Evil, even terrible evil, is felt by God in order to be redeemed by God–partially in history, but fully within the divine nature."[19] It depends on what she means. If she means that God uses what some intended for evil and transforms it into good, this works biblically as well as metaphysically. If she means that unrepentant sinners who have rejected participating in divine love, creativity, and justice are redeemed, then this contradicts her earlier understanding of judgment and New Testament understandings of heaven and hell. Suchocki argues that her understanding of judgment is true because in history we have a choice to go with or against God, whereas in God we do not have that power. "We must be conformed to the divine image, transformed into the insistent depths of a God whose 'nature and whose name is love.'"[20]

What happened to the persuasive God? Apparently, being in the direct presence of divine love is irresistible. Evil is transformed into good. "Redeemed" may not be the right word here. Coleman's understanding of "creative transformation" makes greater sense. God creatively transforms even evil into good to effect God's creation with blessing, in spite of tendencies among entities in the world to violate others. Still, Suchocki's understanding leaves doubts in the minds of many Christians. Divine everlastingness sounds strongly deterministic rather than persuasive. Second Peter 3:13 indicates that God creates "new heavens and a new earth." Biblically, however, there is no reference to redeeming those who experience everlasting life as hell or agony. Theoretically, some Christians have argued, it could be possible. Metaphysically, from a Whiteheadian perspective, it makes some sense, but not enough if suddenly God is strongly deterministic rather than persuasive. Biblically, there is insufficient warrant for this claim. Metaphysics takes us only so far. It is enough to leave this a mystery known only to God and in God's everlasting realm.

Finally, Suchocki does not have a strong doctrine of the Holy Spirit. Understanding of resurrection healing and life is incomplete without attention to the power of the Holy Spirit. The Holy Spirit is the power of healing and resurrection in life everlasting and in temporal existence. The Holy Spirit is not like a genie in a bottle, which is what it has become for some: "Call on the Holy Spirit and all your ills, weaknesses, and money problems will disappear. A true believer, a true Christian, is wealthy, healthy, and fully lives out the American dream of prosperity." This notion of "healing" always means that there is no visible illness or disability remaining. Healing must evidence itself in the utter disappearance of an affliction. Those who suffer are weak in faith or have some hidden sin that keeps them in poverty, illness, or disability. If God does not heal the people in the visible, dramatic way expected, then those people have not prayed hard enough. Their faith is weak. They need to repent more and pray harder. They have not "allowed" the Holy Spirit to work through them. Among those who think in this way the claim to "know" what God *can* do becomes a tyrannical dictation of what God *must* do. This view, like the perspective that God only comforts during the "age of the church," looks for control. Unconsciously, however, this perspective reveals a desire to control God and knowledge of the nature of God. "God must heal *only and always* in the way *I* understand," the believer seems to be saying. Moreover, little attention is given to Paul's experience of asking for healing three times only to accept his difficulty as a gift with the understanding that God's grace is sufficient (2 Cor. 12:1–10). Whether intentional or not, it seems that from this perspective God's grace *is not* sufficient. There is little or no awareness that an individual can rejoice in being alive and performing God's work in spite of disability or lack of wealth.

An opposite perspective goes to a different extreme that ends with the same result of revealing an unconscious desire to control God and knowledge of God. In this view, miracles are mythic accounts of what the ancients could not scientifically explain or, in the case of dispensationalists, they have ceased because God no longer needs to perform them. In this perspective, Christians claim to know what God *cannot* do or, at best, claim to know exactly in which historical period God chooses to do it. This closes off the meaning of the testimonies of persons for whom prayer works according to personal, family, communal, medical, and scientific accounts. Although doctors and scientists generally note they hope for a scientific explanation one day, the studies that demonstrate the effectiveness of prayer in such healing suggests that those who believe in the healing and miracle working power of the Holy Spirit have experienced *something*. They frequently call this something *God*. William James, in his study of varieties of religious experience, called it "the More," not limiting it to Christian experience but always focusing on the transformative effects of a belief in the life of a person of faith. For Christians who believe in the power of prayer to heal, "the More" would be understood as God, Christ, and/or the Holy Spirit, with particular attention to "the movement of the Holy Spirit."

Some translations of Paul's story say that God gave him a thorn or handicap in his side. Other translations are vague. I offer a contemporary illustration that speaks to the assumptions and suspicions of both types of Christian perspectives named above: This author knows a man we will call Anthony who recounts that, as a teenager in the 1970s, he was moved by the Holy Spirit to consciously receive God in Christ. He has a handicap. There is much about Paul's testimony that makes sense to him.

Anthony does not believe God gave him his handicap, but rather that God uses his handicap to help Anthony see God and the world differently, in some ways more clearly than he might if he took able-bodiedness for granted. He is no Paul, but is among those whose witness includes experiential awareness of the transforming power of the Holy Spirit. Shortly after his conversion, at the age of sixteen, Anthony was diagnosed with *systemic lupus erythemetosis*. Lupus is an illness in which the white blood cells of the body go awry and, instead of attacking organisms invasive to the body, attack the immune system. Healthy organs are adversely affected; weakness and arthritic symptoms emerge. Heavy doses of prednisone are administered in severe cases. One of the side effects of prednisone is that it thins the bones of the lupus patient. As a teenager, Anthony, as we shall call him, was told that he would not live beyond the age of twenty-five and that given the deterioration of his hip bones he could either undergo hip replacement surgery or live in a wheelchair until his death. During the 1970s hip replacement surgery was novel and still relatively experimental. It was not the routine type of surgery that it has since become for the elderly. Younger patients, even today, are a puzzlement for orthopedic surgeons, because the prosthetic devices last, on average, up to ten years. For the younger patient, this means a life of multiple hip replacements, which over time weaken the muscles and can lead to severe osteoporosis. This is what happened to Anthony.

To make a long story shorter, when Anthony was diagnosed with lupus and failed to miraculously recover from it, his charismatic teenage peers insisted something was wrong with him, some hidden sin and a failed faith were preventing his healing. This sent Anthony along a lifetime journey of theological questioning in which he eventually entered seminary, earning M.Div. and Ph.D degrees. Contrary to medical predictions, he lived past the age of twenty-five, married, has three children, and celebrated his fiftieth birthday in 2005, outliving several ablebodied peers. The miracle of healing that he received was not immediately apparent, but it is evident in the sustaining grace of the Holy Spirit in his life. Through years of illness, hospitalizations, multiple hip surgeries, and periodic remissions of the lupus, he came to learn the meaning of the saying, "God's grace is sufficient." Experiencing the healing power of God's grace in the Holy Spirit, he learned to help others who despair of their physical or mental disabilities. He also learned to teach and sometimes simply endure those for whom such grace is not enough.

For those who fail to see that God's grace is enough, the weak and the lame must *always* "rise up and walk!" They become *ableists,* viewing the sick and the shut-in as weaker in faith than themselves. They engage in *ableist supremacy,* the belief that persons with physical challenges are less Christian than themselves. Ableist supremacy is nothing less than another form of a very old sin: *self-righteousness.* In the midst of such self-righteousness, insecure Christians fail to appreciate the gift of grace, which is a strengthening gift of God in the midst of weakness.

Recently, after decades of multiple hip replacement surgeries, Anthony's hip bones have been worn down to nothing, the prostheses taking up most of the space where bones once existed. He has been told that the little remaining bone is so thin, that it is best that he employ a wheelchair most of the time to avoid future surgeries that at this point would be precarious. Being in a wheelchair has rendered him in the position that he experienced as a teenager among numerous fellow Christians. Recently, at an airport security checkpoint, a well-meaning Christian agent who wanded him told him that he was praying for God to heal him, because "this," he said, pointing to the wheelchair, "is a fact, but it is not the truth. It is a lie straight from the pit of hell."

The security agent revealed more than his faith in the healing ability of God through the power of the Holy Spirit. He also revealed his insecurities with physical differences. Because he was so certain of what he *knew,* the agent made numerous uninformed assumptions. Therefore, he failed to see the healing and miracle that were already present: that an individual condemned to die at age twenty-five was a fiftyish accomplished scholar, author of five books, composer and minister of music, active father of three children, committed partner to his spouse, a lover of God, and beloved by God in the midst of *all* his circumstances. These many manifestations of God's gift are not immediately apparent. Christians cannot assume to *know* much about the work of the Holy Spirit in an individual's life by whether or not they are fully able-bodied, able-minded, or in perfect health. At best, Christians can engage in more thorough, holistic study of the nature of the Holy Spirit to entertain the fuller possibilities of the work of healing grace than are often popular.

There was no recognition on the part of the Christian airline agent of Paul's wisdom that "God's grace is sufficient." Nor was there awareness of the wheelchair-bound Christian's experience of faith or of the power of God in his life. Pastors with humor call this the "Super Christian" attitude. The agent's pronouncements had little to do with God, Christ, or the grace experienced in the power of the Holy Spirit. To the contrary, he exhibited a form of the very type of Christian pride that Paul discounts. Was the agent truly as well-meaning as he believed himself to be? Was he irritated that it takes longer to wand an individual in a wheelchair at the end of a long day? Or, as one moving closer to old age, was he unhappily reminded of his own mortality and the fact that weakness that comes toward the end of our days? These are the types of questions Christians who move in faith in the healing power of the Spirit of God must ask themselves in their relationships with people who have visible "handicaps."

There is evidence of the power of the Holy Spirit in one's life when one responds to persons with physical or mental challenges, not in condescension, but with respect and joy in the goodness of God in the land of the living. All too often there is a failure to see the gift that God has given to those with visible handicaps. An unwitting, faithless fear of the vulnerability of the human body emerges in its place. This leads to some of the unacknowledged obstacles that people with disabilities face everyday: pity, arrogance, and patronizing attitudes. In the power of the Holy Spirit, one responds instead with an attitude of thankfulness for abundant life. Anthony has prayed for more than healing. He has prayed for a miracle. But once the prayer is made, there is careful waiting and listening along with acceptance of his existential situation and awareness that God's grace is enough. Abundant life is promised and continues. Life has become richer, not less. He has learned to appreciate the gift that Paul writes about. This gift is simply the gift of life, love, and the graceful, gracious dynamic dance of the Spirit in the rhythmic movement of God through Christ who dwells with creation.

The Holy Spirit, by whose power the Jesus of the four gospels heals and performs miracles, is not a genie we can manipulate to make all wishes come true. There is a difference between answer to prayer and the granting of wishes. Prayer may be answered in unexpected ways. Children want to receive their wishes exactly, sometimes to the wisher's disappointment if the wish has been ill-conceived. The answer to a prayer may be, "No," or, "Wait," as well as, "Yes." Prayers are answered according to the greater wisdom and power of a transcendent God through the power of the Holy Spirit who searches the mind of God. It is in the power of the Holy Spirit that God meets the *needs* of believers, not their wishes.

Healing and resurrection power are the particular characteristics of the divine action or revelation of the Holy Spirit. Healing and resurrection power are also the work of the entire Trinity. Healing and resurrection power are revelations of divine love in the world. The Holy Spirit is the power of love, but all three actions or relations of the Trinity are loving. All three relational actions create, recreate, and renew. Scholars know less about the Holy Spirit than the other two persons of the Trinity, because New Testament writers say more about "God the Father" and "Jesus, the Son, the Word, and Christ" than about the "Holy Spirit." Bruce Marshall has written that Jesus witnesses to God the Father and to the Holy Spirit. The Holy Spirit witnesses to the first two persons of the Trinity, but the Holy Spirit does not witness to the Holy Spirit. This makes the Holy Spirit more mysterious than the other two persons of the Trinity.[21] There are clues, however, to the nature of the Holy Spirit in the four gospels and in the Pauline letters. Secondarily, there are clues to the nature of the Holy Spirit in the written and oral accounts of Christian experience throughout the ages. The latter, secondary resources are accountable to descriptions found in scripture and when they fail to give adequate attention to the primary resource of scriptural accounts they tend to distort the nature of the Holy Spirit as noted above. In Genesis 1, many Christians interpret "the Spirit" to be the "Holy Spirit" of New Testament literature. The Holy Spirit, in New Testament literature, is also called "the Spirit" in several texts. Beginning with Genesis, one might offer a contemporary poetic rendering as follows:

In the beginning, there was dance. The Spirit of God hovered over the water. The author of all creation danced with the Spirit and the Word, which sang let there be light, let there be...let there be...Divine, everlasting community said let us create *adam*–earth creature–male and female, in our image, reflecting our creative, communal dance with one another and it was so. An entire interrelational universe freely became through the power of persuasive, divine, creative, loving community, integrating spirit and matter, and it was good. Earth creatures, male and female, became greedy, wanting more than their share of power. Taking the freedom they were created in by persuasive, loving, divine community, they greedily grasped at more than their share of power. This created an imbalance, leaving divine community, which was already eternally creating, creating anew what had been whole and now was broken. The creation that took millennia to become whole spiritually strives to find wholeness again. Some desperately seek wholeness through false, destructive means–the idolatry of grasping at more than one's share of power in the universe. Some find authentic wholeness through the preventing grace of the Author and Parent of the universe, through the redeeming, restoring grace of Word and Wisdom, and the through healing power of the Holy Spirit. Resurrection hope is in the latter.

Divine preventing grace in the providence/nurture of God keeps evil from overcoming the freedom to consciously experience and participate in divine love. Without preventing grace, evil and hatred would overcome the creaturely freedom to participate in divine love. Preventing grace makes it possible for human beings to literally *feel* convicted by omnipresent, divine love. Divine, justifying grace in the Word/Wisdom of God receives the persuaded, convicted hearts of the world to free them from hatred and unnecessary violence. The Word/Wisdom of God frees, justifies, and redeems those who desire to participate in divine love so that they may love others. The sanctifying grace of God, in the power of the Holy Spirit, heals the wounds inflicted by evil actions and perfects the love of followers of the Word/Wisdom of God to make them whole. The entire community of God restores followers of Word/Wisdom to God, freeing them from broken relationship with God and the world. Then heaven and earth rejoice, because God's initial aim is realized on earth as in heaven. This happens day by day and is also a future event as creation moans, groans, and strives towards full redemption, the creation of a new heaven and a new earth in the fully realized reign of God.

The grace of God moves through the entire Trinity. It is present in God who is like a Parent, which reflects God's dynamic, providing, nurturing love. It is present in God's dynamic, creative relation of incarnate, passionate, and redeeming love. This is the power of God in Christ who is the Word and Wisdom of God. It is present in God's compassionate, comforting, and resurrecting love, which is the power of the Holy Spirit. It is the power of the Holy Spirit who unites the first two. This understanding is similar, in one respect, to Augustine's understanding of the Trinity. All three relational actions of the divine community create and love. The Holy Spirit is the power of divine creativity and love, empowering and encouraging divine community into creativity and love.

Referring to 1 John 4:16, Augustine said, "God is love." He understood the Trinity as the one who loves, the one who is loved, and love. In other words, one might describe God as Lover, Beloved, and Love. For Augustine, "the Father and Son and Holy Spirit are one God, creator and ruler of the entire creature." Yet the specific work of each person is not alien to the other in love. The Father is not the Son, nor the Holy Spirit the Father or the Son, he writes, "but...there is a trinity of mutually related persons and a unity of equal substance."[22] He associated the dynamic power of Love itself with the third person of the Trinity. This power of Love, found in the Holy Spirit, he wrote, unites Lover and Beloved. All three persons participate in divine love.

The source of love, for Augustine, always is God, because God in every aspect of God's nature inspires love. This was Augustine's description of the immanent Trinity and how the three persons of the Trinity relate to one another within God's one nature. There are moments such as these, when

Augustine moves toward a relational concept of God, that come close to understandings in process metaphysics. For Augustine, God is Trinity and functions as a type of relational community. Overall, however, most process metaphysicians find that Augustine viewed the hypostases, or "persons," as substances rather than nonstatic, dynamic relations.

There is something powerful, something more than mere flesh and blood. It is the very energy that creates flesh and blood, that makes love in the midst of hate crimes possible. In the experience of existential evil, the temptation to hate in kind, along with the temptations to give in to bitterness, passivity, or nihilism is ever-present. A power greater than flesh alone makes it possible to choose love instead. There is something greater and more persuasive than the impulse to seek revenge that is present in this world. God in all three relational actions or *hypostases* is persuasive. The distinctive action of the Holy Spirit in God's persuasive activity is multiple. Not only is it comforting, guiding, instructing, healing, discerning, and empowering; but it is also encouraging. According to Romans 12:8, encouragement, leadership, generosity, and mercy are all gifts of the Spirit.

Theologians in recent years, particularly Jürgen Moltmann,[23] have given much attention to empowerment through the Holy Spirit. The fullness of the Holy Spirit's grace in the body of Christ is understood only when the gifts are understood in relation to one another. In a world in which many have become apathetic, failing in faith and hope regarding creative transformation, the regenerating gift of the Holy Spirit, encouragement–the strengthening of the heart–helps clarify how the Holy Spirit empowers. The Holy Spirit lifts up the faint of heart, giving them courage to receive other gifts. This encouragement is contagious. It spreads through the body of Christ so that it is able to receive the other gifts to become a fuller realization of the church or *ecclesia,* so that all the gifts–wisdom, understanding, knowledge, mercy, leadership, prophecy, encouragement, discernment, healing, miracles, helps, teaching, apostleship, and, yes, the least of these gifts, which is speaking in tongues (*glossolalia*)–are present in the body of Christ. The Holy Spirit gives different gifts to members of the body of Christ. When one looks at the traditions and denominations within the church universal, there are some traditions and denominations that exercise some of these gifts more than others. Together, they form the holy catholic church in its original meaning, which is simply holy *universal* church.

According to the teachings of John Wesley, we can do nothing without the Holy Spirit. The specific work of the Holy Spirit is sanctifying grace, but the Holy Spirit as grace is present in the prevenient and justifying activities of the first and second persons of the Trinity. For Wesley the sanctifying presence and power of the Holy Spirit is evident in works of mercy. The entire Trinity gives gifts of prevenient, justifying, and sanctifying grace to the world. The Holy Spirit, however, is the specific hypostasis in which we find God's work of sanctifying grace–gifts. The entire Trinity loves because God loves the world enough to send God's only Son that we might have abundant life. Yet, it is in the sanctifying activity of the Holy Spirit that we learn what it means to love. The Holy Spirit is (1) our comforter, who nurtures us like a mother; (2) our teacher and guide who leads us into all truth, which is the Wisdom/Word of God who justifies us in divine grace; (3) our advocate, who with Word/Wisdom advocates for us before God the Parent and in response to the world of profound injustices; (4) the power of life, who, like a mother, bears and births us (Jn. 3:3–8), and in perfect Love; (5) a divine witness to the Word and Wisdom of God; (6) one who intercedes for us with sighs, groans, and moans when words are inadequate for expressing what is in the depths of our hearts; (7) the hypostasis of the One God who makes church a reality.

Those who are wise draw from the sagacious power of the Spirit to create beauty out of ugliness, celebrate life in the midst of suffering, and walk in love in the midst of hate. Womanists attribute the power of love to the Spirit. Womanists and other peoples tend to employ the term "Spirit" in two ways: (1) to refer to God who is a spirit; and (2) among Christian womanists and Christians in general, to refer to the Holy Spirit. The Holy Spirit is a distinctive, relational action or mode of being in the Trinity. Or, to emphasize the dynamic movement of the Holy Spirit, one might say that "she" is the dynamic agent of divine healing revealed by Jesus the Christ. Her constant unchanging nature is to comfort, heal, renew or recreate, and instruct. She is the power through which God "creates a new thing."

A healing comes to mind. A healing big enough to hold anger and turn it into justice seeking, rather than vengeance seeking. A healing big enough to hold bitterness, transforming it into peace. A healing big enough to hold hate and transform it into love. A healing big enough to overcome death and create new life. God is big enough to hold our anger. God is big enough to hold bitterness. God is big enough to hold hate. God is big enough to overcome death. God takes the hotness of anger, the ferment of bitterness, and the sourness of hatred to work with it, creatively transforming it into something sweeter. Existence alone ranges from bitter to bittersweet. Conscious, committed existence in God is more. The very presence of a moment of sweetness, comfort, or joy testifies to the presence of goodness in the land of the living. The Holy Spirit is the power of resurrecting healing. The distinctive work of the relation Christians call "the Holy Spirit" is healing, renewing, comforting, instructing, guiding, and encouraging the people of God; not only healing them, but also empowering them with gifts to go out and heal others.

Concrete Social Manifestations of the Healing Movement of the Holy Spirit

The Holy Spirit inspires the dance of God, calling all to participate in the dance of divine love, creativity, healing, justice, and renewal. Healing is contagious. It is something that those who have experienced healing share with others. In the case of the Byrd Family, the Holy Spirit gave them gifts of finances, love, and teaching that empowered them to create a center for racial healing. In the case of James Byrd, he received gifts of finances, funds, love, teaching, writing, and speaking to create the Black Holocaust Museum in Milwaukee, Wisconsin. Many people such as these around the world find divine courage. They literally take heart and commit their lives to receiving and participating in the grace of divine healing.

In the mid-twentieth century, "the Holocaust" primarily referred to the genocide of over six million Jews during Hitler's Nazi regime. For some, the use of the term "holocaust" to refer to other acts of hatred, torture, and racial/ethnic/religious violence besides the Holocaust of the Jews under Hitler is controversial. For others it makes sense to place this particular holocaust within a wider examination of historical and contemporary similar events. "Holocaust" is an old word, whose first meaning is "destruction on a mass scale"[24] or "a great loss of life."[25] In recent years, the term has become synonymous with "genocide."[26] Many around the world and in the U.S. identify with the word *holocaust* because of both meanings of the term. They employ the term "holocaust" to describe racial-ethnic, ethnic, political, or religious destruction. "Holocaust" for many has become the best term for describing racial-ethnic and religious terrorism.

Holocaust museums commemorate the suffering and genocide of Jews during Hitler's Nazi rule; they exist around the world and in several states, including California, Virginia, Missouri, Florida, New Mexico, and Texas. Of course, the most famous one is the one in Jerusalem. The United States Holocaust Memorial Museum in Washington, D.C., educates the public about the rise of Nazism, the Nazi terrorism of Jews, and the genocide of six million Jews. These museums honor victims and survivors of terror and genocide, and sometimes fall victim to hate themselves. In late 2003, an arsonist set fire to the C.A.N.D.L.E.S. (Children of Auschwitz Nazi Deadly Lab Experiments Survivors) Holocaust Museum in Terre Haute, Indiana, destroying it and much irreplaceable memorabilia. In 2001, an electrical fire destroyed much material in the El Paso, Texas, Holocaust museum which continues to offer education to five school districts in its area. However, firefighters raised money to help rebuild the museum. These museums throughout the United States and around the world are sites of racial-ethnic and religious tolerance that resist hatred. Several of them offer education on the Jewish Holocaust and on global genocide, hate crime, and intolerance. They seek to increase awareness that genocide, intolerance, and hate crimes have been problems for thousands of years and that these problems continue in the present.

The Native American Holocaust Museum in Houston, Texas, not only commemorates those who have suffered or died through colonization, but corrects misinformation regarding the success of genocidal efforts. It celebrates the fact that in spite of the genocide of thousands, today there are 7,876,568 Native Americans belonging to 562 federally recognized nations according to the U.S. census, whereas in 1900 there were just 250,000 Native Americans.. The Houston museum's mission is "to offer comfort, support, encouragement and understanding; and to encourage its visitors to reflect upon the need for dignity of and respect among all peoples."[27] It breaks down the popular myth that colonizers successfully "killed all the Indians" and "only a few are left, so it's hard to find them." Yet the genocide was real. "Genocide" does not mean that an entire people is entirely wiped out, but rather it means the planned systematic killing and extermination of very large numbers of a racial-ethnic, political, or cultural group. It is mass murder of civilians. According to *Wikipedia,* "the term *genocide* was coined by Raphael Limkin (1900–1959), a Polish Jewish legal scholar, in 1943, from the roots *genos* (Greek for family, tribe, or race) and *–cide* (Latin–*occidere,* to kill), to name the mass murder atrocities of the Nazis." He "successfully campaigned" for international laws that forbid genocide.[28] However, the law did not end the practice of the crime. The ethnic cleansing in Bosnia was a form of genocide.

The Spirit of God moves through such museums to heal the problem of human hatred, genocide, religious bigotry, and intolerance of human diversity. The objective of such educational sites is to promote tolerance and respect for the divinely inspired dignity of others.

The Holy Spirit and Social Activism

Mamie Till-Mobley was not simply concerned about the lynching of her own son when she held a nationally attended open-casket viewing and funeral in 1955. She was protesting the entire institution of lynching and racial hatred. As a Christian, she felt led by the Holy Spirit to make the horrific tragedy of Emmett's death an event for protest and a call to righteous, just love. She went on to speak out against racial violence nationally and as an educator.

For this reason the artist Vanessa Baker observes that, "There are many stories that circulate throughout history, then become pivotal in the mind's eye. One is the case of Emmett Till." Baker recalls, "I first heard of him as I listened in on one of the many discussions that went on between my mother and my paternal grandmother. They discussed everything–the past, the present, the future; they discussed religious views: who was in and who was out–politically; and the weather. They debated issues concerning what then typified the current status of society. These were *our* stories." Storytelling, historically, has been an important aspect of African American family life. The elders told stories not simply to entertain, but to educate. They shared, and many still do share, history. Even folk tales carry with them the same intent as the parables of Jesus, to tell truth in a way that anyone of any age in a community can understand. Baker's elders, like many, shared historical stories. Baker observes, "Some, such as Emmett's, were painful. But within that pain, even as a young child, I saw inspiration. Emmett's life stood as an ever-existing mirror angled before the face of humanity. It was placed before us through the agony, yet determination, of a courageous mother, Mamie Till [-Mobley], who helped to teach me that all things–including one's afflictions–are woven into one's wholeness."[29] Baker found wisdom about wholeness in the story of the Till family.

Baker believes that by faith and in divine grace, she is called to provide more opportunities for educational healing through artistic events in which young people and mature adults alike participate. While some experience God, "the Spirit," or, in the case of Christians, God in the power of the Holy Spirit calling them to create centers or museums for human tolerance and the healing of racial hatred, the Spirit gives many more gifts to the world. Vanessa Baker experiences her artistic talents as gifts of the Holy Spirit that she is to use in the work of education and healing.[30] As a Christian artist, Baker's faith in the Holy Spirit to empower and inspire her has led her to respond to a calling to create poetry and dance that tell healing stories of the past. As she puts it:

> My hope is that sincere concern and interest in regard to these stories continue to rekindle in each of us. Maybe we'll see less handcuffed youth, declaring the significance of a "color" while sporting jeans that cup the thigh instead of the waist. Maybe when we reunite as a community of pride-filled people, those who attack us to create an everlasting subservience will cease their tactics of intimidation. The rewards to us for clinging to our legacy are limitless.[31]

Theologians such as Joanne Terrell in the 1990s and myself in the twenty-first century have been moved by the Till story and stories like it to give theological attention to such events in relation to systematic theology, specifically christology. Like the story of Mary, mother of Jesus, the story of Mamie Till-Mobley teaches that the power of faith, drawn from an ever-present God revealed in Christ, inspired by the breath of God's own spirit, brings new life. What we learn from her story is that we need not be overcome by the second death that tries to take the soul. Mother Mobley was contemplating suicide when the phone rang, and from seemingly nowhere–a place that could only be the quiet, nudging voice of God–she found courage to tell a reporter she planned to go back to school. The reporter helped her register for college. After only three and a half years, she became a teacher to what would become, in time, thousands of children. She did not give in to despair.[32] Held by the power of God, she was not overcome by bitterness that kills the soul. In her lowest moment, she found what Katie Cannon, a womanist ethicist from the South, calls "unshouted courage."[33]

"Unshouted courage" comes from that place where God "makes a way out of no way." It is what the old and the wise have in mind when they say

God can “make something out of nothing.” Feeling suicidal is to feel that you are nothing, that there is nothing to hope for, no reason to continue on. Life has lost its meaning. All looks and feels dark when one is in the depths of despair. Yet, in the depths of that abyss, there is a light that shines, a voice that calls, an energy that lures or draws the soul forward from the darkness and into a place of light, where gradually a sense of purpose is renewed. Mamie Till-Mobley’s legacy is her lived testimony to this light that shines in the darkness:

> All things came into being through him, and without him not one thing came into being. What has come into being in him was life, and the life was the light of all people. The light shines in the darkness, and the darkness did not overcome it. There was a man sent from God, whose name was John. He came as a witness to testify to the light, so that all might believe through him. He himself was not the light, but he came to testify to the light. The true light, which enlightens everyone, was coming into the world. (Jn. 1:3–9)

Already a Christian woman, Mamie Till-Mobley experienced this light in her darkest moment. Through divine, preventive grace, the telephone rang; and it came into her mind that she would go back to school instead of jump out of a window.[34] She did not keep the light of God’s presence to herself, but shared it with others. She taught the knowledge that in God each of us has a purpose. She shared this message in one way as a school teacher, encouraging children to live up to their full potential. She shared this in other ways as a community leader and church mother in the Church of God in Christ. Like John, she herself was not the light. Like Mary, she was simply a bereaved mother whose son died a brutal death.

Before she died, Mamie Till-Mobley said to her biographer, “I have come to realize that we are all here for a purpose and we have unique gifts to share with the rest the world.” She knew her time was near and said further, “I have enjoyed a full, rich, meaningful life because I was able to discover my reason for being and to perfect my gifts in fulfilling my purpose, touching so many lives in the process. Hopefully, I have left each one just a little better than I found it. Hopefully, I have made a difference. That is, after all, how our lives are measured. By how many other lives we touch and inspire. By how much of life we embrace, not by what we reject. By what we accept, not by what we judge.”[35] Mother Mamie Till-Mobley acknowledged that even with all the goodness and joy she had come to experience in her life, especially through touching the lives of others, she still cried about Emmett sometimes.

> But I see much more clearly now through my tears, and that is a good thing. Rainy days always help us appreciate the sunny ones so much more, don’t they? Besides, it is in crying that we are able to let go. In letting go, I have experienced what it is like to bring hope from despair, joy from anguish, forgiveness from anger, love

> from hate. And if I can do it, I know anyone can. And if everyone does it, just imagine how much better we all can be.[36]

Indeed the Holy Spirit graces followers of Jesus with many gifts to *edify* or *build up* the church, which is the *body of Christ,* to fulfill its call to participate in God's loving, healing activity with heart, head, and body (1 Cor. 12). Mother Till-Mobley knew that by the grace of God and in the power of the Holy Spirit, she truly could do "all things through [Christ] who strengthens me" (Phil. 4:13). She did not sink into victimhood and wallow in suffering. She became an overcomer and a leader in the civil rights movement before Martin Luther King Jr. became the leader of the bus boycott in Montgomery, Alabama, in 1955, a boycott initiated by another great woman of God–Mother Rosa Parks. Mother Till-Mobley, like Rosa Parks, was a faithful witness to the light, the divine energy that calls us forward into realizing active hope in the full potential of humanity. She knew the wisdom so many African American women have taught their children and practiced: "You have to rise to the occasion!" As a follower of Jesus, she took heart, because she knew the living Christ had overcome the world. In courage she became a leader for righteousness, justice, and tough love. In Christ she became a leader in overcoming a world of crucifixion. She did not ask, "What should I do?" She listened to the Spirit, and she did it! The community knew she was a woman in the Spirit and did not cynically ask, "Well, what should we do?" and wait for a miracle. They listened to the Spirit, too, and in so doing *became the miracle.* An ordinary woman and bereaved mother, Mother Mobley became a prophet and mother to many in her commitment to helping an entire nation understand that it must be transformed...May we all learn not only from her life well-lived, but from her life's testimony to the gracious power of the Spirit to move even the most despairing of believers forward, one dynamic step at a time. Like Coretta Scott King, she walked and she did not faint. She carried the banner for peace, love, and healing of racial hatred. Already led by the Spirit to commit her life to racial healing, she shared the Christian and Gandhi-inspired values of the twentieth-century human rights movement led by Dr. Martin Luther King Jr., Coretta Scott King, Rosa Parks, Ella Baker,[37] and a host of others, female and male, of diverse racial-ethnic, religious groups and nationalities.

Women like Mother Mamie Till-Mobley, Mother Rosa Parks, Mother Ella Baker, and First Lady Coretta Scott King could have hated, but walked in love. They could have sunk to violent rage, but instead they walked in holy indignation and holy dignity. They led others as they followed Christ in the comforting, encouraging, and healing power of the Holy Spirit. God in Christ bore them up on wings like eagles (Isa. 40:31). They showed the world the meaning of resurrection, Holy Spirit power. One step at a time, may we all take heart. One step at a time and by the grace of God, may we all follow Christ's example, Mary's example, Mother Mobley's, Rosa Parks's, Ella Baker's, and Coretta Scott King's examples. One dynamic step at a time, may we all dance with the Trinity in the power of the Spirit! May we do so in love for an entire creation, following the example of Coretta Scott King who, as the first lady of the civil rights movement throughout her adult life, met with freedom and human rights activists of all religions and from around the world as a follower of Jesus. May we who are Christian, like these women of the Spirit, realize that when we truly follow Jesus–with all our hearts, minds, strength, and souls, loving our neighbors as ourselves–we are the miracle. We are the miracle when we live in the wholeness of divine grace toward all creation. This is the good news of Jesus, the Christ! This is the dance with God!

Amen.

Notes

Preface

[1]Delores Williams, *Sisters in the Wilderness: The Challenge of Womanist God-Talk* (Maryknoll, N.Y.: Orbis, 1993).

Introduction

[1]See for example, Thomas Jay Oord, "A Process Wesleyan Theodicy: Freedom, Embodiment, and the Almighty God," and "Wesleyan Theology, Boston Personalism, and Process Thought," in *Thy Nature and Thy Name is Love: Wesleyan and Process Theologies in Dialogue,* ed. Bryan P. Stone and Thomas Jay Oord, 193–216, 379–92 (Nashville: Abingdon Press, 2001). See also Michael Lodahl and Thomas Jay Oord, *Relational Holiness: Responding to the Call of Love* (Kansas City, Kan.: Beacon Hill Press of Kansas City, 2005).

[2]Karen Baker-Fletcher, *Sisters of Dust, Sisters of Spirit: Womanist Wordings on God and Creation* (Minneapolis: Fortress Press, 1998).

[3]Thomas Jay Oord, "Evangelical Theologies," in *A Handbook of Process Theology,* ed. Jay McDaniel and Donna Bowman (St. Louis: Chalice, 2006), 251–54.

[4]Ibid., 252.

[5]See Kelly Brown Douglas, *Sexuality and the Black Church: A Womanist Perspective* (Maryknoll, N.Y.: Orbis, 1999), 1–7, 11–30, 31–59; Karen Baker-Fletcher and Garth Baker-Fletcher, *My Sister, My Brother: Womanist and Xodus God-Talk* (Maryknoll, N.Y.: Orbis, 1997), 259. Overall, many African Americans who are conservative about sexual orientation and abortion and those who are more accepting alike tend to deconstruct campaign platforms to uncover power-mongering political strategies to simply get their vote in each party.

[6]This conserving movement is an inherent aspect of Whiteheadian metaphysics itself, but in Whiteheadian orthodoxy certain aspects of classical Christian theism are deemed as lacking philosophical and metaphysical soundness. I am playing with language here in part to question Whiteheadian discomfort with Trinity, the primacy of scripture, and bodily resurrection, and in part to criticize a lack of depth in the way we use certain terms to maintain political, division, opposition, derision, and cynicism in contemporary U.S. culture.

[7]For an open theist construction see Clark H. Pinnock, *Flame of Love: A Theology of the Holy Spirit* (Downers Grove, Ill.: InterVarsity Press, 1996). The theology of *Dancing With God* shares some things with Pinnock in its emphasis on the relationality of God, but it differs from Pinnock's work in its understanding of omniscience. Moreover, while I find Pinnock's Spirit christology very compelling, my emphasis is on Christ the Word/Wisdom of God, synthesizing the Logos tradition with the Hokmah/Sophia traditions of the First Testament and Intertestamental writings.

[8]John Cobb, for example, references John Wesley, "An Earnest Appeal to Men of Reason and Religion," Bk. 32 and "The New Birth," Bk. II.5, in *The Works of John Wesley*, begun as *The Oxford Edition of the Works of John Wesley* (Oxford: Clarendon Press, 1975–1983); continued as *The Bicentennial Edition of the Works of John Wesley* (Nashville: Abingdon Press, 1945), 11:56–57 and 2:193–94. John B. Cobb Jr., *Grace and Responsibility: A Wesleyan Theology for Today* (Nashville: Abingdon Press, 1995), 97–98.

[9]Oord in "Evangelical Theologies" writes that it is process metaphysics' scientific arguments regarding evidence of internal experience that makes it of some interest to evangelical theologians. See William L. Andrews, *Sisters of the Spirit: Three Black Women's Autobiographies of the Nineteenth Century* (Bloomington: Indiana Univ. Press, 1986); Thomas C. Oden, ed., *Phoebe Palmer: Selected Writings* (New York: Paulist Press, 1988).

[10]Marjorie Hewitt Suchocki, "Spirit in and through the World," in *Trinity in Process,* ed. Joseph A. Bracken, S.J. and Marjorie Hewitt Suchocki, 173–90 (New York: Continuum, 1997).

[11]See Oord, "A Process Wesleyan Theodicy," 193–216, and "Wesleyan Theology," 379–92. See also Lodahl and Oord, *Relational Holiness.* In "A Process Wesleyan Theology," 206, 213, 215, and 216, Oord writes of God's omnipresent and indirect bodily relationship to the universe as a Spirit. Moreover, he develops free will theism in relation to theodicy. He turns

not only to process-relational metaphysics, but also to John Wesley's statement that "God is in all things, and that we are to see the Creator in the glass of every creature; that we should use and look upon nothing as separate from God...who by his intimate presence holds them all in being, who pervades and actuates the whole created fame, and is in a true sense the soul of the universe" (John Wesley, Sermon 23, "Upon our Lord's Sermon on the Mount III," 1.11 in *The Works of John Wesley*).

[12]Howard Thurman, *The Search for Common Ground: An Inquiry into the Basis of Man's Experience of Community* (Richmond, Ind.: Friends United Press, 1986, c1971), 1–41. This is a book that many who are interested in holistic healing and spirituality like to have on their bookshelves.

[13]See Anne Spencer Thurman, ed., and Vincent Harding, intro., *For the Inward Journey: The Writings of Howard Thurman* (1971; reprint, Richmond, Ind.: Friends United Meeting, 1984), back cover.

[14]Gordon D. Kaufman, *In Face of Mystery: A Constructive Theology* (Cambridge: Harvard Univ. Press, 1993), 46. I agree with Kaufman's statement that "in the absence of other well-thought-out alternatives to Whitehead's cosmology many theologians have felt pressed simply to take it over and do the best they can....Doubtless there is much to be learned from Whitehead about contemporary conceptualization of the world, but in my opinion we theologians must do our own work with respect to the question of God, not simply take over someone else's."

[15]Kaufman, *In Face of Mystery,* ix-xii, 36–42.

[16]Ibid., 7–12. While he does not take on Paul Tillich's experience-based understanding of divine revelation, he agrees that the word "God" is the primary symbol of theological discourse. In Kaufman's words, "The symbol 'God' is perhaps the most complex and dialectical of any bequeathed to us by western traditions" (9). See also Gordon D. Kaufman, *The Theological Imagination: Constructing the Concept of God* (Philadelphia: Westminster Press, 1981), 80–95.

[17]A number of theologians have written about this, and space does not allow us to "reinvent the wheel" here. See Paul Tillich, *Dynamics of Faith* (New York: Harper & Row, 1957), 41–54; idem, *The Courage to Be* (New Haven: Yale Univ. Press, 1952), 188–89; idem, *Theology of Culture* (New York: Oxford Univ. Press, 1959), 53–67; idem, *Systematic Theology,* Vol. 1 (Chicago: Univ. of Chicago Press, 1951), 238–47, 61–62, 122–23,286–89. See also Clifford Geertz, *The Interpretation of Cultures: Selected Essays* (New York: Basic Books, 1973), 4–5, 17–18, 45–46; Kaufman, *The Theological Imagination,* 101–130; Sallie McFague, *Models of God: Theology for an Ecological, Nuclear Age* (Philadelphia: Fortress Press, 1987), ix–xv, 3–57; and Elizabeth A. Johnson, *She Who Is: The Mystery of God in Feminist Theological Discourse* (New York: Crossroad, 1992), 3–16, 33–57, 78–103, 113–20, 141–49, 154–56, 170–87, and 205–23.

[18]Alice Walker, *In Search of Our Mothers' Gardens: Womanist Prose* (San Diego: Harcourt Brace Jovanovich, 1983), xi–xii. The term *womanist* has been defined many times in the last two decades by womanist theologians, ethicists, and scholars of religion. Originally, Alice Walker defined "womanist" most succinctly as "a black feminist or feminist of color." She noted that the term comes from the Black folk expression "womanish," which refers to acting grown up, being grown up, wanting to know more than is good for one, loving entire communities male and female, loving women and men sexually and nonsexually, liberating those in captivity to take them to freedom, as belonging to the same color family as feminists but of darker hue and different social-historical experience, as "Loving the Spirit," and as viewing "colored race" like a flower garden with every color in it. Walker's daughter, Rebecca Walker is biracial, black white and Jewish with no commas. Therefore, one assumes Walker meant what she wrote. Over the years in the field of religious studies, "womanist" has come to refer to spiritually empowered Black women who are committed to their survival, thriving, and liberation. Many womanists in the field of religious studies no longer define "womanist" as a "Black feminist." Those who do define "womanist" in this way share my concern to work in relation to a diversity of global feminists and communities. I also resonate with Walker's understanding that God is not absent from creation. I recommend reading works by the following womanists to gain a sense of the breadth of womanist scholarship in religion: Katie Cannon, Jacquelyn Grant, Delores Williams, Diana Hayes, Kelly Brown Douglas, Linda Thomas, Debra Mubashshir, C S'thembilie West, Rosetta Ross, Lynne Westfield, Joy Bostic, Traci West, Evelyn Parker, and Monica Coleman, to name a few. There is some variation in how each womanist scholar of religion defines the term "womanist." No one definition is better than the other. Without those who focus more exclusively on African American women's

experience, as I did in my earlier work, Black women's religious thought is rendered invisible. Not all Black women scholars of religion are "womanists." Some prefer to call themselves Black feminists to clarify identity with global feminism. Others prefer to call themselves Black women scholars of religion. Still others simply identify themselves by their fields of research, writing, and teaching. Womanist community is too much a part of the best of my life to abandon the term "womanist." I intentionally, however, relate and integrate the term "womanist" along with other terms like "relational," "open," "integrative," "conserving," "liberationist," "evangelical," "biblical," "charismatic," "Pentecostal," "Baptecostal," and "Methecostal."

[19]Howard Thurman, *With Head and Heart: The Autobiography of Howard Thurman* (New York: Harcourt Brace Jovanovich, 1979), 144.

[20]See Thurman, *The Search for Common Ground*, 1–7, 8–41, for Thurman's discussion of the human experience of the interdependence of all life, which is our common ground.

[21]This project does not cover the types of interfaith concerns Thurman addressed through his church, although it appreciates the questions that emerge in interfaith dialogue.

[22]Katie G. Cannon, *Black Womanist Ethics* (Atlanta: Scholars Press, 1988), 105–16, 127–41, 143–44, 145–51.

[23]Malcolm X is unique in this group in that he was apparently killed by Black men who may have been assassins from the Nation of Islam paid off by the FBI or other government officials, or assassins appointed by Elijah Muhammad, or both. This is unclear. All others were killed by the Ku Klux Klan and similarly-minded racial hate groups or individuals, except for the Kennedy brothers, whose assassins killed them for any number of political motivations, including their support of racial integration and more. Many African Americans hung photographs of the Kennedys on the walls of their homes next to Martin Luther King Jr.'s, in appreciation for the Kennedy brothers' growing support of civil and human rights. Schwerner and Goodman were two Jewish civil rights workers who were assassinated with James Chaney, an African American, for their support of the movement. Neither Jews nor African Americans, nor Native Americans nor Euro-Americans supporting the civil rights movement were safe from hate crime in Mississippi, Alabama, and other Southern states during this period. Lynchings were common in the South from the late nineteenth century until the last recorded lynching in 1964. More recent lynchings have been more difficult to document, and the traditional hanging from trees is less common, leading legal authorities to employ the term "hate crime" to describe a variety of racialized, religious, nationalist, gender, homophobic, and ableist motivated vandalisms, burnings, rapes, assaults, attempted rapes and murders, and murders. Lynching is one form of hate crime.

Chapter 1: Renewing Our Minds

[1]W. E. B DuBois, "Our Spiritual Striving," in *The Souls of Black Folk* (New York: Penguin, 1996), 3.

[2]Thanks to Cornel West for insights he offered regarding Anna Cooper's optimism in a brief informal discussion I had with him in October of 1995 at a social gathering honoring Preston N. Williams, who was our mentor, at Harvard Divinity School. At that time I had recently published *A Singing Something: Womanist Reflections on Anna Julia Cooper* (New York: Crossroad, 1994).

[3]See, for example, Sharon Welch, *A Feminist Ethic of Risk* (Minneapolis: Fortress Press, 1990), 15–22, 103–22. Welch writes very realistically of the problem of cynicism and despair in middle-class, success-oriented culture that leaves many afraid to take risks for justice. This has left the poor of diverse cultures feeling abandoned by the middle class.

[4]Howard Thurman, *Jesus and the Disinherited* (Nashville: Abingdon, 1949; reprint, Richmond, Ind.: Friends United Press, 1976), 7–8, 14–35.

[5]Marjorie Hewitt Suchocki, *God, Christ, Church: A Practical Guide to Process Theology* (New York: Crossroad, 198), 259. Suchocki explains that "each unit of process is called an actual entity; it is a drop of experience" that emerges in the process of becoming, moving into concrescence, and moving forward into further becoming as the "building blocks" of "the composite world of rocks, trees, and people." The world is made up of drops of experience, dynamically moving subquantum particles of energy and matter.

[6]John Cobb emphasizes that in Whiteheadian metaphysics, one finds that experience is not simply external. It is also internal. Whitehead describes the universe as the body of God.

Also, Sallie McFague has written an ecofeminist theology entitled *The Body of God: An Ecological Theology* (Minneapolis: Fortress Press, 1993).

[7]This is a reference to Whitehead's understanding of "objective immortality" and acceptance of our finitude as creatures. Alfred North Whitehead, *Process and Reality: An Essay in Cosmology,* corrected edition, ed. David Ray Griffin and Donald W. Sherburne (New York: Free Press, 1978), xiii, 29, 32, 347, 351. See also, John B. Cobb Jr. and David Ray Griffin, *Process Theology: An Introductory Exposition* (Philadelphia: Westminster Press, 1976); Suchocki, *God, Christ, Church,* 28–36, 39, 202–205, 257; Charles Hartshorne, *Omnipotence and Other Theological Mistakes* (Albany: State University of New York, 1984), 26–28, 59, 133–35.

[8]Paul Tillich, *Systematic Theology,* vol. 1 (Chicago: Univ. of Chicago Press, 1951), 171. This section of the theology is in agreement with Tillich's understanding that God is not another object among other objects or a being among other beings, but it moves toward an integrative rather than a correlational method. In Tillich's correlational method, he is unclear in his understanding of divine presence, because he lacks an integrative metaphysics in which in salvation and redemption the *basileia* or reign of God, which is yet and not yet, is an integration of Spirit and world. This is the meaning of a new heaven and a new earth, in which God, in the reign that is already at hand and yet to come, is already recreating heaven and earth. God in creating a new heaven and earth is everlastingly in the process of creating a new world, a new cosmos if you will, in our present understanding of cosmos and a transcendent cosmos, which exceeds present imagination. See also John B. Cobb Jr., "Commonwealth and Empire," at Drew University's web site, http://www.users.drew.edu/mnausner/ttc3cobblecture.pdf, , pp. 1–12 for his interpretation of *basileia theou* as the realm of God, which honors divine responsibility and power without suggesting the domineering understanding of God that some imagine, while being consistent with the understanding that God is persuasive, not coercive. Cobb encourages the use of the Greek *basileia* to avoid misunderstandings, as we move into a more accurate understanding of *basileia* as "Commonwealth" and "realm."

[9]Here again, I am revising some of Tillich's particularly influential ideas. See Tillich, *Systematic Theology,* vol. 1, 49.

[10]Augustine, *On the Trinity,* Bk. 9 in *The Trinitarian Controversy,* trans. and ed. William G. Rusch (Philadelphia: Fortress Press, 1980), 164–79.

[11]See for example, Okechukwu Ogbannay, *Communitarian Divinity* (New York: Paragon House, 1994), 13–30, 58–72, 89–90. Ogbannay emphasizes divinity as community in relation to the Christian understanding of Tertullian and traditional African religions.

[12]The words "courage" and "encourage" are derived from the Latin word *cor* or "heart."

[13]See David Tracy and John B. Cobb Jr., *Talking About God: Doing Theology in the Context of Modern Pluralism* (San Francisco: HarperSanFrancisco, 1984), chap. 1, for a sustained discussion of Paul Tillich's correlational method and process theism.

[14]Anselm, *Proslogion,* in Anselm of Canterbury, *The Prayers And Meditations of Saint Anselm with the Proslogion,* trans. Sister Benedicta Ward, S.L.G. (Hammondsworth, England: Penguin Books, 1973), 238–39, 244–47.

[15]See Cornel West, "Prophetic Christian as Organic Intellectual: Martin Luther King, Jr.," *The Cornel West Reader* (New York: Basic Civitas Books, 1999), 425–34.

[16]Paul Tillich, *The Dynamics of Faith* (New York: Harper & Row, 1957), 20.

[17]W. E. B. DuBois, *The Souls of Black Folk* in *Three Negro Classics: Up From Slavery, Booker T. Washington; The Souls of Black Folk, Willliam E. B. DuBois; The Autobiography of an Ex-Colored Man, James Weldon Johnson,* ed. John Hope Franklin (New York: Avon, 1965), 213–21.

[18]"Christ" from the Greek and "messiah" from the Hebrew both mean "anointed one."

[19]This book does not have sufficient space to explore this, nor is it necessary as there are several books that have been written on this subject. Dianna Hayes, for example, a womanist scholar who writes about black religious thought in general and black women's religious thought in particular, writes of these connections, drawing in part on the earlier work of Gayraud Wilmore. Emilie Townes and Albert Raboteau also have written of these connections. See, for example, Diana L. Hayes, *And Still We Rise: An Introduction to Black Liberation Theology* (Mahwah, N.J.: Paulist Press, 1996), especially chaps. 1 and 2; Emilie M. Townes, *In a Blaze of Glory: Womanist Spirituality as Social Witness* (Nashville: Abingdon Press, 1995), especially chap. 1; Cheryl Townsend Gilkes, *If It Wasn't for the Women* (Maryknoll, N.Y.: Orbis Books, 2001) especially chaps. 3, 5, and 7; Katie Cannon, *Teaching Preaching: Isaac Rufus Clark and Black Sacred Rhetoric* (New York: Continuum, 2002); Gayraud Wilmore, *Black Religion and*

Black Radicalism: An Interpretation of the Religious History of African Americans (New York: Anchor, 1973); Lawrence W. Levine, *Black Culture and Black Consciousness: Afro-American Folk Thought from Slavery to Freedom* (New York: Oxford Univ. Press, 1977); Albert Raboteau, *Slave Religion: The Invisible Institution in the Antebellum South* (New York: Oxford Univ. Press, 1980); Milton C. Sernett, *African American Religious History: A Documentary Witness*, 2d ed., (Durham: Duke Univ. Press, 1885; 1999); William Andrews, *Sisters of the Spirit: Three Black Women's Autobiographies of the Nineteenth Century* (Bloomington, Ind.: Indiana Univ. Press, 1986); Margaret Creel, *A Peculiar People: Slave Religion and Community Culture among the Gullah* (New York: New York Univ. Press, 1988); Mechal Sobel, *Trabelin' On: The Slave Journey to an Afro-Baptist Faith* (Princeton: Princeton Univ. Press, 1988); C. Eric Lincoln and Lawrence H. Mamiya, *The Black Church in the African American Experience* (Durham: Duke Univ. Press, 1990; 2001);Evelyn Brooks Higginbotham, *Righteous Discontent: The Women's Movement in the Black Baptist Church, 1880–1920* (Cambridge: Harvard Univ. Press, 1994); Theophus H. Smith, *Conjuring Culture: Biblical Formations of Black America* (New York: Oxford Univ. Press, 1995); Cheryl J. Sanders, ed., *Saints in Exile: The Holiness-Pentecostal Experience in African American Religion and Culture* (New York: Oxford Univ. Press, 1996); Dwight N. Hopkins, *Down, Up, and Over: Slave Religion and Black Theology* (Minneapolis: Fortress Press, 1999), especially chaps. 3–6; Yvonne Chireau, *Black Magic: Religion and the African American Conjuring Tradition* (Berkeley: Univ. of California Press, 2003); and Cornel West and Eddie S. Glaude Jr., eds., *African American Religious Thought: An Anthology* (Louisville: Westminster John Knox Press, 2003), which includes essays by Benjamin E. Mays, W. E. B. DuBois, Howard Thurman, C. Eric Lincoln, Evelyn Brooks Higginbotham, Charles Long, Albert J. Raboteau, Carla L. Peterson, and Elsa Barkley Brown who offer research contributions on pre-twentieth-century and very early twentieth-century black religion. Those interested in comparative religious studies might also examine Linda Elaine Thomas, *Under the Canopy: Ritual Process and Spiritual Resilience in South Africa* (Columbia, S.C.: Univ. of South Carolina Press, 1999).

[20]Marjorie Hewitt Suchocki, "Spirit in and through the World," in *Trinity in Process,* ed. Joseph A. Bracken, S.J. and Marjorie Hewitt Suchocki (New York: Continuum, 1997), 173–90.

[21]Seminarians will find helpful Karl Barth, *Dogmatics in Outline* (New York: Harper, 1959), 9–14, 18–21, 72–77, 79–81; and idem., *Church Dogmatics,* vol. 2, *The Doctrine of God,* ed. G. W. Bromiley and T. F. Torrance (Edinburgh: T&T Clark, 1957) S 26:1, particularly 106–9.

[22]See Karl Barth, *Dogmatics in Outline* (New York: Harper & Row, 1959), 9–14; idem, *Church Dogmatics*, vol. 1.2, *The Doctrine of the Word of God* (Edinburgh: T&T Clark, 1956; 1980), chap. 2, pt. 2, 13:1–2. See also Shirley Guthrie, *Christian Doctrine* (Louisville: Westminster John Knox Press, 1994), 11.

[23]See, for example, Karl Barth, *The Humanity of God* (Atlanta: John Knox Press, 1960), 46–52.

[24]The word "gospel" means good news.

[25]See John B. Cobb Jr., Jeanyne B. Slettom, eds., *The Process Perspective: Frequently Asked Questions about Process Theology* (St. Louis: Chalice Press, 2003), 70–73 for one process theologian's response to questions regarding the infallibility of scripture.

[26]Donald W. Dayton, "The Use of Scripture in the Wesleyan Tradition," in *The Use of the Bible in Theology: Evangelical Options*, ed. Robert K. Johnson (Atlanta: John Knox Press, 1973), 135; see Stanley J. Grenz, "How Do We Know What to Believe," in *Essentials of Christian Theology,* ed. William C. Placher (Louisville: Westminster John Knox Press, 2003), 21–27.

[27]Augustine, *On Christian Doctrine,* trans. D. W. Robertson (Upper Saddle River, N.J.: Prentice Hall, 1958), parts 1 and 2.

[28]See Stanley J. Grenz, *Theology for the Community of God* (Nashville: Broadman & Holmam, 1994), 494–527.

[29]Schubert Ogden, *The Point of Christology* (Dallas: Southern Methodist Univ. Press, 1992), 97–105. Ogden's understanding of scripture, however, was more Bultmannian, distinguishing myths that point to the reality of the divine nature from what one can say is literally true about God. Our theology maintains confidence in the healing miracles attributed to Jesus with reference not only to testimonies throughout the ages, but to scientific evidence that proves when individuals and communities pray for sick individuals they heal faster and more completely than those who are not prayed for. See also William James, *Varieties of Religious Experience* (New York: Penguin Books, 1982), 20, 53–58, 485–523. Through collecting historical and contemporary data for his time (the turn of the twentieth century), the philosophical pragmatist, scholar of religion, and neuropsychologist William James came to the conclusion

that given the preponderance of narrative data on religious transformation, there existed something "more," which is supernatural, and which we call God.

[30]Ibid.

[31]Charles Hartshorne, *Omnipotence and Other Theological Mistakes* (Albany, N.Y.: SUNY, 1984), 22, 27, 39. Hartshorne speaks of divine empathy on pp. 27, 39, 108. See also Marjorie Suchoki, *God, Christ, Church* (New York: Crossroad, 1989), 66–77, 81, 101 for a rigorous and similar Whiteheadian analysis.

[32]Augustine, *On the Grace of Christ*, in *Theological Anthropology*, ed. J. Patout Burns (Philadelphia: Fortress Press, 1981), 105–108.

[33]Cobb and Slettom, *The Process Perspective*, 77–79.

[34]Tillich, *Dynamics of Faith*, 12–16, 28, 106–107.

[35]Tillich, *Systematic Theology*, vol. 1, 155–58.

[36]Theodore Walker Jr., *Mothership Connections: A Black Atlantic Synthesis of Neoclassical Metaphysics and Black Theology* (Albany: State Univ. of New York Press, 2004), 27–28. Alfred North Whitehead, *Science and the Modern World* (New York: MacMillan, 1925), 101–102, 103–105, 108–112. Whitehead writes: "Later on, we find the relations of mass and energy inverted; so that mass now becomes the name for a quantity of energy considered in relation to some of its dynamical effects. This train of thought leads to the notion of energy being fundamental, thus displacing matter from that position. But energy is merely the name for the quantitative aspect of a structure of happenings...There is thus an intrinsic and extrinsic reality of an event" (102–103). In other words, energy and matter are dynamically and integratively related in each organism or entity. Each organism is not eternal. Only God is eternal, but organisms, which perish, endure in a temporal process in response to internal feelings/experiences of the world and external influences as they engage in selective processes of becoming. Life consists of "underlying eternal energy" and "activity" (105). Moreover, "enduring things are thus the outcome of a temporal process; whereas eternal things are the elements required for the very being of the process" (108). In other words, energy pervades physical reality; matter and energy are interrelated.

[37]John B. Cobb, Jr. and David Tracy, *Talking About God: Doing Theology in the Context of Modern Pluralism* (New York: Seabury Press, 1983), chapter 4.

[38]Peter Mwiti Rukungah, "The Cosmocentric Model of Pastoral Psychotherapy: A Contextualized Holistic Model from a Banta African Worldview, a Perspective for Post-Modern Pastoral-Psychotherapy," Ph.D. dissertation, School of Theology at Claremont, 1994.

[39]Theodore Walker Jr., *Mothership Connections*, 31–35, 66–67, 79–80. Theodore Walker carefully explains Hartshorne's redefinition of divine omnipotence, in which God is the all embracing, comprehensive, omnipresent, all-knowing, all-loving, all-inclusive one "to whom all things make partly determinative differences and who makes partly determinative and wholly righteous differences to all things." In other words, God, the all-inclusive one, feels/experiences/knows the world in its entirety. God, "supremely creative," relational, and "social," shares creativity and freedom with all creation, universally and eternally interactive with the many. God shares power in God's relational social response to the world, partly determining our becoming and partly sharing God's own freedom of decision with creation. See also Hartshorne, *Omnipotence*, 79.

[40]Katie Cannon, *Katie's Canon, Womanism and the Soul of the Black Community* (New York: Continuum, 1997), 57–68.

[41]William James, for example, who borrows from the thought of the preacher and philosopher of religion, Jonathan Edwards, misquotes his writings a bit to emphasize that in James's analysis of religious experience, it is the transformative results in a believer's life that lend credence to the authenticity of the professed experience. This is also a biblical concept, found in the New Testament–"you shall know them by their fruits" (Mt. 7:16, 20)

[42]Paolo Freire, *Pedagogy of the Oppressed* (New York: Continuum, 1999), 68–69, 106–109.

[43]See chapter 1, p. 15.

[44]Anselm, *Proslogion*, 244.

[45]Paul Tillich, *Theology of Culture* (New York: Oxford Univ. Press, 1959), 40–51, 53–67.

[46]Whitehead, *Process and Reality*, 21.

[47]I recommend the following books by Gordon Kaufman for this discussion: Gordon D. Kaufman, *In Face of Mystery* (Cambridge: Harvard Univ. Press, 1993), 3–83 and 264–80; idem, *An Essay on Theological Method* (Atlanta: Scholars Press, 1975; rev. ed. 1979); idem, *The Theological Imagination: Constructing the Concept of God* (Philadelphia: Westminster Press, 1981).

Chapter 2: Our Spiritual Striving

[1]Toni Morrison coined the term "disremembered" in her Nobel Prize winning novel, *Beloved.* See Toni Morrison, *Beloved* (New York: Alfred K. Knopf, 1987), 274–75. It refers to a literal history of violent dismembering during the North Atlantic slave trade and slavery, as well to a literal dismembering of historical truth so that traumatic memory is fragmented or dismembered. See also Karen Baker-Fletcher, "Immanuel: Womanist Reflections on Jesus as Dust and Spirit," in Karen Baker-Fletcher and Garth Kasimu Baker-Fletcher, *My Sister, My Brother: Womanist and Xodus God-Talk* (Maryknoll, N.Y.: Orbis, 1997), 90–91. Finally, see Walter Clemons, "A Gravestone of Memories," *Newsweek* (September 28, 1987), 74–75.

[2]See for example, Sheila Greeve Davaney, *God and the End of Modernity* (Philadelphia: Trinity Press International, 1991), ix–xii, 1–16.

[3]Cornel West, "Race and Modernity," *The Cornel West Reader* (New York: Basic Civitas Books, 1999), 67–86.

[4]For seminarians, I recommend beginning with Jacques Derrida, *Of Grammatology,* trans. Gayatri Chakravorty Spivak (Baltimore: Johns Hopkins University Press, 1976) and idem. *Acts of Religion,* ed. Gil Anidjar (New York: Routledge, 2002).

[5]Friedrich Nietzsche, *Beyond Good and Evil,* trans. Walter Kaufman (New York: Vintage Books, 1989) and idem, *On the Genealogy of Morals and Ecce Homo,* ed. and trans. Walter Kaufman (New York: Vintage, 1989). See also Cornel West, "Nietzsche's Prefiguration of Postmodern American Philosophy," in West, *The Cornel West Reader,* 189, 581 n. 1; Friedrich Nietszche, *Twilight of the Idols,* trans. R. J. Hollingdale (Middlesex, U.K.: Penguin, 1968); and Friedrich Nietzsche, *The Will to Power,* trans. Walter Kaufman and R. J. Hollingdale (New York: Vintage Press, 1968).

[6]See David Ray Griffin, *God and Religion in the Postmodern World* (Albany, N.Y.: State Univ. of New York Press, 1989), and idem, ed., *Spirituality and Society: Postmodern Visions* (Albany, N.Y.: State Univ. of New York Press, 1988).

[7]Susan Dolan-Henderson, "Postmodernism," in *Dictionary of Feminist Theologies,* ed. Letty M. Russell and J. Shannon Clarkson (Louisville: Westminster John Knox Press, 1996), 217–18.

[8]Dolan-Henderson, "Postmodernism," 217.

[9]Ibid.

[10]Ibid.

[11]Joerg Rieger, *God and the Excluded* (Minneapolis: Fortress Press, 2001), 8. Rieger's emphasis is on a liberative understanding of God and the poor. He is critical of both modernity and postmodernity, as he develops what he calls "common interest theology." For Rieger, a German liberation theologian in the United States, it is important for the white middle class to understand that liberation theology is common interest theology. Rieger is a student of Fred Herzog.

[12]Rieger, *God and the Excluded,* 9. See also Jean Baudrillard, *America,* trans. Chris Turner (New York: Verso, 1989, [1988]).

[13]Rieger, *God and the Excluded,* 9

[14]David Ray Griffin, *Religion and Scientific Naturalism* (Albany, N.Y.: 2000), x-xiii, 19–23, 43, 83, 87, 133. Alfred North Whitehead, "The Quantum Theory," *Science and the Modern World* (New York: MacMillan, 1925; Free Press Paperback Edition, 1967), 129–32.

[15]Written interview responses by Vanessa Baker, April 20, 2005.

[16]Written interview responses by Vanessa Baker, April 20, 2005.

[17]Sallie McFague, *Models of God: Theology for an Ecological, Nuclear Age* (Philadelphia: Fortress Press, 1987), 25–26, 31–40. See also Sallie McFague, *Metaphorical Theology: Models of God in Religious Language* (Philadelphia: Fortress Press, 1982), 1–66.

[18]Jacques Derrida, *Acts of Religion* (New York: Routledge, 2002), 104–133.

[19]Ada Maria Isasi Díaz, *Mujerista Theology* (Maryknoll, N.Y.: Orbis Books, 1996), 21.

[20]W. E. B. DuBois, *The Souls of Black Folk* in John Hope Franklin, ed., *Three Negro Classics* (New York: Avon Books/Hearst, 1965), 213–21.

[21]Howard Thurman, *Head and Heart: The Autobiography of Howard Thurman,* (New York: Harcourt Brace Jovanovich, 1979), 268–69.

[22]Alfred North Whitehead, *Process and Reality: An Essay in Cosmology,* corrected edition, ed. David Ray Griffin and Donald W. Sherburne (New York: The Free Press/MacMillan, 1978), 85–87.

[23]The theory and method posited here is closest to Paul Lakeland's description of liberation movement's response to postmodernity. According to Lakeland, liberation theology participates in the best of postmodernity while criticizing the worst of it. Here I am critical of postmodernity's dance of death, while I fully engage the best of its deconstructive contributions. Critical thinking similar to deconstruction, however, is present in earlier strategies practiced by oppressed peoples. The movement here is not strictly deconstructive but participates in older movements of critical and constructive thinking in African American traditions. See Paul Lakeland, *Postmodernity: Christian Identity in a Fragmented Age* (Minneapolis: Fortress Press, 1997), 61–64.

[24]David Ray Griffin, ed. *Physics and the Ultimate Significance of Time* (Albany, N.Y.: State Univ. of New York Press, 1986), 1–15. Here I am not entirely wed to Whiteheadian process physics as understood by David Griffin or to Whitehead's understanding of Albert Einstein's quantum physics. I appreciate Whitehead's and Griffin's basic common sense or pragmatic approach to time in which time is inseparable from mind and body. While I also appreciate Einstein's understanding that one might consider time an illusion, at least ultimately, I agree with Griffin and John Cobb that quantum physics does not necessarily lead to the conclusion that time is not real. For Griffin, Cobb, and Whitehead, even Einstein and quantum physicists who succeed him must attend to the unseen, intrinsic dynamics of physics. We can talk about time existentially as part of the intrinsic nature of events, human and nonhuman based on common sense experience.

[25]Here I am employing some of Jürgen Moltmann's language, which emphasizes that God is a spirit and that the Holy Spirit is an important person of the Trinity found in the church's living relationship with Christ. See, for example, Jürgen Moltmann, *The Spirit of Life: A Universal Affirmation,* trans. Margaret Kohl (Minneapolis: Fortress Press, 2001), 17–22, 29–77. On page 19, Moltmann introduces themes of the Spirit of Life and the dancer.

[26]Derived from notes on a sermon delivered by Dr. Renita Weems and Martin Espinosa, "A House Is Not a Home," St Luke "Community" United Methodist Church, Dallas, Texas, June 30, 2002. In this sermon, Weems and Espinosa refer to a rhythm and blues ballad by Luther Vandross in which he sings that "a house is not a home." The point of the sermon is that in a world where even the middle class, of any race, is two or three checks away from homelessness, it is inadvisable to confuse your house with your home. Only God can make a house a home. This is yet another example of the ways in which African American preachers and churches participate in multiple cultural forms, artfully blending the secular and the sacred to communicate the wisdom of the Spirit. Such aesthetic form and content are not approved of or accepted in all African American churches. Churches that participate in such cultural forms for articulating the Christian message, however, are generally very successful in outreach to the masses of African Americans.

[27]W. E. B. DuBois, "Our Spiritual Striving," in *The Souls of Black Folk,* 214.

[28]Paul Tillich, *Dynamics of Faith* (New York: Harper & Row, 1957), 80.

[29]Karen Baker-Fletcher, "Preface," *Sisters of Dust, Sisters of Spirit: Womanist Wordings on God and Creation* (Minneapolis: Fortress Press, 1998).

Chapter 3: The Breath of God

[1]Bruce Marshall, *Trinity and Truth* (Cambridge: Cambridge Univ. Press, 2000; Reprint 2002), 43, for example, writes that "The church believes that the triune God–the Father, the Son, and the Holy Spirit–creates redeems, and perfects the world; these actions and their significance may be attributed to the triune God and to no one else." Marshall's analysis of the Trinity is clear and precise. The only problem I have with it is that from a womanist or feminist perspective, his take on philosophy of language is rather rigid in its emphasis in employing exclusively classical sentence structures and names for God, restricting him to referring to God *always* as Father. "Father" is one of many metaphors one might employ to refer to the first person of the Trinity. Marshall sees it as "God's name." Father or "Abba," which is something like "Daddy," is one way of metaphorically designating the intimacy of a relational God. The Psalms, for example, refer to God as provider, and Exodus and Deuteronomy refer to God as being like a "mother eagle." The term "Father" designates the first agent of the Trinity as the generator of the Son or Word/Wisdom, who proceeds from the first agent of the Trinity. This is important to Trinitarians, because it emphasizes that Jesus as Son of God is of the same substance (*homoousios*) with the first person of the Trinity.

[2]Van A. Harvey, *A Handbook of Theological Terms: Their Meaning and Background Exposed in over 300 Articles* (New York: Touchstone, 1997), 228–29.

[3]Cappadocians include generally Basil of Caesarea (330–379), Gregory of Nyssa (331/40 to about 395), and Gregory of Nazianzus (330–390), leading Eastern theologians who were all born in the ancient region of Cappadocia, now central Turkey.

[4]Harvey, *Handbook,* 244. See also William G. Rusch, "Introduction," and Gregory of Nanzianzus, "Gregory of Nanzianzus's Third Theological Oration Concerning the Son," in *The Trinitarian Controversy,* trans. and ed. William G. Rusch (Philadelphia: Fortress Press, 1980), 23–24, 142–43.

[5]Sallie McFague, *Models of God* (Philadelphia: Fortress Press, 1987), 39. In McFague's words, "we can envision relating to God as to a father and a mother, to a healer and a liberator, to the sun and a mountain."

[6]Ibid., 42–43.

[7]See for example, Harvey, *Handbook,* 99–100, or Gerald Bray, "Filioque Controversy," *The Dictionary of Historical Theology,* ed. R. A. Hart (Grand Rapids: Eerdmans, 2000), 214–17.

[8]Delores Williams, *Sisters in the Wilderness: The Challenge of Womanist God-Talk* (Maryknoll, N.Y.: Orbis Books, 1993), 23.

[9]McFague, *Models of God,* 25, 31–36, 39. McFague's theology is metaphorical and heuristic (experimental). It investigates whether or not the model of God as "mother" can reinfuse some of the shock value of the most oft-used metaphor of "father." She wants to remind the reader of the "is" and "is not" of all metaphors for God. God is and is not a father, a mother, or a parent, she argues. These words are all metaphors from human, anthropomorphic experience.

[10]Marshall, *Trinity and Truth,* 14–16, 34–36. Marshall writes, "Since these words take masculine pronouns in English, and the reflexive character of pronouns has no adequate substitute in ordinary language, masculine pronouns will be used for God....Whether Christians ought to continue to talk to and about God in this way is of course now much debated. It will be evident that I think the answer to this question is yes"(14–16).

[11]"Can a mother forget the baby at her breast and have no compassion on the child she has borne? Though she may forget, I will not forget you!" (Isa. 49:15, NIV).

[12]John B. Cobb Jr. and Jeanyne B. Slettom, *The Process Perspective: Frequently Asked Questions about Process Theology* (St. Louis: Chalice Press, 2003); compare Terrence Fretheim, "El," in *New International Dictionary of Old Testament Theology and Exegesis,* ed. Willem A. Van Gemeren (Grand Rapids: Zondervan, 1997), 1.401: "the meaning of the name remains uncertain. Most often it is linked to mountains (hence, 'God, [one] of the mountain[s]'), as gods often were in the ANE. 'God of the breasts' has also been suggested. The translation "God Almighty' is based on the LXX [Septuagint]; an abstraction of an originally concrete image, this may reflect an educated guess as to meaning on the part of the LXX translators."

[13]I intentionally employ the phrase "mother's bosom" rather than "breast" for evangelical clergy and seminarians who ask, "But how can I share that with my congregation?" "How can I preach that?" "How can I say that in Bible study?" "Mother's bosom" may be a way of saying the same thing, without women feeling the pastor is objectifying women's bodies to speak about God, and it emphasizes the point: *God who is mighty also nurtures.* Candidates for ordained ministry and clergy need to know what the word *shaddai* literally means. Not every congregation member needs or wants to know. They do need to know, however, that "God who is mighty as a mountain" is also "like a nurturing mother who loves her young and draws them to her bosom." This is a sensitive way of saying the same thing and is in keeping with Jesus' later example of speaking in parables. While some liberal and radical feminists will not find this strong enough a statement, the fact is that the same type of feminists may be inclined to side with women who feel offended and accuse male or even female clergy of sexual harassment. So, the truth simply is *that knowledge of sexual imagery in scripture is sensitive knowledge and clergy must be wise in presenting it.* Women might be more comfortable hearing such truth in a women's Bible study, for example, and men in a men's Bible study. One may even have a woman pastor teach the women's Bible study and a male pastor teach the men's Bible study, since many larger churches have several pastors for teaching purposes. "The God of Israel is also like a nurturing mother in Hebrew understandings of God as almighty," is an even safer way for male clergy to speak of this. Thirteenth-century monks even spoke of being fed from Jesus' bosom. See Caroline Walker Bynum, *Jesus As Mother: Studies in the Spirituality of the High Middle Ages* (Berkley: Univ. of California Press, 1982).

[14]See Cobb and Slettom, *The Process Perspective.*

[15]*Hokmah* is the Hebrew term for wisdom, while *sophia* is the Greek term for wisdom.

[16]Elizabeth A. Johnson, *She Who Is: The Mystery of God in Feminist Theological Discourse* (New York: Crossroad, 2002), 86–100, 150–54, 165–69. See particularly Prov. 1:20–33; 4:13; 8:35; Job 28; Mt. 11:28–30; 23:37–39; Jn. 6:51; 7:28, 37; 10:14; 11:25; 14:6; 1 Cor. 1:22–24 and 12:12–26; Col. 1:15. Part of the mystery of scripture is its multiple and hidden meanings, which patriarchal interpreters of scripture have disguised with overlays of masculinized language. Johnson has uncovered a profound mystery, human-made, not God-veiled, in this case. The Jewish writers of scripture were far less hesitant to write of Wisdom in feminine terms, personifying her sometimes as God's first creation (Prov. 8) and at other times as a hypostasis of God. Overall, if Word/Wisdom (Logos) is with God since before the beginning according to John, then this is the Hokmah/Sophia of Proverbs 1, 4, and 8; Job 28, and the intertestamental literature of Sirach and the Wisdom of Solomon. Otherwise, Christians would need to create a new canon in which Genesis, Proverbs, and Job are excluded. Given that this is not an option for biblical Christians, one must learn to appreciate the truth revealed in reading of scripture, including the truth that the *Logos*, which means Word/Wisdom, includes and is Hokmah/Sophia of earlier, Holy Spirit inspired, biblical texts.

[17]While feminist thought informs this discussion, I am not seeking here to appease every feminist argument regarding God-language. My primary concern is authenticity to scripture and tradition, as well as to the diversity of ways of describing the God/Creation relationship.

[18]Specifically, according to Proverbs 8:22–31, Wisdom, who is personified as feminine, proclaims that "The Lord brought me forth as the first of his works, before his deeds of old; I was appointed from eternity, from the beginning, before the world began…I was there when [God] set the heavens in place, when he marked out the horizon on the face of the deep, when he established the clouds above and fixed securely the fountains of the deep, when he gave the sea its boundary so the waters would not overstep his command, and when he marked out the foundations of the earth. Then I was the craftsman at his side. I was filled with delight day after day, rejoicing always in his presence, rejoicing in his whole world and delighting in [humankind]."

[19]Athanasius, "Orations Against the Arians, *Book 1,*" in Rusch, ed., *The Trinitarian Controversy,* 88, 91.

[20]If this understanding appeared only in Ecclesiastes, which is part of the Wisdom literature and given lower rank in Jewish tradition than the Torah, some would argue questioning it. That this understanding also appears in Genesis, which is part of the Torah, gives this understanding significant authority.

[21]Gregory of Nanzianzus, "Gregory of Nanzianzus' Third Theological Oration," in William G. Rusch, *The Trinitarian Controversy* (Philadelphia: Fortress Press, 1980), 132–33, 142–43; and Gregory of Nyssa, "Gregory of Nyssa's Concerning We Should Think of Saying That There Are Not Three Gods to Ablabius," in William G. Rusch, *The Trinitarian Controversy,* 151–52, 154–57.

[22]Gregory of Nanzianzus, "Gregory of Nanzianzus' Third Oration," 142.

[23]Gregory of Nyssa, "Gregory of Nyssa's Concerning We Should Think of Saying That There Are Not Three Gods to Ablabius," 152.

[24]Ibid.

[25]Ibid.

[26]See Alice Walker, *In Search of Our Mothers' Gardens: Womanist Prose* (New York: Harcourt Brace Jovanovich, 1983), xi–xii.

[27]Alice Walker, *The Color Purple* (New York: Harcourt Brace Jovanovich, 1992), 166.

[28]Ibid., 167.

[29]Anthony B. Pinn, *African American Humanist Principles: Living and Thinking like the Children of Nimrod* (New York: Palgrave Macmillan, 2004), 7, 24–25. Pinn describes five principles that revolve around guiding norms of 1) understanding of humanity as fully (and solely) accountable and responsible for the human condition and the correction of humanity's plight; 2) suspicion toward or rejection of supernatural explanation and claims, combined with an understanding of humanity as an evolving part of the natural environment as opposed to being a created being (This can involve disbelief in God[s]); 3) an appreciation for American cultural production and a perception of traditional forms of black religiosity as having cultural importance as opposed to any type of "cosmic" authority; 4) a commitment to individual and societal transformation; 5) a controlled optimism that recognizes both human potential and human destructive activities.

[30]American Humanist Association, "Definitions of Humanism," http://www.americanhumanist.org/ humanism/definitions.htm.. While many ecotheologians might find the term "humanist" lacking in clarity as a precise way of naming Walker's attention to environmental concerns, the AHA is in fact concerned about human values in relation to an entire creation.

[31]Ibid.

[32]Alice Walker, *Now Is the Time to Open Your Heart: A Novel (*New York: Random House, 2004), 1–6, 196–97.

[33]Alice Walker, *The Same River Twice: Honoring the Difficult: A Meditation on Life, Spirit, Art, and the Making of the Film,* The Color Purple, *Ten Years Later* (New York: Scribner, 1996), 43.

[34]Alice Walker, "We Have a Beautiful Mother," in *Her Blue Body Everything We Know; Earthling Poems 1965–1990 Complete* (New York: Harcourt, Brace Jovanovich, 1991), 459–60.

[35]Alice Walker, *Living by the Word: Selected Writings, 1973–1987.* (San Diego: Harcourt Brace Jovanovich, 1988), 146.

[36]Charles Hartshorne, *Omnipotence and Other Theological Mistakes* (Albany, N.Y.: State Univ. of New York Press, 1984), 51–63; Alfred North Whitehead, *Process and Reality: An Essay in Cosmology,* corrected edition, ed. David Ray Griffin and Donald W. Sherburne (New York: The Free Press/MacMillan, 1978), 65–67, 108–9, 165–67, 343–45; John B. Cobb Jr. and David Ray Griffin, *Process Theology: An Introductory Exposition* (Philadelphia: Westminster Press, 1976), 13–26.

[37]Alice Walker, *The Color Purple,* 167.

[38]Karen Baker-Fletcher, *Sisters of Dust, Sisters of Spirit: Womanist Wordings on God and Creation (*Minneapolis: Fortress Press, 1998, 24–25), and Susan Niditch, "Genesis," in *The Women's Bible Commentary,* ed. Carol A. Newsom and Sharon H. Ringe (Louisville: Westminster John Knox Press, 1992), 13. See Catherine Keller, *The Face of the Deep: A Theology of Becoming (*New York: Routledge, 2002), 4–10, 18–24, 39–40, 43–64, 155–38 for a rich discussion of the biblical understanding of *creatio ex profundus* (creation out of the deep) in the book of Genesis in contrast to patristic understandings of *creatio ex nihilo* (creation out of nothing). See also her discussion of *tehom* (the deep) on pp. xiv–xvi, 213–31.

[39]Karen Baker-Fletcher, *A Singing Something: Womanist Reflections on Anna Julia Cooper* (New York: Crossroad, 1993), 64–65, and Anna Julia Cooper, "Equality of the Races and the Democratic Movement," (Washington, D.C.: Privately printed, 1945), 4–5.

[40]Psalm 19:1: "The heavens are telling the glory of God; and the firmament proclaims his handiwork." See Theodore Walker Jr., *Mothership Connections: A Black Atlantic Synthesis of Neoclassical Metaphysics and Black Theology* (Albany, N.Y.: State Univ. of New York Press, 2004), 16–18, 94–96.

[41]Alfred North Whitehead, *Science and the Modern World (*New York: MacMillan, 1925), 192. Specifically, Whitehead writes that "religion is the expression of one type of fundamental experiences of mankind.... Religion is the reaction of human nature to its search for God.... Religion is the vision of something which stands beyond, behind, and within, the passing flux of immediate things; something which is real, and yet waiting to be realized.... The immediate reaction of human nature to the religious vision is worship.... The vision claims nothing but worship; and worship is a surrender to the claim for assimilation, urged with the motive force of mutual love.... *The power of God is the worship he inspires.... The worship of God is not a rule of safety–it is an adventure of the spirit, a flight after the unattainable"* [emphasis mine](190–92).

[42]R. S. Pine-Coffin, trans., *Saint Augustine: Confessions,* (Hammondsworth, England: Penguin Books, 1961), Bk. 1.1–6.

[43]Karen Baker-Fletcher, "Something or Nothing: An Eco-Womanist Essay on God, Creation, and Indispensability," in *This Sacred Earth,* ed. Roger Gottlieb (New York: Routledge, 2003).

[44]Karen Baker-Fletcher, "Nativity and Wildness," *Sisters of Dust, Sisters of Spirit,* 21–25.

[45]Karen Baker-Fletcher, "Nativity and Wildness," *Sisters of Dust, Sisters of Spirit,* 25; compare Susan Niditch, "Genesis," in *The Women's Bible Commentary,* 13.

[46]Niditch, "Genesis," 13.

[47]Keller, *The Face of the Deep: A Theology of Becoming* (London and New York: Routledge, 2003), 4–24, 217–20.

[48]Leonardo Boff, *Cry of the Earth, Cry of the Poor* (Maryknoll, N.Y.: Orbis Books, 1997).

[49]Ibid., 53–54.

[50]Anselm, *Proslogion,* in Anselm of Caterbury, *The Prayers and Meditations of Saint Anselm with the Proslogion,* trans. Sister Benedecta Ward, S.L.G. (Hammondsworth, England: Penguin Books, 1973), 247.

[51]Hartshorne, *Omnipotence and Other Theological Mistakes,* 76.

[52]Ibid., 74–80.

[53]See Delores Williams, *Sisters in the Wilderness: The Challenge of Womanist God-Talk* (Maryknoll, N.Y.: Orbis Books, 1993), 198. Williams writes that God provides Hagar and African American women with "*new vision* to see revival resources where [they] saw none before."

[54]For the original, longer discussion of these issues, see Karen Baker-Fletcher, "Something or Nothing." The present discussion is a significant revision of my earlier publication.

[55]Peter and other Jewish Christians came to understand Jesus as the Christ (Mt. 16:16), because Jesus does only what the promised Messiah can do: forgive sins, save, and redeem. Only the Messiah can do what God does, and Jesus does what God does.

[56]See Karen Baker-Fletcher, *Sisters of Dust, Sisters of Spirit,* chaps. 1–4 for earlier discussions of this material.

Chapter 4: Even the Rocks Cry Out

[1]Charles Hartshorne, *Omnipotence and Other Theological Mistakes* (Albany: State Univ. of New York, 1984), 2–4, 10–26.

[2]Ibid., 14, 62, 106–7.

[3]See the very practical comments of Cathy Peterson, *Call Me If You Need Anything...and Other Things Not to Say: A Guide to Helping Others through Tragedy and Grief* (St. Louis: Chalice Press, 2005).

[4]Seminarians often comment that it is impossible "to preach theology." In point of fact, every preacher presents his or her theology each time they enter the pulpit. What seminarians mean is that they cannot present a formal theology paper from the pulpit. Clearly, one does not preach an academic theology paper from the pulpit. One preaches a sermon that is well informed by careful biblical and theological research. A sermon is not a theology essay. It is always, however, informed by one's theological position on the nature of God. Whether intended to be or not, a pastor's theology is always evident in the sermon's content. Likewise, the theological positions of the laity are always evident in their God-talk, whether given in a Bible teaching group or in an informal conversation. Theology, whether it is sound or unsound, academic or nonacademic, is God-talk. One's theology is exposed in the very process of delivering a sermon, engaging in informal conversation about God, offering pastoral counseling, or presenting a systematic theological essay. Some theologians, like Gordon Kaufman, for example, refer to this as "first order theology." See Gordon D. Kaufman, *In Face of Mystery: A Constructive Theology* (Cambridge: Harvard Univ. Press, 1993), 18–31.

[5]Ibid., 1–49.

[6]Ibid., 2–4, 6–27.

[7]Alfred North Whitehead, *Process and Reality: An Essay in Cosmology,* corrected edition, ed. David Ray Griffin and Donald W. Sherburne (New York: The Free Press/MacMillan, 1978), 27–28.

[8]John Calvin, *Institutes of the Christian Religion, II,* trans. Henry Beveridge (Grand Rapids: Eerdmans, 1983), chaps. 21, 22, 24.

[9]See Theodore Walker Jr., *Mothership Connections: A Black Atlantic Synthesis of Neoclassical Metaphysics and Black Theology* (Albany, N.Y.: State Univ. of New York Press, 2004), 55–59 and 62–63.

[10]Marjorie Hewitt Suchocki, *God, Christ, Church: A Practical Guide to Process Theology* (New York: Crossroad, 1982; rev. 1989), 259.

[11]Hartshorne, *Omnipotence,* 1–32, 45.

[12]Ibid., 44–49.

[13]Suchocki, *God, Christ, Church,* 17–19, 27, 220–23; and idem, *The Fall to Violence: Original Sin in Relational Theology* (New York: Continuum, 1995), 16–30, 31–79.

[14]Suchocki, *God, Christ, Church,* 210–15.

[15]I am deeply indebted to Suchoki, *God, Christ, Church,* 66–73, for Suchoki's keen integrative and relational analysis of divine feeling, knowledge, and possibilites for becoming here.

[16]Anselm, *Proslogion,* in Anselm of Canterbury, *The Prayers And Meditations of Saint Anselm with the Proslogion,* trans. Sister Benedicta Ward, S.L.G. (Hammondsworth, England: Penguin Books, 1973), 244–45.

[17]Suchocki, *God, Christ, Church,* 15–24, and *The Fall to Violence,* 16–30, 31–79.

[18]See Suchocki, *The Fall to Violence,* 16–65, 82–100.

Chapter 5: Your Brother's Blood

[1]Written interview response by Vanessa Baker, April 20, 2005.

[2]Ibid.

[3]Gayraud Wilmore, *Black Religion and Black Radicalism: An Interpretation of the Religious History of Afro-American People,* 2d ed. (Maryknoll, N.Y.: Orbis, 1983), 7–8, 12–13, 15, 238–241.

[4]W. E. B. DuBois, for example, refers to the Negro Spirituals as "sorrow songs," although some were also celebrative. See W. E. B. DuBois, "The Souls of Black Folk" in *Three Negro Classics: Up From Slavery, The Souls of Black Folk The Autobiography of an Ex-Colored Man,* ed. John Hope Franklin (New York: Avon, 1965).

[5]Delores S. Williams, "Sin, Nature, and Black Women's Bodies," in *Ecofeminism and the Sacred,* ed. Carol Adams (New York: Continuum, 1993),24–29.

[6]Marjorie Suchocki, The Fall to Violence: Original Sin in Relational Theology (New York: Continuum, 1995).

[7]Ibid..

[8]Coleman, "Walking in the Whirlwind: A Whiteheadian Womanist Soteriology," Ph.D. dissertation, Claremont Graduate University, 2004, 27. See also Henry James Young, *Hope in Process* (Minneapolis: Fortress Press, 1990), 130–32.

[9]Augustine, *Confessions* (New York: Image/Doubleday, 1960), Book I.1 and 5–6, Book II. 1–10.

[10]Augustine, *Confessions,* Book I.1 and 5–6, Book II.1–10, Book VI.16, Book VII.1–5. Reinhold Niebuhr, *Moral Man and Immoral Society* (New York: Charles Scribner's Sons, 1932;1960), 51–60, 66–67. 69–70. Note, however, that Niebuhr applauds Augustine's realism while criticizing a "note of defeatism" in Augustine's theology, which in Niebuhr's view "creeps easily into a rigorous religion, with its drift toward dualism." Reinhold Niebuhr, *The Nature and Destiny of Man* (New York: Charles Scribner's Sons, 1943; 1964), 30, 40–41, 43–44, 115–16, 134–40. Marjorie Suchocki, *The Fall to Violence* (New York: Continuum, 1995), 12–13, 14, 16, 18–19, 21–29, 31–32, 95, 164.

[11]Paul Tillich, *Systematic Theology,* vol. 2 (Chicago: The University of Chicago Press, 1957), 36–39, 44–59. See also Paul Tillich, *Systematic Theology,* vol. 3 (Chicago: The University of Chicago Press, 1963, 285–86; Paul Tillich, *The Courage to Be* (New York: MacMillan, 1984), 52–54, 75–77, and 125–27; and Paul Tillich, *Biblical Religion and the Search for Ultimate Reality* (Chicago: The University of Chicago Press, 1955), 55–56.

[12]See for example, Augustine, *Confessions* in *Saint Augustine: Confessions,* ed. R. S. Pine-Coffin (Hammondsworth, Middlesex, England: Penguin Books, 1961), Bk 8:7–12; Reinhold Niebuhr, *The Nature and Destiny of Man,* vol. 1 (New York: Charles Scribner's Sons, 1941, 1964); Marjorie Suchocki, *The Fall to Violence,*16–29, 29–46.

[13]Ibid.

[14]Andrew Sung Park, *The Wounded Heart of God: The Asian Concept of Han and the Christian Doctrine of Sin* (Nashville: Abingdon Press, 1993), 15–30.

[15]Ibid., 15.

[16]Ibid., 15–20.

[17]Ibid., 38–40. Here, Park employs Carl Jung's understanding of "unconscious," in which the unconscious is a source of archetypes, memories, relics of the past, and symbols. Park goes beyond Jung to note that in his own usage of the term "collective unconscious," this *han* takes over only "the structure of han-memory," not "the content of the han of previous generations."

[18]Ibid.

[19]Ibid., 40.

[20]Delores S. Williams, *Sisters In the Wilderness: The Challenge of Womanist God-Talk* (Maryknoll, N.Y.: Orbis, 1993), 161–67.

[21]Karen Baker-Fletcher, *My Sister, My Brother: Womanist And Xodus God-Talk* (Maryknoll, N.Y.: Orbis, 1997), 75–82.

[22]Ibid. and Williams, *Sisters In the Wilderness*, 161–67.

[23]See James Cone, *The Spirituals and the Blues* (New York: Seabury Press, 1972; reprint, Maryknoll: Orbis Books, 2004), 1–7, 20–31, 53–77, and 97–127 for a strong and sound discussion of the Negro spirituals as a cultural form that expresses the relationship between God and black suffering as well as an equally strong and sound discussion of the blues as a cultural form that might be called "secular spirituals." In other words, both forms of music express one set of common, plaintive blue notes in the midst of hope against hope in human experience from the souls of black folk.

[24]Keening in Irish culture is "to cry out or wail in grief." It is a form of lament. *Webster's Dictionary of the English Language, Second Edition, Encarta* (New York and London: Bloomsbury, 1999; 2004).

[25]Ricardo Ainslie, *Long Dark Road: Bill King and Murder in Jasper, Texas* (Austin: University of Texas Press, 2004), xi–xiii, 1–10, 234–35.

[26]Korean theologian Park Seong Joon, a doctoral candidate at Perkins School of Theology and a student in the Advanced Feminist Theory class Dr. Martha Satz and I taught, emphasizes that *han* also includes love. Specifically, Park observes, there is "jeong" in *han*. *Jeong* is a form of compassion particularly, but not exclusively, experienced by women in Korea who are among the *minjung* of the *minjung*, the sinned against of the sinned against, or the oppressed of the oppressed. Similarly, the blues of Bessie Smith and the spirituals as sung by black women in America, represent the lament, hope, love, and resentment of the oppressed of the oppressed in African American experience and culture. Globally, women and children are among the poorest of the poor and the most afflicted among the afflicted by murder, assault, abuse, and the grief of loss (of loved ones, homes, and family). No doubt, this was true during Jesus' lifetime as well, which is why he emphasized not only love of neighbor–male and female–but also liberty and healing of the poor, the brokenhearted, and the bruised (Lk. 4:18). The author of the book of James understands "pure religion" as "care for the fatherless and widows in their affliction" in keeping with Malachi 3:5 and Psalm 10:14.

[27]From 1882 through 1968, 4,743 documented lynchings occurred in the United States, predominantly but not exclusively in the South. Of these, 3,446 lynchings were of African Americans, while 1,297 were of white Americans. Southern lynchings accounted for most of the reported lynchings of African Americans from 1882 to 1968. The Web site http://www.law.umkc.edu/faculty/projects/ftrials/shipp/lynchingsstate.html, based on statistics from the archives of Tuskegee Institute, claims that there were 4,743 total lynchings, including 3,446 lynchings of African Americans. The statistics for lynchings of African Americans in Southern states are as follows: Alabama 299, Arkansas 226, Florida 257, Georgia 492, Kentucky 142, Louisiana 335, Mississippi 539, South Carolina 156, Tennessee 204, Texas 352. In border states, some of which many would call Southern, the statistics are: Maryland 27, Missouri 69, North Carolina 86, Virginia 83, and West Virginia 28. In addition, there were 2 in California, 3 in Colorado, 1 in Delaware, 19 in Illinois, 14 in Indiana, 2 in Iowa, 19 in Kansas, 1 in Michigan, 4 in Minnesota, 2 in Montana, 5 in Nebraska, 1 in New Jersey, 3 in New Mexico, 1 in New York, 3 in North Dakota, 16 in Ohio, 40 in Oklahoma, 1 in Oregon, 6 in Pennsylvania, 2 in Utah, 1 in Washington, and 5 in Wyoming, from Only 7 states had 0 documented lynchings of African Americans: Arizona, Idaho, Maine, Nevada, South Dakota, Vermont and Wisconsin (six states are not included in the online statistics–Alaska, Connecticut, Hawaii, Massachusetts, New Hampshire, and Rhode Island). See also Jacqueline Jones Roster, ed., *Southern Horrors and Other Writings: The Anti-Lynching Campaign of Ida B. Wells, 1892–1900* (Boston and New York: Bedford Books, 1997) for Ida B. Wells-Barnett's early research, statistics, and writings in her publications: *Southern Horrors: Lynch Law in All Its Phases,* 1892; *A Red Record,* 1895; and *Mob Rule in New Orleans,* 1900. Royster's volume includes all three of these primary publications by Wells-Barnett in their entirety. Finally, see Emilie Townes, *Womanist Justice, Womanist Hope* (Atlanta: Scholars Press, 1993), 131, for a theo-ethical analysis of Wells-Barnett's thought and work in the wider context of the historical anti-lynching campaign and for womanist ethics today. Townes observes that one of the striking features of the statistics that the National Association for the Advancement of Colored People (NAACP) documented for the years 1889 to 1919 is a 5.6 percent rate of "no crimes charged" in the cases of documented lynchings. They also documented a 12 percent statistic for "miscellaneous crimes" that people were lynched for, 35.5 percent for accusations of murder, and 28.4 percent for accusations of rape and attacks on women. Much of Wells-Barnett's work, as well as that of others, was to shatter the myth that so many black men who were lynched had actually raped white women. Some researchers, Townes observes, refer to the myth of black men as rampant, ravaging, rapists of

white women, requiring the protection of white women from all black men, as "folk pornography."

[28]Jana Evans Braziel, "History of Lynching in the United States," Table 2–5, ACLA Syllabi & Documents & Documents, obtained through www.umass.edu Web site.

[29]The Federal Bureau of Investigation releases a regular report on *Hate Crime Statistics,* explaining, "Each year's edition of *Hate Crime Statistics* presents data regarding incidents, offenses, victims, and offenders in reported crimes that were motivated in whole or in part by a bias against the victim's perceived race, religion, ethnicity, sexual orientation, or disability." Federal Bureau of Investigation, *Hate Crime Statistics,* http://www.fbi.gov/ucr/ucr.htm#hate.

[30]Rape, Abuse, & Incest National Network, *http://www.rainn.org,* based on the U.S. Department of Justice's 2002 National Crime Victimization survey and statistics.

[31]I refer here to the highly acclaimed, richly researched, trial-based, and interview-based work of Joyce King, *Hate Crime: The Story of a Dragging in Jasper, Texas* (New York: Anchor Books, 2003) While there are other books about the Byrd case, Joyce King's volume is the most original and accurate. The Byrd Family, Sheriff Billy Rowles, and other Jasperites have endorsed King's research and writing on the Byrd case as 100 percent accurate..King is an African American native Texan.

[32]Augustine, *Confessions,* book 3, chap.7.

[33]King, *Hate Crime,* 16–17, 21–22.

[34]Ibid.

[35]Ibid., 23.

[36]Ibid., 23–24.

[37]Ibid., 24.

[38]Ibid.

[39]Ibid., 25.

[40]Ibid.,26.

[41]Ibid., 26–27, 158

[42]Ibid., 167.

[43]Ibid., 26–27, 125.

[44]Joyce King, *Hate Crime,* Ricardo Ainslie, *Long Dark Road,* 42–43. Ainslie's analysis is thin, largely because, as Ainslie admits, "John William King wants to be remembered as an "enigma" and will not allow anyone to look too deeply into his psyche. I have attempted to note overlap in Ainslie's largely derivative work with Joyce King's earlier work as much as possible. Ainslie's psychological analysis of John William King, however, has some kernels of insight regarding how a troubled youth might become a notorious murderer.

[45]King, *Hate Crime,* 19, 128.

[46]Ibid.

[47]From http://www.cnn.com/US/9807/06/dragging.death.02, and Joyce King, *Hate Crime,* 25, 43–44, 119–120.

[48]King, *Hate Crime,* 5–7, 13–22, 24–25, 88–89, 94–112.

[49]Ainslie, *Long Dark Road,* 79–80. Ainslie's findings through his interviews with John William King are fairly consistent with Joyce King's earlier findings documented in *Hate Crime.* It is impossible to join a gang and find protection from other gangs without first proving you will stand up and fight. Moreover, newcomers must fight back to avoid even worse attacks, including being raped. See Joyce King, *Hate Crime* 128, 110–11.

[50]King, *Hate Crime,* 110–11, 128, 210. King writes (p. 210): "nonviolent offenders do not belong in prison units with inmates with a higher propensity for violence. They all too easily become immovable targets. It would not hurt Texas to modify its classification system for inmates, which helps officials determine where offenders will be housed and what kind of jobs they will be assigned. John William King, despite his defiant attitude and criminal mistakes, was one burglar who did not belong at the Beto Unit." See also Ainslie, *Long Dark Road,* 79–81. Ainslie finds that not fighting back would have made King vulnerable to further attack by other prisoners in the Beto Unit. New prisoners must prove they will stand and fight.

[51]Ibid., 96.

[52]Samuel Beckett, *Waiting for Godot: A Tragi-Comedy in Two Acts* (New York: Grove Press, 1954; 1982.) This play, which comes under the genre of "theater of the absurd," is about two men who wait continually for "Godot," who never comes, in the midst of a mundane existence that never changes. Prisoners were said to understand this play by Beckett more deeply than general audiences.

[53]I encourage readers to read Victor Hugo, *Les Miserables* (New York: Signet Books, 1987) in its entirety or to view the film version, which is much shorter and based on the play that is often performed in theaters.

[54]Fyodor Dostoevsky, *Crime and Punishment* (New York: Bantam Classics, 1984). For those who are not familiar with this classic text, I recommend reading this carefully-researched, in-depth psychological study in its entirety.

[55]Thomas Harris, *The Silence of the Lambs* (New York: St. Martin's Paperbacks, 1991). Ricardo Ainslie, *Long Dark Road,* 8–9.

[56] King, *Hate Crime,* 97–112.

[57]Stephen Dove, "Byrd Son Fighting for Life of Killer," *Houston Chronicle,* 2002, posted March 10, 2004, http://www.chron.com/cs/CDA/ssistory.mpl/special/jasper/latestnews/1482477.

[58]Karl Barth, *The Humanity of God* (Louisville: Westminster John Knox Press, 1960), 37–68.

[59]King, *Hate Crime,* 209.

[60]Park, *The Wounded Heart of God,* 40.

[61] Joyce King, *Hate Crime,* 210..

[62]Associated Press, "Byrd Family Relieved Act Passed," http://www.chron.com/cs/CDA/ssistory.mpl/special/jasper/latestnews/907487.

[63]David Ray Griffin and Donald W. Sherburne, eds., Alfred North Whitehead, *Process and Reality, Corrected Edition,* (New York and London: Free Press, 1978), 346.

[64]Coleman, *Walking in the Whirlwind,*47.

[65]Tammerie Spires, presentation on "Racial Healing," for Karen Baker-Fletcher's course "Feminist, Womanist, and Mujerista Theology: Women and Theology," October 18, 2005.

[66]Ainslie, *Long Dark Road,*8–9, 234–35.

[67]Paul Tillich, *Systematic Theology,* vol. 3 (Chicago: University of Chicago Press, 1963), 102–6. Tillich refers to and discusses "the demonic" in relation to distortions of divine revelation and self-transcendence sporadically throughout his three-volume *Systematic Theology,* offering a more clear and sustained discussion in vol. 3. For Tillich, the "demonic" "distorts self-transcendence by identifying a particular bearer of holiness with the holy itself" (102) and "suppresses honest obedience to the structures of truth" (106). See also Paul Tillich, *The Courage to Be* (New Haven and London: Yale University Press, 1952), 33–34, 39, 58–60, 128–30 for an earlier, but less clear understanding of what Tillich means by the term.

[68]My emphasis on "God in Christ in the power of the Holy Spirit" throughout this book is derived only in part from Jürgen Moltmann, *The Church in the Power of the Spirit: A Contribution to Messianic Ecclesiology* (San Francisco: Harper, 1977), in which Moltmann emphasizes the unifying, ecclesial, empowering work of the Holy Spirit that is revealed through Christ, the head of the Church, who is the messiah promised to Israel and proceeds from the first person of the Trinity. I share a similar understanding with Moltmann simply because of my communal reading of scripture, Wesleyan background, and Charismatic evangelical Christian experience, in which the first person of the Trinity so loves the world as to send Christ into the world and Christ sends the Holy Spirit to empower, to encourage, to teach, and to comfort. See Jn. 1:1–14; 3:16–21, 31–36; 14:25–31; 15:26–27; 16:7–15. Moltmann is one of the few theologians of the twentieth century to take such understanding, which was already present in the book of John and in Christian experience, seriously. For this reason, it is not unusual for Charismatic evangelical and Pentecostal Christians to find some areas of common ground and opportunities for meaningful dialogue in Moltmann's work.

[69]Ainslie, *Long Dark Road,* 93–97, 126. Ainslie refers to the depth of King's violent rage and turmoil as "self-loathing."

Chapter 6: The Pulse of God

[1]Elizabeth Johnson, *She Who Is: The Mystery of God in Feminist Theological Discourse* (New York: Crossroad, 1992), 87–88, 90–91, 241–45, 246–54.

[2]An excellent introduction to this material is available in William C. Placher and Robert W. Jenson, "How Does Jesus Make a Difference?" in *Essentials of Christian Theology,* ed. William C. Placher (Louisville: Westminster John Knox Press, 2003), 183–91, 197–200. See also Serene Jones and Paul Lakeland, eds., *Constructive Theology: A Contemporary Approach to Classical Themes* (Minneapolis: Fortress, 2005), 167–69.

[3]Robert W. Jenson, "How Does Jesus Make a Difference?" 199–200.

[4]The problem for Gentile or non-Jewish Christians reading the gospel of John is a historical interpretive tendency to assume that the fourth gospel endorses anti-Jewishness. It is important to understand that this gospel represents internal dialogue in the same way that Americans, for example, might have an internal discussion of the strengths and weaknesses of Americans or the ways in which Christians challenge one another today across diversity of Christian traditions and denominations. Contemporary Christians must remember that Jesus and his disciples, as well as the first crowds Jesus preached to, *were Jewish*. Moreover, the first Christians in Acts as well as many in Paul's letters were Jewish.

[5]Alice Walker, "A Name Is Sometimes an Ancestor Saying, Hi I'm with You," in Walker, *Living by the Word: Selected Writings 1973–1987* (New York: Harcourt Brace Jovanovich, 1998), 97–98.

[6]Sojourner Truth, *Narrative of Sojourner Truth,* ed. Margaret Washington (New York: Vintage Books/Random House, 1993), xxii–xxvix, 49–53, 87–88.

[7]Billy Abraham, *The Logic of Evangelism* (Grand Rapids, Mich.: Wm. B. Eerdmans, 1989), 97–135, 174–78.

[8]Truth, *Narrative,* 86–88. See also Karen Baker-Fletcher, "Truth, Sojourner," in *Dictionary of Biblical Interpretation,* ed. John H. Hayes (Nashville: Abingdon Press, 1999), 592–93.

[9]Anthony Pinn, *Why Lord? Suffering and Evil in Black Theology* (New York: Continuum, 1995), 9–10.

[10]Ibid.

[11]Ibid.

[12]Ibid.

[13]Ibid., 141, 157.

[14]Ibid., 157.

[15]Ibid. There are black evangelical Christians who are alternately angered or troubled by Anthony Pinn's work. One imagines that evangelicals generally would be critical of his work. Given my own evangelical leanings, which are moderate, I understand the shock Pinn's work has created for some. The shock value of Pinn's work is good. If there is a Christian answer to the problem of hatred and evil, other than the notion that suffering is redemptive, then we need books that shock well-meaning Christians into communicating our faith around issues of theodicy more clearly. I look at Pinn's work as the honest reflection of a theologian who, like some of his ancestors, is weary of asking "Why Lord?" His questions are not so different from Job's in the Hebrew Bible, or from Jacob's, who tested the strength of an angel until he received a blessing (Gen. 32:24–32). While Pinn's conclusions are different from Job's and Jacob's in that he denies the existence of God, challenging "God" with human achievement like Nimrod (Gen. 10:8–9; 1 Chr. 1:10; Mic. 5:6}, one wonders if Job may have done likewise without his whirlwind experience of the Divine. It is important to take Pinn's questions seriously enough to look for Christian responses that are credible and concretely viable. Moreover, his work is important for understanding why some who know suffering cannot reconcile the existence of evil with a theistic, let alone Christian, worldview. The questions such men, women, and children raise are the questions Christians are accountable for answering in a world of crucifixion.

[16]Ibid., 146–47.

[17]In the novel, Celie knows no other name for husband except Mister. This is a literary device that Alice Walker employs and is in keeping with the genre of nineteenth- and early twentieth-century slave narratives, as well as women's narratives in general during the same historical period.

[18]Alice Walker, *The Color Purple* (New York and London: Harcourt Brace Jovanovich, 1982), 164–65.

[19]Evelyn C. White, *Alice Walker* (New York and London: W.W. Norton & Co., 2004), 18–21, 334–38, 359.

[20]Alice Walker, *In Search of Our Mothers' Gardens* (New York: Harcourt Brace Jovanovich, 1983), 265.

[21]Ibid.

[22]Alice Walker, "Womanist," in ibid., xii.

[23]Alice Walker, *The Same River Twice: Honoring the Difficult* (New York: Scribner, 1996), 25.

[24]Howard Thurman, *Jesus and the Disinherited* (Friends United Press: Richmond, Indiana: 1981), 13–35; Howard Thurman, *With Head and Heart: The Autobiography of Howard Thurman* (San Diego and New York: Harvest Books, Harcourt Brace and Company, 1981).

[25]See, for example, Abraham Smith, *Comfort One Another: Reconstructing the Rhetoric and Audience of 1 Thessalonians* (Louisville: Westminster John Knox Press, 1995) and Abraham Smith, "Unmasking the Powers: Toward a Postcolonial Analysis of 1 Thessalonians," in *Paul and the Roman Imperial Order,* ed. Richard Horsley (New York and London: Continuum, 2004). In Smith's interpretation and analysis, Paul is critical of the pro-Roman aristocracy in Thessalonica.

[26]Alice Walker, "The Only Reason You Want to Go to Heaven Is That You Have Been Driven Out of Your Mind," in *Anything We Love Can Be Saved* (New York: Random House, 1997), 18.

[27]Walker, *Anything We Love Can Be Saved,* 25.

[28]I am playing on Johannine and early Christian understandings, particularly in the writings of Athanasius, of Jesus as *Logos. Logos* means word or knowledge. It is associated with wisdom. See John 1:1 in any translation of the New Testament. See also Athanasius, "Orations Against the Arians, Book I," in *The Trinitarian Controversy,* ed. and trans. William G. Rusch (Philadelphia: Fortress, 1980), 87–88. Also, see Alice Walker, *Living by the Word: Selected Writings, 1973–1987* (New York: Harcourt, Brace, Jovanovich, 1980), 1–2. Walker's understanding of what it means to "Live by the Word" comes from a dream of a "two-headed woman" or root worker who she believes to be a healer and a wise woman. In the dream, the woman told Walker to "Live by the Word and keep walking." I am playing on Walker's understanding, deliberately contrasting it with a specifically Christian understanding in which Jesus the Christ is the Word, the Logos, the very knowledge that is with God at creation. For a Christian womanist, living by the Word means to walk with Jesus. In Walker's work the meaning is deliberately vague and may very well be something else entirely. My argument here is that if Jesus' message of love is true as Walker acknowledges, then there is no good reason *not* to follow the living Word or Logos incarnate in Jesus. My goal here is not to "make" Walker Christian or a follower of Jesus, but to note some of the ambivalence in her work, re black people who follow Jesus and the contradictions in her work regarding the value of biblical literature.

[29]Countee Cullen, "Christ Recrucified," in *Witnessing Lynching: American Writers Respond,* ed. Anne P. Rice and Michele Wallace (New Brunswick, New Jersey, and London: Rutgers University Press, 2003), 222. The authors note that this poem was first published in *Kelley's Magazine,* October 1922. See also Countee Cullen, *The Black Christ and Other Poems* (New York: Harper and Brothers, 1929) for Cullen's lengthier poem "The Black Christ."

[30]Jonathan Markovitz, *Legacies of Lynching: Racial Violence and Memory* (Minneapolis and London: University of Minnesota Press, 2004), 21. Markovitz includes the photograph of Ms. Nelson, giving credit to the Allen-Littlefield Collection, Special Collections Division, Robert W. Woodruff Library, Emory University.

[31]Ibid., 137–38.

[32]W. E. B. DuBois, "Jesus Christ in Texas," in *Dark Water: Voices from Within the Veil* (1920; reprint, New York: AMS Press, 1969), 123–33.

[33]Ibid., 129–33.

[34]Ibid., 133.

[35]Lynching totals from http://www.law.umkc.edu/faculty/projects/ftrials/shipp/lynchingsstate.html. More such statistics are cited in chapter 5.

[36]Written interview response by Vanessa Baker, April 20, 2005.

[37]See Markovitz, xxv–xxviii and 26–28. Also, written interview responses by Vanessa Baker, April 20, 2005.

[38]Markovitz, *Legacies of Lynching,* 138–41.

[39]A reprint of the full poem may be found in Anne P. Rice and Michele Wallace, eds., *Witnessing Lynching,* 269. Rice notes the primary sources for the poem as *Contempo* (December 1931): 1; reprinted in *Scottsboro, Limited* (New York: Golden Stair Press, 1932) n.p.

[40]Ibid.

[41]Go to TheBlackMarket.com (http://www.theblackmarket.com/ProfilesInBlack/JCameron.htm) for an interview, biography, and news report on James Cameron's story. Cameron is also author of *A Time of Terror* (Baltimore: Black Classic Press, 1994). In this

volume, Cameron discusses his experience and the historical context of the lynching of African Americans in detail.

[42]Ibid.

[43]H. Richard Niebuhr writes of the relationship between Christ and culture as an enduring problem. He then goes on to present five types of christologies or representations of Christ. Here, I refer to the cross as an enduring symbol that highlights the tensions between Christ and human culture with its invented tools of destruction, derivative from nature, in a world of crucifixion or unnecessary violence. See H. Richard Niebuhr, *Christ and Culture* (New York: Harper & Row, 1951), 1–11.

[44]J. Denny Weaver, *The Nonviolent Atonement* (Grand Rapids, Mich.: Wm. B. Eerdmans, 2001), 1–7, 12–69, 166–68, 210–28. On pp. 12–69, Weaver focuses on the understanding of Christ overcoming evil in the New Testament and its connection with First Testament understandings of divine victory over evil. On pp. 210–28, Weaver compares the early church's Christus Victor doctrine with Anselm's much later, twelfth-century theory. See also Gustaf Aulen, *Christus Victor: An Historical Study of the Three Main Types of the Idea of Atonement,* trans. A.G. Herbert (New York: Macmillan Publishing, 1969). Gustaf Aulen was a retired Swedish Lutheran bishop when he published his work on the Christus Victor doctrine of Atonement, finding this doctrine represented by Luther, neglected texts in the New Testament, and in the thought of early Christians before Anselm.

[45]The word *satan* means adversary. All that is adversarial to God is "satan" or "evil."

[46]An ethic of risk clarifies the actual meaning of "sacrifice" and what it means to be willing to give something valuable to the world knowing that it may reject the gift or try to destroy the gift and the giver. Therefore, the terms "risk" and "sacrifice" become synonymous. See Sharon Welch, *A Feminist Ethic of Risk* (Minneapolis: Fortress Press, 1990).

[47]See for example, Joanne Terrell, *Power in the Blood? The Cross in the African American Experience* (Maryknoll, N.Y.: Orbis, 1998), 105–44.

[48]Weaver, *The Nonviolent Atonement,* 15.

[49]Ibid., 16–17.

[50]Lk. 23:34, Mt. 6:12.

[51]Mamie Till-Mobley and Christopher Benson, *Death of Innocence: The Story of the Hate Crime That Changed America* (New York: Random House, 2003), 130–200.

[52]Written interview responses by Vanessa Baker, April 20, 2005.

[53]Ibid.

[54]Ibid.

[55]Till-Mobley, *Death.*

[56]See Evelyn Parker, *Trouble Don't Last Always: Emancipatory Hope Among African American Adolescents* (Cleveland: Pilgrim Press, 2003), 141–44, for a discussion of holy indignation.

[57]Lyrics and music by Lewis Allan, 1940. According to a Public Broadcasting Station (PBS) Web site on the PBS film, also entitled "Strange Fruit": "While many people assume that the song "Strange Fruit" was written by Holliday herself, it actually began as a poem by Abel Meeropol, a Jewish schoolteacher and union activist from the Bronx who later set it to music. Disturbed by a photograph of a lynching, the teacher wrote the stark verse and brooding melody under the pseudonym Lewis Allan in the late 1930s. Meeropol and his wife Anne are also notable because they adopted Robert and Michael Rosenberg, the orphaned children of the executed communists Julius and Ethel Rosenberg." See http://www.pbs.org/independentlens/strangefruit/film.html.

[58]See chapter 7.

Chapter 7: More than Suffering

[1]See also Howard Thurman, "Whither Shall I Go From Thy Presence" and "If I Ascend Into Heaven, Thou Art There!" in *For the Inward Journey: The Writings of Howard Thurman,* ed. Anne Spencer Thurman (Richmond, Ind.: Friends United Press, 1984), 106–7. The NRSV translation was not available to him.

[2]John B. Cobb Jr. and David Ray Griffin, *Process Theology: An Introductory Exposition* (Philadelphia: The Westminster Press, 1976), 49.

[3]"When the day of Pentecost had come, they were all together in one place. And suddenly from heaven there came a sound like the rush of a violet wind, and it filled the entire house where they were sitting. Divided tongues, as of fire, appeared among them, and a tongue

rested on each of them. All of them were filled with the Holy Spirit and began to speak in other languages, as the Spirit gave them ability" (Acts 2:1–4).

[4]Diana L. Hayes, *And Still We Rise* (New Jersey: Paulist Press, 1996), 178.

[5]Ibid., 178.

[6]Ibid., 173.

[7]Ibid.,178.

[8]Ibid.

[9]Delores Williams, *Sisters in the Wilderness: The Challenge of Womanist God-Talk* (Maryknoll, New York: Orbis, 1993), 179–84.

[10] See Cheryl Townsend Gilkes, *If It Wasn't for the Women* (Maryknoll: Orbis, 2001) for a discussion of Mamie Till-Mobley's influence as a Christian activist as a church mother in the Church of God in Christ. Comparing Mother Till-Mobley with the late Mrs. Lilian P. Benbow, also of the Church of God in Christ and a former president of Delta Sigma Theta sorority, Gilkes finds, "Mrs. Mobley is not the only "saint" to have an effect on the ethical and political culture of the black experience. Mrs. Benbow urged black sororities and fraternities to abstain from their annual dance and give the money they usually spent on "The Dance" to benefit the larger black community instead.

[11]This spiritual is influenced by several scriptural sources, including Psalm 16:8 and New Testament literature, particularly the synoptic gospels, regarding Jesus' crucifixion on the cross. One line, for example, proclaims steadfastness and unmoveability even when one's cross is heavy. The spiritual emphasizes that in the face of injustice one must stand strong, "like a tree planted by the water."

[12]"Sister" in African American colloquial expression is not limited to biological sibling relationship. Generally, it refers to a woman who is part of the community. In a church it refers to a woman who is a member of that church and a fellow Christian.

[13]Cheryl Townsend Gilkes, *If It Wasn't for the Women* (Maryknoll: Orbis, 2001), 1, 4, 7–8, 15–27,43–117, 196–211. Elisabeth Schüssler Fiorenza, *Searching the Scriptures: A Feminist Introduction* (New York: Crossraod, 1993), 1–24.

[14]See also Katie Cannon, *Katie's Canon: Womanism and the Soul of the Black Community* (New York: Continuum, 1996), 113–21 for a discussion of preaching that is uplifting for women.

[15]Ibid. Also, see Marjorie Suchocki, *God, Christ, Church: A Practical Guide to Process Theology* (New York: Crossroad, 1992), 205–6, 244. For Suchocki, "God, and only God, can feel the entirety of the other. Thus the flow of feeling that takes place as God prehends the other is a flow of the full subjectivity of the other into the full subjectivity of God. This is subjective immortality for the world within the life of God...There will be a new heaven and a new earth, but the locus of both is God's own being through God's power of resurrection. This resurrection is spiritual, not material." Suchocki derives this understanding from Whitehead's understanding of God as "feeling of feeling," in which God alone feels, experiences, or prehends all others in their entirety. For Whitehead, the temporal, finite world experiences only "objective immortality." Suchocki argues that given divine feeling of the feelings of the world, in the everlastingness of subjective resurrection in God there is also *subjective immortality*. This is not only logical, but satisfying in contrast to Hartshorne's nearly exclusive turn to *objective immortality*. See Alfred North Whitehead, *Process and Reality*, (New York: The Free Press/ Macmillan, 1978), 211–12, 246.

[16]Monica A. Coleman, "Walking in the Whirlwind: A Whiteheadian Womanist Soteriology," Ph.D. dissertation, Claremont Graduate University, 2004, 36.

[17]Marjorie Suchocki, "The Last Word?" in *Strike Terror No More: Theology, Ethics, and the New War*, ed. Jon Berquist (St. Louis: Chalice Press, 2002), 219, and Suchocki, *God, Christ, Church*, 208–10, 211–16. God, in God's justice and judgment, is for Suchocki the "overcomer of evil."

[18]Ibid.

[19]Ibid.

[20]Ibid.

[21]Bruce Marshall, lecture notes, "Interpretation of the Christian Message I," Fall 2002, and Marshall, *Trinity and Truth* (Cambridge, U.K.: Cambridge University Press, 2000; reprint 2002), 180–81, 254–56.

[22]Augustine, "Augustine of Hippo's On the Trinity, Book 9," in *The Trinitarian Controversy*, ed. William G Rusch (Philadelphia: 1980, Fortress Press), 164–177.

[23]See for example, Jürgen Moltmann, *The Church in the Power of the Spirit: A Contribution to Messianic Ecclesiology* (San Francisco: Harper, 1977).

[24]From *Ask Oxford.com,* at http://www.askoxford.com.

[25]From *Wikipedia,* at http://en.wikipedia.org/wiki/Holocaust.

[26]Ibid.

[27]The Native American Holocaust Museum Web site at http://www.nahm.org/AboutUs.html.

[28]"Genocide," in *Wikipedia,* at http://en.wikipedia.org/wiki/Genocide.

[29]Interview responses from Vanessa Baker, April 20, 2005.

[30]Ibid.

[31]Ibid.

[32]Mamie Till-Mobley and Christopher Benson, *Death of Innocence: The Story of the Hate Crime That Changed America* (New York: Random House, 2003), 217–18.

[33]Katie Cannon, *Black Womanist Ethics* (Atlanta: American Academy of Religion, 1988) 143–48.

[34]Till-Mobley, *Death.*

[35]Ibid., 283.

[36]Ibid.

[37]Ella Baker is known as the "Mother" of the Student Non-Violent Coordinating Committee (SNCC) and was a leader in the Southern Christian Leadership Conference (SCLC), which helped young people found SNCC. Members of SNCC initiated the "sit-ins" in restaurants and diners that discriminated against people of color and Jews. As far as I know, she is not related to myself and my family. Still, however, given the disruption of family relationships during slavery and all she stood for, I feel kinship with her as a Baker in name and simply as an ancestor that should be admired by all of us as one of our spiritual mothers in the communion of saints.

Name Index

Subject Index

K

L

M

N

O

P